BREAK THE WEIGHT LOSS BARRIER

BREAK THE WEIGHT LOSS BARRIER

DR. JIM MESCHINO
DR. BARRY SIMON

FOREWORD BY
NADIA COMANECI
& BART CONNER

with Recipes by Rose Reisman

PRENTICE HALL
Englewood Cliffs, New Jersey 07632

Library of Congress Cataloging in Publication Data

Meschino, James.
   Break the weight-loss barrier / James Meshcino, Barry Simon,
  with recipes by Rose Reisman.
     p. cm.
   Includes index.
   ISBN 0-13-745407-4 (cloth)
1. Weight loss—Psychological aspects. 2. Reducing diets
—Recipes. I. Simon, Barry, M.D. II. Reisman, Rose. III. Title.
RM222.2.M463 1997
613.2'5—dc21   97-4342
                                                  CIP

Printed in the United States of America

10 9 8 7 6 5 4 3 2 1

ISBN 0-13-745407-4

Every reasonable effort has been made to obtain permissions for all articles
and data used in this edition. If errors or omissions have occurred,
they will be corrected in future editions provided written notification
has been received by the publisher.

ATTENTION: CORPORATIONS AND SCHOOLS
Prentice Hall books are available at quantity discounts with bulk purchase for
educational, business, or sales promotional use. For information, please write to:
Prentice Hall Career & Personal Development Special Sales, 113 Sylvan Avenue,
Englewood Cliffs, NJ 07632. Please supply: title of book, ISBN, quantity, how the
book will be used, date needed.

PRENTICE HALL
Career & Personal Development
Englewood Cliffs, NJ 07632
A Simon & Schuster Company

On the World Wide Web at http://www.phdirect.com

Prentice Hall International (UK) Limited, *London*
Prentice Hall of Australia Pty. Limited, *Sydney*
Prentice Hall Canada, Inc., *Toronto*
Prentice Hall Hispanoamericana, S.A., *Mexico*
Prentice Hall of India Private Limited, *New Delhi*
Prentice Hall of Japan, Inc., *Tokyo*
Simon & Schuster Asia Pte. Ltd., *Singapore*
Editora Prentice Hall do Brasil, Ltda., *Rio de Janeiro*

Contents

Part 2 James Meschino's Plan 67

Part 3 Recipes   201

Foreword

As Olympic Gold Medal gymnasts competing for different countries in different years, little did we know that we shared the same training philosophy. Eat smart; live well; look great—this was our secret to winning a total of 11 medals in the Montreal, Moscow, and Los Angeles Games.

Because training was a way of life for us back then, finding the time to balance a healthy lifestyle came easily. We had trainers, team doctors, and personal physicians to recommend ideal diets, aerobic exercise regimens and vitamin supplement plans. We now know, however, that the everyday demands of work and family make healthy living a challenge. From talking with the many people we meet around the country and around the world, we see that we are not alone in our search for a practical health and nutrition program that fits in easily with our hectic lifestyle. That is why we were intrigued when we first read *Break the Weight-Loss Barrier*.

In this book, Dr. James Meschino provides readers with the keys they need to unlock a future of looking good and feeling good. What we like best about Dr. Meschino's plan is that you don't have to be an athlete to achieve positive results. Anyone can use this blueprint for healthy living and be successful at it.

Most of the programs we have heard about over the years offer a "band-aid" approach to wellness. Instead of taking a total body approach, they focus on only one area such as losing weight, lowering cholesterol, or toning muscles. So while some people may diet, they are doing nothing to lower their cholesterol or become more physically fit. Likewise, people who head straight from the gym to the donut shop are negating the positive effects of exercising.

By focusing on the body *and* mind, *Break the Weight-Loss Barrier* offers a comprehensive, yet simple, formula for healthy living. This includes the right balance of carbohydrates, proteins, and fat; an optimal intake of protective vitamins and minerals; and gentle aerobic exercise. Just 30 minutes a day will do! Dr. Meschino shows how incorporating practical nutrition and fitness strategies into a daily routine enables the body to maintain its ideal weight and protect itself against degenerative diseases such as cancer, osteoporosis, and heart attacks.

And because Dr. Meschino knows that a good road map is useless if you cannot get started, he has teamed up with Dr. Barry Simon to break down the psychological barriers that can stand in the way of your success. By identifying the external triggers and inner conversations that guide your behavior, Dr. Simon will help get you started on the road to healthier living. With the right mind-set, you can—and will—make this program a natural and automatic extension of your life and achieve long-term success while you are at it!

Being Olympic gymnasts required a deep commitment to our goals. Outside the world of competition, however, we've found that it is difficult to define goals for health and nutrition and even harder to stick with them. Sure, many people know what they would like to weigh or, at the very least, that they would like to fit into the pair of blue jeans hanging in the back of their closet. Few, however, clearly define the fitness and nutrition strategies they will use to reach their goals. That is where *Break the Weight-Loss Barrier* enters into play.

After providing you with the information you need to understand the principles of nutrition and exercise, Drs. Meschino and Simon give you the tools you will need to tailor the program to your individual needs. Using the Goal-Setting Wellness Planner outlined in Chapter 10, you can set specific goals for *your* body and health, identify the obstacles that may stand in *your* way, and develop personal strategies to overcome them. This Wellness Planner will help keep you on track, much like our coaches did during our Olympic years.

Drs. Meschino and Simon believe, as we do, that the recipe for a lean, fit, healthy body starts with reducing dietary fat. But who has the time to read all of the nutrition labels on the foods they buy? Not only does *Break the Weight-Loss Barrier* provide lists of vitamin-enriched foods necessary for a healthy body, it also provides easy-to-follow recipes for healthy and tasty dishes.

An expert in health and nutrition, Dr. Meschino works as a wellness coach, helping patients map out a lifetime journey toward healthier living. Having educated more than 250,000 people on the vital role nutrition, exercise, and vitamin supplementation plays in maintaining good health, he understands the obstacles that real life presents and describes ways to circumvent them. He even allows you to cheat now and then, offering a list of solution substitution foods that can be less damaging than the high-fat treats you may crave.

A noted psychiatrist, Dr. Simon counsels many weight-loss patients who have failed in the past due to underlying psychological or emotional issues attached to food. In *Break the Weight-Loss Barrier*, he shares his secrets for helping patients establish a new and healthier lifelong relationship with food and activity.

With the weight loss and fitness industry now accounting for more than $30 billion each year, there are a lot of conflicting messages. James and Barry's practical and proven approach, however, stands out from the rest. *Break the Weight-Loss Barrier* provides you with an immediate solution and fast results. But more importantly, it's a commitment for a better body, and healthier and longer life. We're happy to see a program on the market that teaches the cutting-edge research for body fat reduction, health promotion, and disease prevention.

We hope you'll do more than just read this book. We hope you'll live it.

Nadia Comaneci & Bart Conner

Introduction

When we decided to write *Break the Weight-Loss Barrier,* our goal was to provide a solution to a common problem: to develop an effective program that would provide long-term success at weight loss. When we first began designing health programs, more than a decade ago, our programs included three key elements: proper diet, exercise, and vitamin supplementation. And our clients enjoyed initial successes on these programs. They lost weight, toned up, reduced their body fat, and enjoyed exercising or recreational sports. Over the long term, however, some of these clients suffered setbacks, lost interest, and regained the weight they had lost.

We began to examine the reasons that people fail to experience long-term successes in their weight-loss endeavours. We asked ourselves the following questions. Why do people cheat at their health program? Why do they eat when they shouldn't? Why do they procrastinate about exercising even when they understand that it is an essential component of health and weight loss? And why do people bargain with or berate themselves for not meeting their eating or exercise expectations? Our answers to these questions resulted in a shift in focus. We realized that we no longer needed to develop a program that simply combined the perfect combination of carbohydrates and protein with the necessary amount of exercise, but instead we needed to create a program that focused on the unique needs of each individual.

Our clients began to enjoy real and lasting successes when we addressed two key issues: How could the program meet their individual taste preferences, lifestyles, and personal goals? And how could they begin to recognize that their feelings and thoughts affected what they were about to eat or do? This was the turning point. The program must meet the needs of each individual, rather than the individual trying to somehow fit the program's requirements. We recognized that an individual's thoughts and feelings determine his or her actions, so the program had to address these key elements. Although the reasons that people failed were not their fault, they were inevitable. This shift from the best program that fits all, to the program that fits you — your feelings, your tastes, your lifestyle, and your goals — led to 10 years of clinical experience based on an unlikely friendship and collaborative effort between Dr. James Meschino and Dr. Barry Simon.

Dr. Meschino, with his chiropractic and nutrition training, regularly saw patients who were out of shape, tired, and on the road to disease. Yet he believed that most people could become healthy once they understood how to apply the basic principles of health to their lifestyle. He created sound, easy-to-follow nutritional plans and fitness programs for his patients. He was young and enthusiastic. His office was located in the same complex as a health club so he could work out with his clients and provide them with personal direction. By providing these services, Dr. Meschino began to realize the need to accommodate each patient's unique needs rather than designing generic programs that apply to everyone. He noted that although many of his patients experienced successes, others were stuck and felt even more hopeless and resigned.

During their first meeting, Dr. Simon, who was training to

be a psychiatrist, brought clarity to the concerns of the stuck, anxious clients who felt like they were in a rut. Dr. Simon had been the stereotypical chubby teenager himself. He had struggled with his weight as he tried every new weight-loss plan. Self-conscious about his weight, Dr. Simon understands the emotional components that go into that moment when you very much want to eat the treat but you feel guilt about that inevitable "extra pound" on the scale. In his practice with clients in psychotherapy, Dr. Simon discovered that emotional and psychological components are the real underlying obstacles to breaking the weight-loss barrier. As a psychiatrist and psychoanalyst, he brings a deep understanding of the inner emotional experiences that lead to overeating, compulsive dieting, and binging.

Since that first meeting, we have spent 10 years developing a program that helps you to identify and modify the only important moment of change: this moment. If you waste time chastising yourself for what you did yesterday, you lose the momentum of this moment, which could lead to change. Instead, you begin to feel worse about yourself and inevitably end up cheating. Another futile approach is to swear off a food for life. You promise to be good forever and avoid bad foods. Ironically, the very act of swearing off bad food results in your eventual failure.

Success on our program means being the best possible you. This doesn't mean that today's best possible you is the same as tomorrow's you. The best possible you includes not only how you look physically but also how you feel. After all, you can't behave in a way that is not in keeping with your inner feelings and thoughts. If you believe that you can't succeed or that hunger will drive you to eat, you will be unable to turn away from that big snack. Those deep, everyday feelings, taste preferences, and needs also determine your daily health choices. During this program, you will discover these feelings and thoughts and learn how to respond to them.

Break the Weight-Loss Barrier makes this program available to you. It will help you set realistic goals. And, by taking your weight, exercise, food tastes, and lifestyle into consideration, it will show you how to design your own lifetime plan. In Part I, Dr. Barry Simon shows you how to listen to your inner conversation. You will discover why you can sometimes pass by certain foods while other times you are drawn to them or feel an impulsive urge to indulge. Once you have determined the reasons for this, you will discover how to transform these health moments into more health-promoting, body-thinning decisions. In Part II, Dr. James Meschino helps you to stop "putting it off" and start "taking it off." His Two-Staple System allows you to eat according to your personal tastes and to experience the joys of food while burning fat and improving your health. In Part III, nutritionist Rose Reisman shows you how simple it is to put this program into practice without sacrificing life's tastes and fragrances. Her recipes provide great taste and good nutrition.

Every Monday morning millions of Canadians make health resolutions. Yet 70 percent of us are overweight, at any time 25 percent of us are on a diet, and approximately 50 percent of us will die from a heart- and stroke-related problem. Isn't it time to stop promising to go on someone else's diet and begin to create your own plan? *Break the Weight-Loss Barrier* succeeds where other programs fail because you are at the centre of the plan.

Besides the information available in this book, the authors also provide additional resources and information. If you are overweight and struggling to lose weight, Dr. Simon offers a 10-session audiotape program based on his office-practice weight-loss sessions. This self-directed program is designed for those who need added psychological guidance in conquering their cravings, emotional eating, and staying on track with weight-loss goals. For further information about this program, you can call 1-888-889-3305 or 416-921-6500.

Dr. Meschino also offers various nutritional resources and information. For example, he provides a series of audiotapes covering topics ranging from wellness for women to nutritional and athletic performance. In addition, he has developed a comprehensive program entitled "The 20/20 Vision of You," which combines education with food supplements to improve personal health and lifestyle. For further information about these programs, contact Dr. Meschino at 1-888-MESCHINO.

Break the Weight-Loss Barrier provides a map for a lifetime journey toward healthier living. It does not provide therapeutic diets or nutritional therapies for particular ailments and is not intended to replace the advice of a personal physician or medical specialist. Since no program can consider the health needs of every reader, we strongly recommend that you consult your doctor before beginning to follow our nutritional, exercise, and psychological strategies for success. A complete examination is the first step in identifying your starting point and it will help you modify our program to suit your individual needs. Many people have developed eating disorders during their lifetime. If you have suffered anorexia or bulimia nervosa, you should not use the program without the guidance of a therapist or physician.

Dr. Barry Simon
Dr. James Meschino

Acknowledgments

In addition to our efforts, many people contributed both directly and indirectly to the development and production of *Break the Weight-Loss Barrier* and deserve our recognition and appreciation. First, we thank all of our patients who taught us so much over the past decade and who proved that the principles outlined in this book can provide lifelong success at weight loss. Second, we extend our appreciation to Barry's wife, Susan, for her continued encouragement and support throughout this project. The authors would also like to thank Rose Reisman for her enthusiastic support and contributions to Part 3. We also acknowledge the theoretical and clinical ideas of Dr. Aaron Beck (cognitive therapy) and Dr. Roberto Assagioli (psychosynthesis), which provided the inspiration as well as the principles for Part I of *Break the Weight-Loss Barrier*. Finally, we thank the editorial and production staff at Prentice Hall Canada for their creative ideas, helpful editorial suggestions, and continued belief in the worthiness of this project.

Dr. James Meschino
Dr. Barry Simon

Barry Simon's
Plan

Making the most of the moment

Every day each of us makes choices. We decide between eggs or cereal for breakfast, between a doughnut or a raisin bagel at coffee break, between cream or tomato sauce on our pasta, and between cherry cheesecake or fruit salad for dessert. We have all experienced that universal dilemma — "I really want the cheesecake but I'm watching my weight." At that moment we feel the pull between our desire for cheesecake and the knowledge that we should choose fruit salad. At these moments, and only at these moments, can we make changes to our weight and health. We might have only three or four of these moments in a day, but the decisions we make in them add up. Excess pounds, high cholesterol, low energy, and unfit states of health are the results of hundreds of these little moments.

Your Health, Your Life

Your health is the foundation of your life. Most of us don't think about it daily, but our health is at the centre of our existence. There isn't any event in our lives that being healthy does not enhance — time spent with loving families and devoted friends, community involvement, successful careers, travel, retirement. Feeling and looking our best makes every day better. Being trim and fit and enjoying high energy improves how we present ourselves in the world and how much we enjoy our physical being.

Keeping fit and healthy can also help postpone serious diseases. The statistics are frightening for North Americans – one of every nine women develops breast cancer; one of every nine men over the age of 60 develops prostate cancer; one in 20 people develops colon cancer; approximately 50 percent of people die from heart and stroke problems. How we feed our bodies strongly affects our health potential and the likelihood that we will live longer. With odds like these, we must succeed.

The Many Roads to Failure

Each of us has made thousands of resolutions to change – on Monday mornings, at the beginning of each month, and at New Year's. Procrastinating until tomorrow is the main way we avoid living in this moment. One patient captured this universal sense by saying, "I wish every day was Monday." We also waste time criticizing ourselves for what we did yesterday, and have little energy left to make changes today. Instead, we feel worse and inevitably end up cheating.

Another destructive method is to swear off a group of foods forever. We promise to be good and to avoid bad foods. Ironically, the very act of swearing off bad food results in our eventual failure. When we join a health club, travel to a spa, or follow a rigid diet with no view of who we are, we set ourselves up to fail. Within three weeks, our inner desires and suppressed thoughts break through and we are back at the beginning – just somewhat more demoralized.

For many people, a diet is a punishment for their eating sins. Diets often begin with a promise to start "being good" today. The dieter's strength, creativity, and vision are lost in a last-ditch effort to conform to some program that offers false hope.

The biggest problem with following someone else's diet is that it is someone else's diet. Following a diet plan that someone else sets out means that we give up controlling how we plan meals, choose recipes, and organize our day. Carrying around diet books, weighing foods to the ounce, measuring ingredients to the teaspoon – we soon feel our spirit being depleted.

Whenever we subordinate ourselves to an outside force, we eventually rebel against it and return to our old ways. We rebel for many reasons, but usually we are disappointed that the diet failed to fulfil its promise of a magic solution. Similarly, joining a health club with no sense of "why" other than that we "should" is as unlikely to succeed as is following someone else's diet. If exercise is not part of who we are and if we don't have conviction, our goal will not stick.

There is no single ingredient or secret that will lead to easy weight loss or permanent health. For most people, keeping weight down, exercising regularly, watching fat intake, and keeping up with the latest nutritional information are difficult endeavours. In addition, the demands of work, children, finances, and time affect our ability to eat right and exercise.

Beginning the Journey

You cannot adopt a successful weight-loss and wellness plan today and expect it to remain the same forever. A lifestyle, exercise program, or eating plan that does not take into account your taste preferences, schedule, and previous exercise program will not last.

True success begins by answering the question "How are your feelings and thoughts determining what you're about to eat or do?" In every situation, external events and internal thoughts, feelings, and beliefs dictate how you respond. Each response is personal and unique to you. There are no right responses, just many possibilities. You may not be aware of the external triggers and inner conversations that guide and direct your behaviour.

To succeed, a wellness plan must make you aware of these triggers. Our plan does just that. It helps you to know the outer events and inner conversations that lead to your actions.

Stop and Begin to Listen . . .

As human beings each of us is unique. Unlike animals, which live by the stimulus-and-response model, as human beings we can stop and consider the consequences before we leap into action. Our program is based on this potential — on our ability to stand back and get to know our feelings and thoughts, as well as the people and situations that cause us to act in a repetitive, fixed way.

Only by getting to know yourself can you change your regular responses. You can rekindle your lost love affair with your health, beginning right now. Life is a series of moments and, in every one of them, you choose your commitments — choosing to exercise or not, choosing a lower- or higher-fat food. By catching these moments and slowing them down, you will ultimately change your thoughts and make health-promoting, enlightened choices more often.

Living in this moment means making a choice that is in keeping with where you are right now, not where you think you *should* be. Your "shoulds" include your ideal weight, your perfect diet, your athletic performance, or your vitamin regime. Nothing makes a person more anxious and therefore more prone to failure than trying to be someone he or she is not.

In the following chapters, you get to know your inner voices

— forecasting your feelings, and using all-or-nothing thinking, self-justifying, self-blame, and procrastination. From there, we will look at the places, people, and events that lead you to cheat. You'll discover the situations, people, or feelings that make you most vulnerable to overeating or choosing high-fat foods or to neglecting exercise. We outline a number of strategies you can try once you've slowed yourself down enough to listen to what you say to yourself as you are deciding whether to exercise or to eat. Once you know your inner conversation and external triggers, you can then embark on a series of steps leading to permanent change. You must change from the inside out. There is no other way.

Success on the Program

Break the Weight-Loss Barrier is designed with continuous change in mind. We help you set realistic standards that you can gently raise each week. On our program, you will know you've succeeded after the fact. You may not remember the day you gave up red meat or ice cream or cake or chocolate. Real change occurs when you realize, usually months later, that these foods are no longer part of your lifestyle. Real change is no longer craving or desiring a food. You can achieve this kind of change by beginning where you are right now.

This book is about making changes in the moment. Together let's begin the journey toward better health, fitness, and weight.

1. We don't want you to walk around *hungry*. We want you to walk around *healthy*.

2. As a population, we are not succeeding in being fit and well. Seventy percent of the population is overweight. At any given time, 25 percent of North Americans are on a diet — 95 percent of whom will regain all the weight they lose and more within two years. The reason

is that people are unrealistic in their goals. They adopt an unrealistic program and expect to attain their goals in an unreasonably short period.

3. Being the best possible you is all you can possibly be.

Recognizing the barriers to success

We spend a great deal of time living in the past or hoping to be somewhere in the future, and very little time actually experiencing the present. Living in this moment means making a choice that is in keeping with where you are right now, not where you think you *should* be in terms of your weight, diet, exercise plan, or vitamin regime. To do this, you need to find out where you are at this moment, not where you were yesterday or even this morning. *Nothing makes you more anxious than trying to be someone you're not.* By seeing where you are now, you will be well on your way to making a decision that fits this moment.

Living in the moment is about taking a deep breath and jumping in with the biggest stretch that you can honestly live with right now. By doing this every day, you will find yourself moving closer to a healthier lifestyle.

Your Inner Conversation

Have you ever felt drawn to the refrigerator, unable to keep yourself from opening it and eating a piece of coffee cake? No wonder you sometimes feel weak, ineffectual, and hopeless.

Your personal journey to successfully meet your wellness goals starts with recognizing the negative comments you tell yourself. These comments lead you to gulp down food while asking yourself, "What am I doing?"; to drive to a fast-food restaurant and angrily eat the food, cursing yourself the entire time; to lie aimlessly on the couch eating a bag of cookies with no recognition of your actions. These ongoing thoughts, reactions, and feelings are called your "inner conversation."

Each of us has an inner conversation about food and exercise. Some people are consumed with guilt about the way they eat. They feel uncomfortable in their enlarged bodies. They know that by maintaining negative lifestyle habits they are risking their health, and they therefore have negative feelings about themselves, which, in turn, cause them to berate themselves unmercifully. Once you become aware of these inner conversations, you can reflect upon them. Then you will find it easier to make a healthy new choice, and to feel better about your future ability to choose. Later you'll begin to shift the negative, overwhelming conversation to a compassionate, committed one.

Listening to Your Inner Conversation

Your first step, however, is to identify what makes you feel anxious and helpless.

Whether you are relating to your loved ones, a task you need to do, or the act of eating, you are involved in a relationship. During these times, you feel differently about yourself — tired, strong, wilful, disciplined, powerful. How you feel will affect how you experience things. For example, if you are riding a stationary bike when you are tired, you might experience the bike as a great resistance and say to yourself, "I really need to stop and rest." You might then respond, "But I really should get my full 30 minutes of exercise." If you stop, you might feel that you're undisciplined and chastise yourself, or you might be sympathetic to your feelings and say, "I've had a hard day and deserve a rest." Regardless of your response, you are in the midst of an ongoing, observable conversation.

Let's focus on this inner conversation and your relationship with the outside world. You can react to outside stimuli in various ways. Perhaps you've been on a diet or exercise plan and recall that on some days you felt invigorated, powerful, and able to follow the plan easily. At other times, you longed for a special food that would ease your loneliness or frustration. On some days, you could eat a chocolate-glazed doughnut or neglect your exercise with no emotional reaction toward your body or how you look. From this changing relationship, you can see that it is not the *program* that is crucial for success, but rather your *relationship* to food and exercise. And this changing relationship determines your daily ability to succeed.

Helen's Ice-Cream Struggle

Helen, a therapist, came home after a long day, feeling the anger of her clients as tension in her neck and back. Opening the front door triggered her urge for a bowl of ice cream. Avoiding the kitchen led to a mild sense of discomfort in her cheeks and forehead. As she began to salivate, she excused herself with the thought, "I've had a long day and I deserve a treat." Her facial tension increased and her breathing sped up slightly. At that moment she thought, "I cannot believe I'm thinking about doing this again. It's winter and I'm just getting worse and worse. I'm pathetic." Neither taking a five-minute break nor watching television helped the situation. Instead, her decision not to eat the ice cream simply caused her tension to resurface. She worried that she wasn't really helping her client and fantasized about him quitting therapy. She immediately blamed herself for him not improving and berated herself for hoping he might quit – leaving her feeling helpless and inadequate. Most of her inner conversation happened in a split second. Helen failed to tell herself that she'd helped two people that day or that she could be really hard on herself. Instead of soothing herself with these thoughts, she made a deal with herself: she would throw out the remaining ice cream *after* tonight's snack. After eating two bowls of ice cream, she regretted her actions and still felt guilty about eating the food. This inner conversation was not only about food – it was about guilt and humiliating behaviour.

During these inner conversations, *Helen's self-abuse created an overwhelming, tension-filled moment.* Only when she recognized what was happening in that moment was she more successful in guiding her choices.

Overwhelming Moments

Each of us experiences overwhelming moments – times when we feel weak, sad, upset, frightened, guilty, and ashamed. There is nothing empowering about these feelings. During these times of apprehension or anxiety, as in Helen's ice-cream struggle, we often feel incapable of doing things differently. During these moments, anxiety causes us to lose a skill, ability, or habit.

For example, if I am speaking to a group of people and notice that someone has fallen asleep, I might wonder if I'm boring everyone – not just that person. Then I might stammer or lose my train of thought. This reaction then confirms for me that I really haven't prepared well enough, causing my anxiety to rise even more. In this moment, my usual skills and clear head are lost to a series of emotions and inner conversations.

Examples of Overwhelming Moments

"The toughest part of the day for me is the late after-noon. Tired, hit by a wave of weakness, I turn to choco-late or cookies to give me a burst of energy. Holiday time is the worst; there's food everywhere." – Joe

Joe's feelings of weakness and of losing a sense of direc-tion identifies an overwhelming moment. His feelings of inevitability and urgency are typical parts of these moments.

"Pasta, frozen cakes, creamy desserts – that's the cure for a bad date or, worse, a good date that goes nowhere." – Sarah

Sarah's inner conversation fails to acknowledge her feel-ing of apprehension that she will never form a satisfying personal relationship with someone. Her apprehension causes a sense of hopelessness and loneliness, and the overwhelming feeling of loneliness makes food a neces-sary antidote. Once she realizes that loneliness results in an inability to cope well, she will be able to respond instead with a compassionate conversation with herself.

"It's not worth it. My wife and kids love me. I work late. Pizza's out on the table during tax season. So I eat a few slices. Big deal! I feel guilty. So that's my problem." – Peter

Peter feels compelled to eat the pizza. His comment, "Big deal," really means that he feels that eating the pizza is significant but that he feels helpless to do much about it. His anger is actually frustration that he feels unable to do anything else.

"Once I'm home, I don't even take off my jacket. Dinner is all that's on my mind. I open and close the refrigerator door, sometimes five or six times. I really think I expect to find something different in there each time." – Frank

Frank automatically goes to the refrigerator, indicating that he feels out of control. This tension is accompanied by the thought that the food is unnecessary, yet he automatically opens and closes the refrigerator door repeatedly.

"I feel tired each time I imagine getting up at 6:30 a.m. and working out on my cross-country-ski machine. Lying in bed, I can't imagine taking more than a couple of steps without sitting down." – Vivian

Vivian has the same inner conversation every morning. Each night she plans to exercise in the morning, and each morning when she doesn't follow through, she feels regret and disgust. This repetitive inner conversation of hope and regret keeps her not only from exercising in the morning, but also from exercising at a different time of day.

Anxiety

Anxiety is a response to danger and threats. It can be triggered by what you imagine might happen or by an actual treat. Being afraid to fail a test or standing in front of a Doberman pinscher can both trigger the same anxiety-response system. Anxiety can also produce positive effects: fear of failure might motivate you to study; fear of the dog might make you cautious.

During overwhelming moments, however, anxiety goes beyond being motivational and can undermine success. At these times, you are no longer trying to solve the challenging situation but have a single goal — to get away or to return to something safe. You accomplish this by doing what is most familiar. For example, if you're anxious about exercising when you're tired, you respond by not exercising. Or when you're afraid you can't refrain from eating ice cream, you eat it and the anxiety vanishes. These safe responses, however, leave you hopeless and unchanged, which creates more anxiety.

RECOGNIZING ANXIETY

How can you recognize overwhelming moments? Like the people in the examples, you will experience apprehension – a subtle nervousness that leaves you with a sense of urgency, a need to act, or a feeling that something is not right or safe. During these times, your thoughts may move rapidly or you may mull over worries – worries about money, performance, lack of success, feeling alone or needy, and so on.

Anxiety also manifests itself in physical sensations: a feeling of bodily discomfort; a tenseness in your shoulders, neck or back; a feeling that you are breathing deeply or are even holding your breath. Mild apprehension is evident in tension in the cheeks, mouth, or forehead, or as a sense of not feeling comfortable in your skin or an awareness of how fat you are or how warm you feel. With this bodily feeling comes a sense of needing to do something. Most people fail to recognize this mild physical apprehension until they look for it. Other people do not experience these physical aspects of anxiety. Instead, they feel unsure or not quite right.

ANXIETY AND CHANGE

Even if you sincerely want to change your eating and exercise habits, you may worry that you'll fail once again. Ironically, this anxiety often leads to the very failure you fear. Your anxiety erodes your self-confidence and self-esteem and, hence, your ability to follow through with your fitness goals. This response results in a further loss of self-esteem and more anxiety.

Most people who start a weight-loss plan worry that they are too weak to succeed. During your first moments on a weight-loss plan, you may also be concerned. You may blame yourself for needing to improve. If you've failed many times before, you may feel anxious about failing again. You may repeatedly ask yourself, "What if—?" questions. "What if I still stop for doughnuts?" "What if I can't commit to a high-fibre diet?" "What if I can't manage my out-of-control cholesterol?" You may also be apprehensive about whether you can make lasting changes.

These anxieties may actually prevent you from beginning your journey to better health. When you commit to change, perhaps to a weight-loss plan, how you feel about yourself — your self-confidence — is at stake. You are likely to judge your ability to control all your actions by your ability to not eat when you've told yourself that you shouldn't. You may feel ashamed if you cannot do what you feel you should do, especially after setting a clear goal for yourself.

Connected to weight loss is your sense of how you rank with the rest of the world. Fat people and people who are out of shape often feel that they are less important than others. Many feel incompetent. If you're afraid that you are unlovable or unwanted, you will experience these thoughts each time you fail. If you have these fears, you will feel them even more strongly when you are angry, self-critical, and ashamed.

On the other hand, people who feel competent rarely feel threatened. Boxers don't appear frightened because they feel competent at what they do. A boxing match can be a threatening situation, but boxers who feel prepared to face their opponent will remain relatively calm. However, a boxer who has lost many fights or who is unprepared will lack confidence. Similarly, your success on a health-promotion or weight-loss plan will depend on your past experience. If you have failed many times before, you won't feel competent. Memories of your past inability to keep away from the cupboard, refrigerator, or late-night food store reinforce your feeling that you lack the skills to meet your goals. The resulting shame and guilt you experience make you feel even more incompetent. It's not surprising you become anxious. The inability to cope with these deeper worries gets in the way of true success.

Breaking the Anxiety-Failure Connection

As we have seen, our early warning system is anxiety, which generally leads to failure. Let's apply this understanding to your weight-loss efforts. You are trying something new so you are both excited and nervous. You wonder whether you are prepared or if you have a strong enough character to succeed. Your mind and body reduce the threat by returning to the familiar — what you've done before. You do the safe thing, which could be the repetitive acts of eating the chocolate, not exercising if you are tired, choosing the high-fat treat, and so on. Inevitably, self-preservation and safety win out.

Let's look now at some kinds of inner conversation:
- feeling forecasting
- all-or-nothing thinking
- self-blame
- procrastination
- self-justifying.

Feeling Forecasting

Anxiety has its own style of conversation. During overwhelming moments, you may talk to yourself in a devastating way, typically expecting the worst to happen. You may even view the situation as catastrophic and believe that something is seriously wrong. Typically, you may feel that you will be permanently anxious. This is called "feeling forecasting." It occurs when it seems that your present situation will continue and may even worsen.

Common thoughts include "I know that if I get on the bike, I won't feel like riding for 30 minutes," or "I know I'll never wait the recommended 15 minutes before eating the chocolate bar. I just don't have the willpower." These thoughts are predictions of *future* feelings. Even though you know that all experiences rise, plateau, and fade, during moments of feeling forecasting, you expect the feelings to last, and, feeling that the situation is hopeless, you give in to them. This anxiety can make you feel physically tired and weak, and can support the belief that you can't cope. Despite the fact that the physical weakness will vanish as your anxiety level lessens, you predict the opposite. Thoughts such as "I don't have the strength" have a major effect on you and become a powerful focus for all that follows. If your back aches while biking, you do not view it as an everyday ache — rather it supports your belief that you lack the strength to exercise and that it makes you feel even more tired and hopeless. If you believe that desires for foods last forever, every urge you feel will support your belief in the permanence of the desire. Again, you will be left feeling hopeless and destined to give in to the urge. As you can see, this series of thoughts is especially devastating because every neutral piece of evidence — your regular aches, the urges of everyday life — supports the idea that you'll never succeed.

All-or-Nothing Thinking

Anxiety also causes your thinking to be very narrow and focused. It removes other possibilities, leaving safety as your only choice. This is called "all-or-nothing thinking." Your only choice seems to be a safe action or what feels like a giant, dangerous risk. There is no room for creativity, and even less sense of possibility. This lack of compromise — the need to do something just right or not at all — comprises the perfectionism that stems from these anxious moments. Perfectionist thinking means we must do everything just perfectly. For example, a perfectionist whose goal was 30 minutes of jogging might berate herself for doing "only 18 minutes." After harshly judging her partial effort, she is more likely to put off trying again until tomorrow (procrastination) when she might feel more able to do the "expected amount" of 30 minutes.

This dangerous thought pattern can take you from a small slip of eating one cookie to eating half a dozen. If your "perfect" image (all) disappears with a little slip, you easily fall into the land of "doing nothing" for your health. Half a row of cookies disappears with this belief. You cannot simply accept that one cookie was a treat, nor can you consider compromises or alternatives such as eating a no-fat cookie instead.

Self-Blame

"Shoulds" are inner comments that tell us how we ought to behave. They trigger feelings of weakness, inability, procrastination, or rebellion. Throughout each day, we all have many of these fleeting thoughts and feelings. Our "shoulds" and "oughts" tell us what we believe and feel about things. For example, during a wellness or weight-loss program, we believe that we *should* have urges or desires only for foods that fall within our program. Sometimes simply the thought of a non-healthful food or, even more devastating, the desire for such a food, results in an inner conversation. We become anxious and begin to feel the urge to give in. Self-criticism follows our thought and soon we are anxiously indulging in the food.

Self-blame results from contradicting an inner "should." Our self-critical voices harshly criticize us about some inadequacy with comments such as "You can't even choose tomato sauce; you have to have the cream sauce. You're such a loser." This self-criticism leaves us feeling anxious, weak, guilty, or ashamed. Telling ourselves that we shouldn't feel a certain way leads to our failure, since once we experience the forbidden feeling, we surrender in self-defeat.

Pauline had lost 25 pounds on our program. She was exercising daily, and participating in yoga twice a week. A success story? Wrong. She felt that she *should* be doing a lot better and slowly this sense of falling short – of not being good enough – led her to lose motivation. Unfortunately, instead of blaming me, she blamed herself. For a month she stopped attending the program, then returned three pounds heavier and feeling dejected. The facts had nothing to do with how she was doing; her self-blame and "shoulds" were her final judge and jury. They certainly dealt with her harshly.

Self-blame and falling short of our "shoulds" reinforce our negative self-image. For example, if we crave ice cream, we accuse ourselves of being weak, ineffective, and undisciplined. This reaction to our conscience's criticism is a way of saying that we *should* be acting differently. Personally speaking, when I am tired, I feel hungry. Since I don't think I *should* be tired, I assume that I need nourishment. In the past, when eating did not alleviate my tiredness, I assumed that I was still hungry and ate more. I ate because I wouldn't accept that I might actually be tired – something that would interfere with the goals I had set for myself. For me, fatigue is part of a negative self-image.

Another response to "shoulds" is to rebel against them. Consider the example of Andrew, a 45-year-old dentist, who would "forget" to do his paperwork on patients. At the end of a long day, he'd say to himself, "I really should do my paperwork." But, feeling tense, he'd procrastinate by saying, "I'll get to it later." By disregarding the "should," he felt free and spontaneous. This type of conversation accounts for much of the procrastination or "starting tomorrow" attitude that some people adopt toward their health program. These people develop intense "shoulds" regarding their journey to better health and fitness, which cause them to feel confined and tense, and eventually they break away by doing the exact opposite. This moment of "doing the opposite" is very liberating. Even though they abandon the program, they are not actually rebelling against the program's goals, but rather against their own self-generated "shoulds."

A similar case involved one of my patients. For one month

he did not follow my suggestion to write down his thoughts during overwhelming moments. He was so desperate to avoid the task that I thought he might buy a dog just for an excuse that the dog had eaten his homework. Although I pointed out that I believed that his avoidance was his way of rebelling, only when he saw how subordinate he felt when he followed instructions did he finally give it a try.

Underlying most rebellions of this type is usually a negative self-image or negative feeling such as humiliation or embarrassment at having to do the "demeaning task." Once we further explored this patient's feelings, we found that his rebellious response also emerged in other areas of his daily life in which he did not want to subordinate himself to someone else's suggestions.

Procrastination

Procrastination is closely connected to this pattern. Wellness is an area in which we believe we can procrastinate or deviate. After all, what's the worst thing that will happen if you eat one high-fat meal? Not much. But combine a hundred or thousand of these decisions and the effect can be quite significant — sometimes even devastating. Your inner conversation for making this type of decision might go something like this: "I really should have the pasta dish with the tomato sauce, but I'd prefer the cream sauce. It's not such a big deal." The thought of the tomato sauce leads to some inner tension, which generates a feeling of constraint and a desire to refuse the tomato sauce. This inner tension is followed by putting off the decision to choose the tomato sauce until you feel less tense and anxious. Your hope that a calm moment will arrive tomorrow is a form of procrastination. For now, you choose the cream sauce, not only for the taste difference but also to avoid an uncomfortable, inner tension. Here's the catch: feeling tense is an inevitable part of any new decision. You might end up repeatedly procrastinating as you wait for just the right calm moment to begin your health plan.

Furthermore, in this process you begin to link your desire for the cream sauce with the freedom to do what you want. Self-justifying comments such as "It's not the end of the world" or procrastinating statements like "Just this once" follow the tense moment. These comments provide justification for choosing the cream sauce. If you procrastinate regularly, try to have two or three wellness conversations daily. Take a deep breath, choose the tomato sauce, and listen to the unfolding inner conversation. It will be filled with tension, sadness over the loss of the cream sauce, pride in your health-promoting choice, and a bit of longing for the cream sauce. Beware of the urge to undo your success by having a dessert.

Consider how you feel if you say, "It will be a big deal to choose the pasta with tomato sauce. I really want the cream sauce." By doing this you decrease the anxiety by acknowledging that it *will* take significant effort to make the healthful choice. Once you are aware of this tension and the effort involved, you can gain control over your response or actions.

Let's consider an example outside the food context. How many times have you said to yourself, "I'll just run this red light. It's not a big deal"? Because a high risk is involved, your answer is likely, "Not often." We don't run red lights because the devastating results — a ticket or, worse, an accident — are so immediate. We do, however, break our diet rules because there is no immediate consequence — except our enjoyment of chocolate cake or cream sauce.

Self-Justifying Voice

We have seen how we respond to our critical inner voice with feelings of helplessness and futility. You may also recognize another response — one that justifies and explains our behaviour. Harangued by self-blame, we often justify our actions with thoughts like "I've been good all week" or "I deserve a treat." This response answers the inner critic that is telling us not to eat the treat or encouraging us to get on the exercise bicycle.

Although self-justifying conversations sometimes decrease the force of the self-blaming inner voice, at other times that voice returns even stronger. Self-justification may let us temporarily escape our inner critic and allow us to indulge. Unfortunately, the long-term result is that any setback from our health and fitness plan is met with a sense of hopelessness, guilt, or shame. Many times this final sense of regret causes us to abandon our goals.

Let's look at one final case.

John's Inner Voice

John is a 35-year-old financial analyst who quit his job to work freelance. Both he and his wife work long days before coming home to their three children. Although John has become financially more successful in his new freelance position, his direct contact with clients' demands puts him on edge. At times, he feels badgered as his pager rings throughout the day.

Recently, John has gained 25 pounds. In the evenings, he now relaxes in front of the television before helping his children with their homework or doing his own paperwork. He lives his life stressed out. Although he understands the importance of good nutrition, his tight schedule usually leads him to grab a doughnut rather than stop for a more nutritious snack. Often when he is tense and upset after meeting with a client, he feels slightly hungry. Seeing a doughnut store, he goes in, but before ordering, he grabs the roll of fat around his waist between his thumb and index finger and squeezes it. He

experiences a conflict between his desire for the doughnut and the fat he feels between his fingers. He feels the
tension in his chest and throat as well as a fleeting sense
of nausea. He responds by thinking, "I know I shouldn't
do this but I really am working hard today and I need
a break..." (justification) followed by "I've taken two
of these breaks this week ... I'm so bad ... I have no
willpower. ... " (self-blame). He immediately responds
to this tension and inner criticism by buying a muffin.
He eats it, feels some sense of fullness, followed by a loss
of tension. Driving away, he berates himself again for
being weak, helpless, and unable to even avoid eating a
muffin. This final decrease in tension caused by eating
simply reinforces this type of behaviour for the future.

The Beginnings of Change

Everyone has the potential to change. Change may be painful,
but remaining the same can leave you in a state of silent des-
peration. You cannot expect to change immediately, however. It
takes time to absorb new ideas and to see how they apply to
you.

As a psychoanalyst, I spend a great deal of time helping
people get "unstuck" from the conversations, beliefs, and feelings that guide and create meaning in their lives. The first step
is always the same – to reflect on and to become aware of the
inner conversations that guide our actions. By taking the
opportunity to ask ourselves "why," we can discover the pre-
conceived beliefs we have about ourselves.

Since most of your inner conversations happen very quickly in the back of your mind, you may not yet be able to relate to
what is described in this chapter. The next chapter is about
slowing down your inner conversations, just enough that you
can begin to speak to yourself in an empathetic and compas-

sionate manner. It is not a question of needing more willpower. That's the diet solution. To succeed you must get to know what you say to yourself, what effect your comments have on your chance for success, and how to slowly rewrite the inner dialogue, using what we call your "inner compassionate voice."

1. Remember, the biggest problem with going on someone else's diet is that it is someone else's diet. The foods you choose to eat must be based on your habits, taste preferences, and desires.

2. By getting to know your inner conversation, you will be able to stop and listen instead of simply reacting and failing.

3. It is not the event but what you say to yourself about the event that determines what you think, feel, and eventually do.

4. First you make your habits and then your habits make you.

Listening to
your inner conversation

Just as we often have trouble really listening to others, listening to our inner conversation can be difficult in the face of life's distractions. In this chapter, we show how you can listen to and begin to change your inner conversation. To do this, you need to do the opposite of what you have probably done instinctively many times before. In the past, you may have tried to force yourself into shape with the help of the latest diet plan, regimented exercise program, or well-meaning nutritionist, but since these methods failed to take into consideration the inner you, they ultimately failed. Only when you make change from the inside out will you succeed in directing your thoughts and emotions. Only when you listen carefully to your inner conversation will the way you feel and think change. Only with self-compassion and self-understanding will you create the opportunity for a new you.

Knowing Yourself: The First Step

Self-knowledge gives you both the freedom and the power to make choices. Let's examine some of the reasons why you may have failed in the past and how you might be less overwhelmed now. To do this, we will use two techniques: meditation and deep breathing. These techniques do not require that you become a guru or invest hours learning and practising them. They require only a small amount of your time during which you will move your mind to a place in which you can begin to make the choices you want.

Ellen – "I want to be different, now!"

One day, Ellen walked into my office, sat down, and immediately reached for my couch pillow to cover her stomach. Obviously uncomfortable, with the pillow hiding her anxiety, her first comment was that one of my paintings was hanging crooked on the wall. Ellen asked if I had noticed it. Suddenly I felt on edge. At this point I did two things – I checked my inner conversation and was aware that I felt guarded and had a brief urge to defend myself. I resisted this urge and looked at the painting. Ellen was right: it was crooked, but only slightly so.

As our conversation progressed, Ellen explained that during her twenties, weight was not an issue for her. She jogged regularly and even became a marathon runner. In her early thirties, after the birth of her first child, however, her weight began to haunt her. Finding it hard to be a working mother and still have time to run, she stopped exercising altogether. By then she had gained 30 pounds.

As she spoke, Ellen repeated certain expressions, telling me what she "should have done" and how "wrong" she was to have done certain things and how now it was "too late" for her to change. I slowly repeated her statements back to her and asked her how she felt. She replied that she felt sad and a little hopeless. I then asked where she felt sad and hopeless. "What does that mean?" she barked back. Again, I listened to my inner voice. As I took a breath, I was aware of feeling attacked. I soon realized how wrong Ellen felt about herself when she didn't know how to do something that may be an obvious solution.

Although I had not had an opportunity to ask Ellen about her diet, I could guess how she would speak to herself on any weight-loss plan and how she would start any structured program. Her inner conversations would be critical, focusing on what she believed was wrong with herself, and her inner conversations would be fearful in moments of uncertainty. Unless she recognized her self-critical, perfectionist inner conversation, the plan, program, or nutritionist wouldn't make any difference — Ellen would fail. At overwhelming moments, her thoughts of hopelessness and sadness would lead her to her usual food choices. She would be trapped.

Ellen's natural response was to pummel herself into shape. She hoped that through self-criticism and self-attack she could change her ways. Instead, by learning to actively watch and bend her thoughts, rather than passively letting her thoughts guide her life, Ellen soon began to take charge of her health and fitness goals.

How Meditation Helps

Automatic inner conversations are like flies in a room. Although we can hear them buzzing around us, we get only a brief glimpse of them as they zoom by. To catch a glimpse of inner conversations, we must slow them down. Although we cannot stop our inner conversations midstream, we can try to transform them from flies into butterflies. Butterflies may not remain still for long but at least we can follow their rhythmic patterns. One way to gently slow down our inner conversation is through meditation.

Meditation is an ancient method of watching or focusing on something so that you can experience your true being. Although this may sound very spiritual and esoteric, it is not. It is a powerful tool that allows you to relax, turn down your inner conversation, be calm, and gather insights into how you view the world. Meditation is effective for times when you feel overwhelmed by thoughts. It is just as powerful when you are unmotivated, unconcerned, or uninterested in your health. Meditation creates an inner space in which you can slow down and observe your inner conversation. By pausing, you can choose how to react to your inner conversation instead of simply repeating old responses to thoughts and feelings. This moment of opportunity allows you to respond in a new way.

How to Meditate

To begin, sit in a comfortable chair, loosen any tight clothing, and focus on your breathing. Start by simply paying attention to the coming in and going out of your breath. You might find it easier to follow your breath as it passes by the tip of your nostril, or to follow the movement of your chest or stomach. Take a few moments to find what works best for you.

As you being to focus your attention inward, notice what distracts you. You may feel mildly overwhelmed and sense some pressure in your throat or chest. Simply watch this shift. It might be only a brief, faint recognition of your breathing. If you find that it is difficult to find your breath or that you are too tense, take two or three deep breaths and then go back to watching your breathing.

Now count your breaths. A breath has three parts — an inhalation, a pause, and an exhalation. Begin by saying the word "Inhale" as you breathe in, and counting on the exhalation: "Inhale... one." As you take in your next breath, say to yourself, "Inhale," then exhale "two." "Inhale... three... inhale... four... inhale... five...." Try to let the words last most of the breath. For example, as you're breathing in, say to yourself, "I...n...h...a...l...e...," spreading it across the entire breath. As you exhale, spread out the number. Allow your breath to guide how quickly you count and say "Inhale." There is no right speed, only your speed.

What else are you aware of as you count? Maybe you feel the tickle of your nose hairs. Try to be aware of your attention shift. If your attention goes elsewhere, and you miss counting a breath, go back to your counting, starting again at the beginning – "Inhale... one... inhale... two..." and so on. It is natural for your mind to jump around, so gently go back to your counting as your mind shifts. Try to do this exercise for one minute. Then, work up to five, 10, or even 15 minutes a day. You choose how long you want to meditate.

While you are counting, you will notice your inner conversation. You might notice that you are asking yourself questions at the same time as you are counting your breaths. Take note of this. Sit for a minute or two. Continue counting. You don't need to look for your inner conversation; you will become aware of it. Take each moment as it comes. It might bring an awareness of anxiety, fear, sadness, loneliness, joy, pleasure, or desire (even for food). Don't try to change things. Simply sit and follow each moment with an active awareness.

Ellen's story continues

Ellen found it easy to meditate in my office. But when she tried to meditate at home, her inner critic left her feeling upset and frustrated, telling her how she was failing in some sense. As a result, Ellen felt she wasn't learning and wasn't good enough. Feeling inadequate, she considered quitting meditation. All this time, she was missing the fact that the measure was inside herself.

Being Aware... Not Being a Judge

You may find that when you begin to watch and count your breaths, you begin to breathe quickly. Or you may notice a pressured feeling in your chest — an anxiety in your mind. You are simply seeking an awareness of these automatic experiences. Your experience is now expanding. These same feelings may precede any of your overwhelming moments. By getting to know them, you will be able to respond in a new way. For example, you can respond by using a simple shift in language. Instead of saying "I am anxious" or "I am sad," you can say, "I am aware of anxiety" or "I have sadness." This language shift is effective to use during overwhelming moments since it enhances your ability simply to observe an emotion and not to judge it.

By using meditation and the technique of stating your awareness of certain urges, you can begin to step back and observe your experience. This technique allows you to keep your perspective. By focusing on this moment and recognizing that you're aware that you want some chocolate, you acknowledge the urge directly. Often, simply by acknowledging it, you will lose some of this desire or feeling. You might also find it helpful to say your acknowledgments aloud.

At other times, you can use meditation to observe your inner conversation. When you feel the urge to eat, to not exercise, or when you experience any other overwhelming moment, simply count your breaths. Regardless of the situation, by counting, you ground yourself in the moment. Once you are counting your breaths, you can begin to watch your inner conversation. Meditation is not just a practice to use for five to 15 minutes a day but rather it is an opportunity to stop and observe where you are in any moment at any point during the day.

Be Patient

Don't give up if you find meditation awkward at first. Any time you take a lesson or learn or practise something new, you are awkward at first and stumble over things. Don't be impatient with yourself. Resist the urge to flip ahead in the book and find the diet, rationalizing that all this breathing seems overwhelming. The urge to flip ahead and find the answer is your diet-seeking voice. Acknowledge it for what it is, and label it by saying, "I am aware of my diet-seeking voice."

When you try something new, many of your questions are based in uncertainty: "Will this help?" "Am I doing it right?" "What else could I do?" You can expect to have these inner conversations when you start any new activity — whether you are dieting, lowering your fat intake, exercising, or trying to lower your cholesterol or blood pressure.

Deep Breathing

To attain your health-promoting goals, you cannot force yourself to change — you can only gently bend through experience. By telling yourself how you *should* be, you are denying how you *are* in this moment. This difference between who you are and who you think you should be will inevitably make you tense and insecure. By changing the way you breathe, you can change the way you feel, think, and act. Diaphragmatic or deep breathing can be an effective technique to use when you are about to act in a way that makes you feel ashamed or self-destructive. Whether it is a tension-filled, overwhelming moment or a moment in which you lack interest or motivation to make a healthy choice, this technique can help you stop and choose to act differently.

Deep breathing clears away all the stale carbon dioxide from your lungs and gives you a fresh supply of oxygen. This process clears your mind, lowers your anxiety, and gives you a burst of energy. You can then either continue with the deep breathing or turn to meditation and counting your breaths and become aware of your inner feelings and thoughts. These two techniques help you become a witness to your experience. They will also create a pause in which you can change your response.

How to Practise Deep Breathing

To learn this technique, lie on the floor, a bed, or a hard, flat couch. Place your right hand on your chest and your left hand on your stomach just above your navel. Take in a deep breath through your nose, imagining your lungs filling up. Your left hand should rise while your right hand should move only slightly. This movement indicates that you are using the most neglected lower part of your lungs. As you breathe in, you may become aware of a tightness in your throat or a tenseness in your chest or back. This feeling will come and go. Breathe out through your mouth, making sure that you blow out all the air. Continue this process but as you breathe in through your nose, say to yourself, "Cool air in." Each time you slowly breathe out through your mouth, say, "Warm air out." Saying these words slowly will regulate your breathing. When you are starting out, try to take four seconds on the breath in, pause, and then take at least four seconds on the breath out. Take only one or two deep breaths to start. At first you may find it difficult to blow out all the air. The trick is simply to keep blowing out until you can't do it any more.

When you can perform this exercise in a reclining position, you are ready to use it in other situations. One of my colleagues uses this technique each time she stops at a red light. She uses the time to practise three or four deep breaths. You can practise anywhere, although you shouldn't take more than three deep breaths when operating equipment such as a car.

When you are aware of your breathing and can practise

watching your inner conversation, you are living in the moment. Start by doing this exercise for one to five minutes a day and then increase the frequency as needed. Once you master this technique, even one or two deep breaths clear away your anxiety.

Find Your Anchor

Meditation and deep breathing are the anchors that will keep you on course. The waves of your inner conversation will inevitably rock your inner attention. For example, you will be drawn into not simply watching your inner conversation, but actually becoming involved in it. Simply take a few deep breaths, or simple meditative, counting breaths.

Sometimes late at night you might be lonely or frustrated that you can't sleep, or are feeling tense about work. At these times you might be drawn to food. By practising your chosen anchor – deep breathing or meditative breathing – you will not be forcing yourself to change, nor will you be repeating the destructive past. Instead, you will be watching your present unfold in that moment or witnessing the experience. By using your breathing as an anchor, you will witness yourself in action and will experience the thoughts, feelings, images, and ideas that cross your mind in that moment. You can watch yourself become overwhelmed and your inner conversation shift. This witnessing is what you are trying to achieve.

Back to Ellen's Story

As you recall, Ellen's independent attempts at meditation were unsuccessful. She found it difficult to observe her inner conversation in a non-judgmental manner, and became anxious or fatigued during the first moments of her meditation.

When she tried deep breathing, however, Ellen began

to experience less concern over whether she was doing it right. Calm periods began to intersperse with her sense of judgment and urgency. At other times, she'd be caught off guard by some thought, concern, or image. Gently, she'd return her focus to following her breathing.

After three weeks of practising deep breathing and meditation daily, Ellen noticed how much time she spent each day wondering whether she was doing something right. She recognized her constant sense of urgency to get somewhere in a hurry. Ellen was demonstrating the enlightenment step. She was now actively listening to her inner dialogue. Ellen recognized that her fatigue was linked to a growing sense of hopelessness about being able to do anything. Her fears that she'd never get it right were followed by the urge to escape into sleep.

Getting to know your inner conversation is not a process that has a conclusion. Rather, it is an ongoing, unfolding experience much like long-term success at weight loss, exercise, a career, or a relationship.

In terms of Ellen's situation, we had yet to discuss her eating habits. Now that she knew the inner conversation that led to her failures, it was time to have this discussion. Ellen's homework was to make notes on her inner thoughts during a binge or a meal. At the next session, Ellen referred to having had a cookie binge the previous week. She had forgotten to do her note-taking, however, and could remember very little of her inner conversation. I suggested that she keep a pad of paper in her pocket and write down her inner conversation. The following week she referred to having had a double portion of chili, rolls, and a chocolate bar for dinner as well as other binges but just a brief thought that she should record them.

Now it was time for her to bring her deep breathing into her daily life. I explained that, unlike meditation, deep breathing is a much more direct approach. She would take slow, deep breaths in and out, reciting "cool air in and warm air out." Five consecutive breaths were usually enough to help her slow down during overwhelming moments. During the next week, she wrote the words "cool air in, warm air out" on a piece of paper and attached it to her fridge and cupboard doors. As she felt herself slipping into an overwhelming moment, she immediately took five deep breaths. I also suggested that she practise deep breathing during the day — on her way to a meeting, while talking on the phone, or working on her computer.

Over the next week, Ellen added deep breathing to her daily activities. On one occasion, she noticed that she had been feeling frustrated with a document she was trying to finish. Realizing that she was feeling tense, she feared she would not complete it on time. Earlier she had attached a note to her computer on which she had written "cool air" as a reminder to deep-breathe. So she took five slow, deep breaths. Still feeling some tension, she noticed that her breathing had become shallow. With a further release of her tension, the thought "I'd like a bowl of ice cream" flashed through her mind. The deep breathing had slowed her down and placed her in the witnessing position. Ellen had just witnessed how her anxieties about finishing work could be temporarily relieved by eating ice cream. By breathing and observing her inner conversation, she was able to link her impatience with herself at completing her work and the act of eating ice cream. She recognized that the soothing, cool food would calm her inner fears and uncertainties.

In the past, Ellen would have failed to recognize this link. All she knew was that she often ate ice cream while she was working. She also knew that she felt bad about herself and that she "should" be stronger. Self-blame, "shoulds," and regrets hid her feelings of uncertainty and fears about her document. Only when Ellen discovered her impatience with herself did she begin to choose between eating or reducing her work tensions with alternatives such as phoning a friend, doing sit-ups, taking a quick aerobic break, or reassuring herself that "This is the rate at which I work and I have succeeded in the past."

During the week, she noticed other elements of her conversation — "What a long day ... I'll just order a pizza and watch television." In the past, she would have accepted this moment of permission. Now she wondered if she could reward herself in another way. At other times, she experienced less success. Impatient, depleted, and worried, she angrily ate a bag of potato chips. Although she was better able to listen to her conversation, she was still too overwhelmed to change her final action.

Your *Groundhog Day* Can Be Every Day

The movie *Groundhog Day* tells the story of a man who relives the same day over and over. The turning point occurs when he begins to look at what has gone wrong in his day and tries to determine what else might work. By observing his errors and discovering what he must change, he is freed from this repetitive pattern.

You might also find yourself in the same situation day after day. Think of your health struggles as your personal "Groundhog Day." Every day you wake up and turn off the alarm instead of getting up to exercise; you eat the same late-afternoon snack; you smoke "just one more cigarette" when you're in a bar; you eat an extra serving of dinner for the third time this week; and so on. All of these activities repeat themselves each day or several times a week, and you react with the same surprise, regret, and promises for the future.

Activators

Activators are moments that awaken or activate the same over-whelmed or tense feelings and lead you to impulsive eating. An activator can be a situation, a person, or a feeling. By discovering your activators, you can then develop early warning systems that will give you time to make other choices. For example, if you can predict that going to a buffet leads to overeating, you can prepare for and change your reaction.

Freud once said, "Sometimes a cigar is just a cigar." However, food is rarely just food. Every snack situation awakens inner feelings, thoughts, needs, memories, and concerns. Each overwhelming moment has the typical characteristics of an inner conversation — "shoulds," justifications, and anxiety. Listen for them in your inner conversation.

THREE ACTIVATORS:
SITUATIONS, PEOPLE, AND FEELINGS

The three main activators for your automatic way of eating are situations, people, and your feelings. Ask yourself what your activators might be and take note of them. Later, we'll discuss how you can change your actions.

Let's first examine situation activators. A situation is an event that awakens memories. For example, as you get out of bed on a cold winter morning to exercise on your stationary bike, the cold floor triggers the thought, "I'm too tired to work out" — and you give in and go back to bed. Recognizing that this happens each day challenges you to accept that this process is how you always begin your work-out.

Another example of a situation that might activate your eating is a visit to your parents' home. As soon as you enter the house, you automatically open the refrigerator door and snack on a few items. Events such as visiting your parents awaken feelings and memories. By opening the refrigerator door and indulging, you reawaken your sense of belonging — of feeling safe, wanted, and cared for. In these situations, not eating means denying yourself more than a snack — it means depriving yourself of the other good feelings that accompany it.

Some other examples of situation activators that can cause automatic negative reactions include sitting at home feeling lonely; making dinner for the family and tasting everything; watching certain television shows; attending a celebration; paying bills; or doing laundry. By becoming aware that these situations cause an automatic reaction such as turning to food, you can begin to change your actions.

Let's now look at how some people contribute to your need to eat. Here are some examples that our clients have given us:

- "Jogging with a friend who is in much better shape. After working out with this person I feel inactive and a failure."
- "My boss, when he yells at me."
- "My mother, who makes me angry."
- "My overweight bridge group."
- "My ex-spouse, whenever we talk on the phone."
- "My best friend, who is always doing things better than me."

These examples refer to people who trigger inner conversations. In your life, who awakens feelings of anger, frustration, or sadness? By learning to recognize those people who activate concerns about your competency or value, and by getting to recognize the link between the feelings and the urge to eat, you will be prepared to deal with these situations by applying the strategies in Chapter 4. Often it is preferable to settle struggles with people by using assertiveness techniques that will leave you feeling competent instead of frustrated and in search of a food reward. You can learn these techniques from books such as *When I say no, I feel guilty* by Manuel J. Smith (Bantam 1975).

Finally, feelings can lead you to eat poorly or to ignore your exercise goals. For example, you may eat bread to ease feelings of loneliness or indulge in ice cream when you are bored or feeling deprived of fun. By soothing the feeling with food, you create a temporary, damaging solution to a deeper difficulty.

Everyone has feelings they don't tolerate well. These feelings can be joy, love, or closeness, or the more "negative" feelings such as loneliness, anger, or envy. If you don't believe that you should have a certain feeling, you will be quick to eliminate it.

If you don't feel you are allowed to be angry with someone, you may eat instead of expressing your feelings. One of my clients cannot experience intimacy without feeling as if he is on the verge of humiliation. When he feels close to another person, he imagines the foods he will eat when he gets home and thereby psychologically separates himself from the intimate situation. When he arrives home, he indulges his urges.

Often, we eat to eliminate painful feelings such as anger or hurt. However, by trying to push away these unrecognized wants and acting impulsively, we never truly get what we need. As a result, we are not satisfied. By watching for activators, we can begin to identify and listen to the fears, concerns, and needs that lead to our eating choices.

Your feelings affect not only your weight loss but also your overall health and fitness plan. Commitments to exercising regularly, increasing your fibre, getting enough calcium to decrease your risk of osteoporosis, or even eating cruciferous vegetables such as broccoli and cauliflower, are actions that you might avoid because of your feelings while making these choices. J.B.'s story provides such an example.

J.B.'s Choice

J.B. always ate at meetings, buffets, weddings, or any other occasion where food was available. At first he would make a healthful, weight-loss choice, but soon he would desire high-fat food, experience tension, and, eventually, eat the food. When he stopped to examine his feelings after making the healthful choice, he realized that he always noticed someone else, usually an overweight person, eating the high-fat food. In response, he would feel tense and experience cravings for the food, until he'd indulge. Using deep breathing, his tense feelings calmed and he began to watch his feelings. He recognized that he felt jealous and greedy and that he wanted the high-fat food because others had it. To help himself stand back and witness this, he did deep breathing and said to himself, "I am aware of being jealous and greedy." Once he recognized this experience, much of his frustration for wanting the high-fat food began to dissipate. Then, he challenged himself to make a 15-minute commitment to not indulge and see how his feelings evolved. Again, using deep breathing, he lowered his tension level and followed this by watching and labelling the unknown feeling that, in the past, had led to his eating.

Identifying Real Needs

Knowing what you need frees you to consider alternatives to eating. By recognizing that eating is a way of eliminating a painful feeling or of dealing with a deeper need, you free yourself to choose non-food solutions. You no longer face a question of just eating or not eating. Eating is simply one of many solutions.

By practising meditation and deep breathing, you can develop a tension-reduction switch that will slow you down enough to look deeply into your inner conversation. There you will find deeper needs and desires than those for food. For example, Barb described how when she got off the phone with her mother, she was often quite angry. Not knowing how to deal with her feelings, she found herself in the kitchen with her hand in the cookie jar. Taking a deep breath, she recognized that she had no conscious recollection of picking up the cookies, nor did she know why she was going to eat them. A few meditative, counted breaths and she was able to say, "I'm not hungry." She added, "I'm not going to eat so I don't feel angry. It's okay to just be angry."

Once you discover what needs, fears, concerns, or desires make you eat, you can begin to consider alternatives to eating. For example, if you realize that you eat when you are lonely, you can ask yourself if eating is the best solution to lonely feelings. What are your alternatives? There may be one that is in your better interest. Next time you find yourself reaching for a snack, you can slow down your inner conversation with your breathing, then stand back and make your best choice. You will no longer face the overwhelming feeling that you must either meet your desire to eat or feel deprived.

During these tense inner conversations when you try to identify what you need, take a few deep breaths and ask yourself these questions:

- What do I need?
- What am I afraid of?
- What are my desires at this moment?
- Can I think of three alternatives that might satisfy this need?
- What will I need to do to satisfy this need?

See whether a thought or idea flashes through your mind. Consider it for a moment. Take a deep breath and try again. The right answer will feel right or close to being accurate. Let it settle in for a moment and then begin to think of solutions or alternatives. For example, food is only one option to satisfy loneliness. A good book or movie, a warm conversation, or a visit with a friend, are other options.

To better understand your feelings, use your breathing and ask yourself questions such as:

- What frightens me about this feeling?
- Where in my body do I feel it?

- What can I do to change the feeling?
- If I don't eat, what is the worst thing that will happen?
- What do I imagine I'll start to feel if I don't eat?

Then, try something completely different from eating and see how you feel.

These questions may help you identify your real needs and spark possible alternatives or solutions. Let your breathing anchor you.

1. What do I need? You might find out by completing the statement,

   "What I really need right now is _____."

2. What do I wish would happen? Let yourself imagine various situations.

3. How do I want what's happening now to be different?

4. Is there an unpleasant feeling I want to eliminate? What is it?

5. What are two other ways I could satisfy this need?

6. I don't think I'd be feeling this way if _____ were happening. Look at your answer. See what need is hidden within it.

Dr. Simon's Patient: Who Was Late?

Let's end our discussion about inner conversation and its effects with an example. A patient once forgot that we had changed the time of our session to 15 minutes later than usual. When he accused me of being late, I reminded him about the change. He then told me that while he was waiting, he began to feel that no one cared about him.

"As each minute passed outside," he explained, "I was deciding what to have for lunch." I pointed out that his need to be "cared about" was not the same as his urge for food. He replied that if it was the same, he'd be the most cared-for person in the world! His urge for food passed. Instead, he was left with a deeper sense of longing to be special in someone's eyes. This was the need behind the food solution. Sometimes insights and wisdom leave you sad.

1. A gentle bend, not a forceful break leads to permanent change.
2. Stop and listen to your inner self — not with the goal of doing but with the goal of being with yourself.
3. The stillness of your conversation will vary over time. It is critical to remember that who you are is not the same each moment — who you are changes. This is a key to enlightened health. To fit yourself into a box is to force yourself to break out.
4. You cannot control a feeling once it has taken hold, but you can be sure that it will rise in intensity, fall, and then vanish.
5. The first step of enlightenment is witnessing and listening for your conversation — finding out where you are, not where you think you should be.
6. Deep breathing complements your daily counting meditation. You can use it to reawaken your meditative state when you are being confronted by your daily challenges with eating, exercise, and disease prevention.
7. The Deep-Breath Stress-Breaker
   • Take a single deep breath and hold it for five to seven seconds.
   • Blow it out completely to relieve your tension.
     (If you suffer from heart disease, stroke history, or severe hypertension, don't do the deep-breath stress-breaker.)
8. Gentleness and compassion are the great lessons in meditation. Our minds wander without any encouragement so we must gently let go of the focused thought and return to breath-counting. In many of our experiences, we force and demand when a gentle move is all that is necessary. In overwhelming moments, a compassionate

recognition of our desire goes a long way to easing the force of our inner demand.

9. You can't buy a fire extinguisher and expect to use it effectively after the fire has started. Similarly, if you wait until you are in an overwhelmed place to try deep breathing, it will not work very well. You must be familiar with this practice and how to do it. Find times throughout your day when you can practise taking three to five deep breaths or a couple of stress-breaker breaths.

10. Some Critical Activators that Lead to Overeating

feeling unloved

feeling anxious or restless

feeling happy

feeling angry or jealous

feeling tired

feeling disappointed or rejected

feeling depressed

Creating Your Own
Success Formula

In Chapter 3, you learned how to listen to your inner conversation and how to identify situations, people, or feelings that awaken your tendencies to feel overwhelmed. You learned to slow your inner conversation using meditation and deep breathing so you could listen to your inner concerns, fears, and needs. Having done this, you are now better prepared to discover other ways to satisfy your desires. This chapter will teach you to gently bend and stretch your mind so that you are psychologically prepared to make new wellness choices. This process will bring you one step closer to breaking through the barriers that keep you from making these concrete changes in your life.

Breaking these barriers is not something you do only once. Remember that the only moment in which you can truly change is the moment you are in right now. Regardless of how clear your inner conversation becomes, you will always have choices: "Will I eat the high-fibre cereal or the scrambled eggs?" "Will I exercise or watch television?" To live in this moment, you must first recognize it. Feeling "day-after guilt" or promising to "start tomorrow" don't help. Neither does beating up yourself psychologically because you gave in to your old

ways. These responses only leave you feeling hopeless and pow-
erless to change. We are creatures of habit; we often react to
situations without a second thought. We may have an urge for a
food and, before we know it, we are indulging. When this happens — and it will — it is important to remember that such laps-
es do not make you a bad person. You simply need to keep
trying to overcome your habits.

Tools for Change

To overcome your habits, you need subtle and sometimes not-
so-subtle reminders of your goals. First, visual reminders can
be very effective. For example, a ribbon attached to the door
handle of your refrigerator or cupboard can remind you of
your weight-loss goals, or a ribbon tied to your exercise bicycle
can remind you to exercise. Initially, when you notice this
reminder, take two or three slow deep breaths to overcome the
desire of the moment. (If you are self-conscious about what
others might think of these visual reminders, relax. Most people don't even notice them or, if they do, they simply ask if
they work.)

Second, deep breathing is another powerful tool to overcome desires. An anxious inner conversation often evokes automatic actions. By taking a slow, deep breath, you awaken your
conscious ability to modify your actions by placing yourself in
a slowed-down state. You will then be better able to successfully change your actions.

Third, visualization is a powerful tool for change. It is the
act of creating a source of hope and renewal through an internal vision of a realistic, hoped-for you. It is a concerted effort to
renew your love affair with your body. When making health
decisions, a calm, realistic, and confident image becomes a battery of hope from which to draw in emergency blackouts of
direction. Instead of just thinking about your goals, plans, and

solutions, you create a detailed blueprint for success in your mind.

Visualizing is also the natural complement to setting goals. Goal setting strengthens your thinking while visualizing encourages your emotions and enthusiasm. Visualization helps to fuel your hard work — whether your goal is running a marathon, becoming a vegetarian, improving your game of tennis, or remembering to take your vitamins.

VISUALIZATION

Visualization is performed in a relaxed, meditative state. Whether you begin with meditation, deep breathing, or the deep-breath stress-breaker, visualization is achieved through the release of tension. You can practise visualization anytime or anywhere just by taking a few deep breaths.

How to Visualize

Find a comfortable chair, sit outside on the grass, or lie on the carpet. Begin by doing your deep breathing. Take in a deep breath through your nose, making sure the lower part of your lungs expands. You'll know if you've achieved this if your stomach comes out as you breathe in. Don't force it. Just notice if it seems to move gently outwards. To assist this, focus on the area just above your belly button and imagine it filling up, expanding, and your belly expanding downward. If you find it difficult to focus on your stomach, place your hand above your belly button and watch it rise. As you breathe out, blow out through your mouth. Use the saying, "cool air in, warm air out" as a timing technique. Five slow, deep breaths begin to break the tension and place you in a more receptive state.

Begin by focusing visually on an image of a place or a person you know. As you breathe out, allow the image to come to mind. Don't force it. Pause for a few moments and try to bring the image to mind. Don't be discouraged if at first you cannot perform this step. Even if the image is unstable, fuzzy, or fades, this is still a useful exercise. If you find yourself forcing this image, return to your deep breathing or the big breath. The image may change or disappear.

If you find it hard to imagine a place or a face, focus instead on a number. Think of the number seven. Close your eyes and try to see it in your mind's eye. You will likely experience an outline — a grayness, a shadow of the number.

If you find this exercise difficult, try this alternative, which uses the kinesthetic sense. Try to develop an awareness of your body — your posture or movement. Close your eyes and begin by becoming aware of where your feet are resting. Feel them touching the floor. Notice your back leaning against the chair, your head's position on your neck, your chest, and your stomach. Now, return to your inner visualization and imagine your body standing up. Focus on the position of your head, neck, back, chest, stomach, thighs, calves, and feet. Go to your breathing as required during this early stage. This step brings the pleasure of newness and self-focusing.

You can use either the visual or kinesthetic means of visualization, drawing from whatever seems easier for you. Remember that there is no right way to do it. Visualizing is just one way of focusing mental energy on a specific task. The journey, rather than the destination, enables you to change.

What Is a Realistic Wellness Image?

Your wellness image is like a movie clip that captures how you hope to look, feel, and be. An unrealistic or exaggerated image will leave you feeling unsatisfied regardless of your success. A realistic wellness image, however, can lead to your success.

To choose an image, focus on a time when you were striving for a greater sense of well-being and success. It might have been in high school, at the top of a ski lift, or after a major achievement. If the image isn't positive, don't use it. Focus on a time when you felt good about yourself. You may be able to develop this image in detail. If the image is invigorating and reminds you of a physically possible you, it can become your wellness image.

Dr. Simon's Wellness Images

My two wellness images are dated in both time and context. In the first image, it's 1984 and I'm riding my stationary bike, wearing a pair of wine-coloured sweat pants, T-shirt, running shoes, and white socks. Sweat is pouring down my face as I push to reach the 55 km/hr mark on the speedometer. Bruce Springsteen music is blasting through my earphones, pushing me to travel the extra distance. My shoulders are pulled back, my chest is firm and my stomach is flat except for a small ridge around my middle where my shirt is tucked into my pants. My thighs and calves are firm and well developed. I have a satisfied smile on my face and a sense of accomplishment, pride, and power runs through my body. This image is more than 10 years old. Notice that while my upper body is not perfect, the image is in keeping with my wellness goals for that period of my life. This visualization was a realistic symbol — it was attainable. This is an important part of a successful visualization. This image focused my wellness desires for a year. Then I began the process of redefining my goals and my wellness image.

After five years on the program, my wellness image changed considerably. In this image, I'm wearing mirrored sunglasses, a black T-shirt, faded blue jeans, and high-cut jogging shoes that are encrusted with pine needles from the forest floor. My backpack is filled with trail mix. I jog up the hill. My pectoral muscles outline my chest, my shoulders are firm, and there is a V-shape to my upper body! My stomach is mostly flat but there is still a small area that bulges. My legs are firm and evenly developed. I feel a sense of calmness and serenity as I run up the hill. Reaching the top, I breathe deeply and smile as I look out on a still lake that reflects the surrounding mountains. This image is tied to my own personality. Although this image is quite different from my original visualization, both images reflect realistic, personal goals. The second image has a greater sense of holistic wellness that I could not have achieved without first attaining other intermediate plateaus of change.

I will not disclose my present image, which was developed in 1994, since I believe that it would lose energy and personal strength if I wrote about and discussed it. Once I decide that it no longer represents me or my evolving wellness commitment, I will change it.

FORMING A POSITIVE SELF-IMAGE

Your wellness image is a healthy, attainable picture that you have of yourself. To develop your wellness image, relax in a comfortable chair with a clipboard and pen in your lap and follow these steps:

Begin by imagining the setting for your wellness image. It could be a room, gym, special beach, skating rink, or forest — your own fantasy land. Don't spend too much time consciously developing an image. Simply allow an image to form. Choose the image that seems to be most harmonious with your goals. Open your eyes and briefly write down your wellness setting.

Next, imagine the body you are going to develop on your wellness program. Be realistic! Accept that you will never look exactly like Sharon Stone or Arnold Schwarzenegger. Instead, commit yourself to developing the best possible *you*. Be specific about this image. Become aware of your flexibility, the straightness of your back, your relaxed neck muscles, your expanded chest, your upper arms, your stomach, and your hips. View your thighs, calves, and buttocks in a realistic way. Remember that bulges, tummies, and thighs are all a part of being human. Imagine the clothes you would like to wear. Write down, in as much detail as you can, the physical aspects of your wellness image.

Note your facial expression. In your wellness image, hold your head high and smile with a glow of inner peace. Feel the energy and sense of wellness that radiates from you. Imagine your eyes reflecting your new sense of direction and accomplishment.

Establish how you feel physically. Follow the lines of your chest and feel it expanding as you take slow, deep, revitalizing breaths. Notice the contour of your back. Get up and move around. Feel the flexibility and strength in your legs and the gentle bounce in your walk that symbolizes a healthy new you. Feel your muscle tone, your body's flexibility, your slowed heart beat, and your fresh skin. Experience the sense of wellness when your body is in top physical shape.

Imagine how you will feel when you achieve your wellness goals. List the words, phrases, and thoughts that capture the new you: "alive," "serene," "joyous," "directed," "committed," "sensual," "centred," and so on. Write some affirmations about how good you feel.

Collect together all of these images, and create a unified wellness image. Remember to set a realistic, attainable image. Also remember that you will reset your wellness image as you attain your goals. If part of the image makes you feel anxious, stop and consider whether it is realistic. Some anxiety, however, may stem from your excitement at the prospect of change.

How to Use Your Wellness Image

With regular practice, you will be able to contact this calm, committed self at any time. Whenever you are anxious and overwhelmed, or find yourself drawn into a disease-promoting activity with overwhelming intensity, step back and focus on your wellness image. The more often you practise visualizing your wellness image, the more power it will have to calm and direct you. By discovering the power of visualization, you will have a powerful rudder.

At various times each day, you may be faced with mild uncertainty. This might happen while you are waiting in line in a cafeteria or a gym. You might be mulling over a menu looking for a healthful choice or deciding whether to walk for an extra 15 minutes. You can counter any moment of mild uncertainty or tension by taking a deep breath and focusing on your wellness image. Take a deep breath, smile, and visualize a "possible you" during these moments of indecision, and then pull it all together by making a health-promoting choice. Your deep breathing and visualization bring together both the inner and outer you, and the decision you are going to make.

Greg and the Hamburger Attack

Greg, a senior executive at a major corporation, found that he would regularly have the urge to order a hamburger and french fries to eat at his desk while working. Initially resisting this urge, he'd feel a sense of sadness as he ordered the vegetable platter and chicken sandwich. Giving in to this tension, he'd change his order. He would then feel ashamed but satisfied with his burger and fries. After learning to recognize the mild apprehension he experienced in this situation, Greg began his deep breathing and focused on his wellness image. He would continue to take slow, deep breaths, focusing on the image until his food arrived. Smiling, with his wellness image still strong in his mind, he would dig into his meal. By repeating this process, Greg was able to develop his wellness image and use it whenever he ordered food, thereby taking active control over this important aspect of his life.

The Next Step – Self-Talk

Self-talk is the step beyond simply observing your inner conversation. In this step you start to respond to your inner conversation. This section addresses how to permanently break free from a negative, self-degrading mindset. Like meditation, self-talk begins with the ideal of acceptance – what you think, feel, imagine, fantasize about, or even do, is what you are at this moment. Even if you attack yourself, that also is you.

It is important to recognize that acceptance and resignation are very different states. Resignation means feeling resigned to the fact that you will act on your inner conversation. Acceptance is standing back and seeing that it is simply how you feel now.

An Example of Acceptance

When I started doing yoga, my teacher would often call out from the back of the class, "Barry, straighten your leg." I heard this comment so often I began to think it was my last name. Each time I tried a new posture, I would end up having to bend my leg to copy what the teacher was doing. Finally, the instructor advised, "Barry, you aren't getting anything out of the posture if you bend your leg." But if I didn't bend my leg I'd barely be doing the posture, which was unacceptable to me since the rest of the class looked like pretzels in comparison. Even though I was only a beginner, I felt that I should be able to do the posture as well as an experienced person could. My ego – or more accurately my pride – was getting in the way. I was unwilling to accept what I was: a neophyte with little flexibility.

The same principle applies to any aspect of your wellness plan. If you believe that you should suddenly be free of old desires and urges, you will become discouraged and quit. Does this sound familiar? Imagine that you're eating a small order of French fries and you think, "I know I shouldn't be eating this," accompanied by a wave of tension and a flushed feeling. Then you think about the cookie you ate yesterday, and you feel even more guilty and ashamed, and believe that you'll never be able to follow a healthy diet. Your action has triggered a whole series of personal failings and experiences of yourself as weak and guilt ridden. You end the entire action, not with enjoying the fries, but with the thought, "I'll never succeed." Instead, if you accept where you are, you will be able to move ahead since your failure is typically based on non-acceptance, self-attack, and self-blame.

Revisiting Inner Conversations

To experience acceptance, say to yourself, "I am willing to accept this lapse but I truly want to learn from it." The next step — instead of self-blame or self-attack — is to determine what triggered this lapse. Was it a feeling, a person, or a situation? What inner conversation followed the lapse? What can you decide to do now if the same situation arises? Beware of simply saying, "It won't happen again." If it happened once, you can be confident that it will happen again. If it is a very common situation, write down a few strategies to keep in your wallet and take them out when the moment arrives. Always sign your name to your strategies; it increases your commitment.

One strategy I recommend is to keep a no-fat, ice-cream substitute with fewer than 50 calories per serving in the freezer as a substitute for more serious indulgences. Another strategy is to write down what you might say to someone who hurts your feelings or to call him or her and discuss the issue. Just don't fall into the trap of believing that one or two strategies will change everything right away.

By continually revisiting inner conversations you can begin to develop strategies that will help you change.

A common inner conversation involves going to the gym. You tell yourself, "I really should go, but I am a little tired." An image of all of those energetic people bouncing around flashes through your mind and a deep sense of fatigue sets in — "Why am I always pushing myself to go? Why can't I ever relax?" The image of physically fit people working out leaves you feeling weaker by comparison, left out, and not measuring up. You want to escape your feeling of inadequacy. Instead, choose an alternative — take a deep breath and say, "I recognize my fatigue but I am committed to my exercise plan."

Commit yourself to going to the gym. Before you get there, score your energy level on a scale from one to ten. When you are finished, repeat this exercise. You'll be surprised at how your renewed energy contradicts your earlier advice that "tired is no way to go to the gym."

If you are afraid that others will be more energetic than you, then commit yourself to letting the others energize you. If you hear the voice of embarrassment saying that everyone will be evaluating you with critical eyes, be assured that the only critical

A character we call self-righteous Sam provides another example. At lunch he says to himself, "I really want a hot dog. I'm doing pretty well. I already ran five miles this morning." He reaches under his jacket and feels his stomach. "I'm better off than 99 percent of the population. I can allow myself just one hot dog at lunch." Sam feels good about occasionally indulging in special treats for lunch. Slowly, however, this indulgence becomes more frequent — a couple of times a week. "There's nothing like sitting outside with one of these hot dogs," he says to himself. What is important here is not whether Sam indulges but that he justifies his actions by comparing himself to others, and by giving himself permission using superficial criteria. Sam fails to consider that a hot dog is filled with nitrates that damage his cells, which has little to do with physical appearance.

Sam has just used rationalization. His story also shows how a thought leads to an action and how it soon becomes a habit of eating a hot dog every day. Sam is a typical, healthy-on-the-outside person who uses only one indicator, his abdominal fat, to rationalize ignoring his health. Weight is never the only indicator of success.

eyes are your own. No one in a gym is looking just at you; they're too busy having their own inner conversations.

Julie and the 100 Percent Solution

Probably the most common inner conversation involves perfectionism, or living with an idealized expectation of yourself. Julie's story provides such an example. Her attitude was "If you can't do it 100 percent, then why do it at all?" She wished that every day was Monday because she imagined it would help restart each day and get it just right. As a first step to a better way, she began to generate a list of perfectionist, or all-or-nothing thinking. Then she identified several comments that fit into this category. We discussed setting smaller goals: 20 minutes of exercise a day instead of 30. Without hesitation, Julie commented that this seemed like a short period of time. In her mind, 20 minutes was not enough. Her inner conversation had convinced her what she *ought* to do, and it affected her ability to set small goals. Hearing herself, she took a deep breath, stood back, and listened to these thoughts.

We found many other examples such as: "I need to exercise first thing in the morning or else I won't bother," or "I try to figure out what's the right time ... " with the unspoken idea "...or else I don't do it." These comments all have an all-or-nothing characteristic. I suggested that she consider what the second or even the third best time would be. Later she commented, "If I don't eat right in the morning, I feel lost and lose my enthusiasm." I suggested that the "lost" feeling was a result of no longer being perfect. After we identified several other incidents, she joked, "Being perfect is a full-time job." In later sessions we worked to shift Julie's thinking so she could develop a positive self-image and have a realistic response to these inner conversations.

SIMPLE STRATEGIES FOR STAYING AWARE OF YOUR INNER CONVERSATION

Be aware of your thinking style. Take a deep breath or, if you're too tense, take a big breath and say to yourself, "I am aware of _____," filling in the blank with the way you're thinking. You might choose one of the following:

> — I am aware of "all-or-nothing" thinking.
> — I am aware of having perfectionist ideals.
> — I am aware of the voice of procrastination.
> — I am aware of blaming myself.
> — I am aware of feeling weak and tired.

To identify your thinking style I recommend that you begin by smiling. Take the exercise seriously but don't take yourself too seriously. To distance yourself from your inner conversation you might find it helpful to write down:

My inner conversation:

The thinking style:

Once you have labelled your thinking style with a tag such as "blaming myself" or, in Julie's case, "all-or-nothing thinking," count how often you use this thinking style each day. You may do it while writing a letter, speaking to a group of people, talking to your children, or during intimate moments. By counting the number of times it happens, you will help to place further distance between the thought and the automatic action.

Now develop two *other* ways of thinking about the situation such as the following:

"It might not be perfect but overall it seems quite good. There aren't any complaints."

"That's not perfect but it certainly is a good attempt. It's a lot better than doing nothing."

A good alternative thought is one that offers a compromise and supports the positive but also acknowledges that nothing is perfect.

Combine deep breathing with the "I am aware of" exercise to help you recognize and stand back from other inner experiences, besides those already mentioned. Use this technique for unrecognized needs, feelings, images, desires, or urges. Next time you find yourself picking up a chocolate bar, take a moment to ground yourself in this moment. Take a couple of slow, deep breaths and say to yourself or out loud (try both options to see which one works better for you), "I am aware of..." Answers can be as simple as:

- I am aware of anxiety...
- I am aware of a desire for...
- I am aware of a tired feeling...
- I am aware of a chocolate bar in my hand...
- I am aware of an urge to order a pizza...

Staying on Your Journey to Health and Fitness

Feeling that you lack direction or the ability to guide yourself is a common experience when it comes to promoting your health. One way to change your course is to imagine that you are the captain of your own health ship. Pretend that you are the captain of a ship in rough waters and the crew is frightened. When you start to hear the waves of "anxiety" or the "thoughts" of rough waters ahead, call out commands with conviction. Think of what you would say to reassure your crew that everything is under control. As you listen to your inner conversation, or head for the snack or veer away from exercising, you might make comments such as:

- "You can do it."
- "Stay with your breathing."
- "Just walk away from that refrigerator. You can do it."
- "I'm anxious and worried now, but it will pass."
- "Feel the fear and do it anyway."
- "Of course you're nervous. This is all new for you."

This exercise is a good motivational step when you feel you

can't follow your program. You may also find that it is a fun way to break tension. Some people take it one step further, seeing themselves as the captain of a pirate ship with a patch over one eye and a peg leg. If they start heading for the cookies, they walk with a limp!

Changing Your Response

Once you've recognized a part of your inner conversation, repeat it to yourself when it crosses your mind. Do not ignore it. Only by repeating will you learn to recognize it. For example, if you frequently think, "I don't have the energy to exercise," repeat the thought until you recognize it as simply an opinion that leads to the next thought: "I just need to go home and rest," followed by a sense of relief and greater fatigue. This recognition takes the thought out of the realm of automatic inner conversation. From here, you can use any of these exercises:

- Go to your wellness image to determine what you're looking for in terms of health.
- Hear the thought, ignore it, and just go and work out.
- Repeat the statement "I don't have the energy to work out" ... four or five times aloud.
- Challenge the statement by asking yourself:
  - "Is this true?"
  - "Do I need a certain energy to work out?"
  - "Do I ever get energy when I work out?"
- Choose an alternative – perhaps a modified version of your workout.

Many times when you feel overwhelmed and unable to stand back it is because your inner conversation has a physical component – perhaps as tension in your throat, chest, or back. Begin to rephrase by taking a few deep stress-breaking breaths to change your body's inner climate and make yourself more receptive to change. If your inner conversation tells you to put off a healthy choice until tomorrow, say to yourself, "I *could* do it tomorrow, but if I do part of it today I'll get a head start," or "But by doing it now I'll be one day ahead." By acknowledging you could start tomorrow, you don't set up an inner conflict. You acknowledge that option but then focus on the benefit of the new choice. Or say something more forceful, such as "I could do it tomorrow but I think I'll just do it now." There is no right way. It isn't the correctness of your wording that determines your outcome. The critical part is to stop and listen, and to consider alternatives. This step allows for the moment of choice.

If you regularly tell yourself how weak or pathetic you are, stop and ask yourself:

- "What are things I've done that show I'm not pathetic?"
- "What would someone else do in this very moment?"
- "I know I could do it. Am I willing to try?"

Write your responses in a small notebook. On another page, write your answers to the feeling you're having. By doing this, you challenge and diffuse your negative thoughts. You guide your health ship.

Many times you will find yourself struggling with something — opening the refrigerator, eating a Danish, using the treadmill. To help reframe your thoughts, you may need to ask yourself:

- "Are there other ways of looking at this situation?"
- "Are any of my typical ways of thinking during overwhelming moments crossing my mind or guiding my behaviour at this moment?"
- "What is another way to think about this?"

Dr. Simon's Self-Talk

Here is my favourite self-talk exercise. When I encounter a potentially overwhelming situation, such as the familiar surroundings of a fast-food restaurant, I say to myself, "My old friend McDonald's, where have you been? I know your food tastes great but I'm on my wellness program." Although this may seem like a silly comment, the crucial part is to greet the temptation like an old friend. It took one of my clients 18 months to do this step. He thought it was silly, and it is. But perhaps that's why it works.

If talking it through doesn't work for you, then maybe a visualization exercise will. By exaggerating the outcome, you see yourself carrying out the action, but you take it to an extreme. For example, if doughnuts or chocolates are your weakness, imagine yourself gobbling down a truck-load of them. Imagine yourself becoming fatter, buttons popping, clothes tearing, until finally you explode. Carry the situation to a ridiculous extreme – to the point where you smile and giggle. As a further example, when I exercise on my ski machine, I often don't feel up to the work-out. Tired or aggravated about something else, I just want to stop. But then I imagine myself with a huge pot belly, unsuccessfully trying to get up off the couch. I imagine myself trapped like a turtle on its back – legs flailing in the air. I smile and finish the work-out.

Developing Your Willpower

Probably the most underrated technique to change how we feel and think is to act differently – to make a conscious decision to change. Nowhere is this technique more successful than in a wellness program. Exercising, eating healthful foods, and taking vitamin supplements build a sense of confidence, well-being, and certainty. By actively choosing small tasks, we avoid two of the typical health-promotion failure situations:

- blindly accepting someone else's health plan – either the latest diet, prepared foods, or weight-loss clinic.

- the passive sense of helplessness that there is nothing we can do to help ourselves.

Both of these situations fail to develop our willpower — our own ability to direct, not impose, a way of life on ourselves.

Two things can develop your willpower: 15-minute commitments and action.

FIFTEEN MINUTES AT A TIME

Forever is a long time, but you can manage 15 minutes! When you decide to make a final and absolute change, each failure will make you feel resentful, angry, and disappointed.

Instead, make a 15-minute commitment. Every time you successfully complete a commitment, you build the foundation of your success story. You will also feel differently about yourself. Once you gain a sense of trust, you can move to a 30-minute, hour-long, or morning, afternoon, or daily commitment. Move slowly. Each successful commitment block is a powerful moment of building your willpower.

LIGHTS, CAMERA, ACTION

Your ability to direct your actions is like a muscle. The more you use it, the stronger it becomes. By taking even small steps, you show yourself that you can succeed. Doing something — anything — proves that you can be in control if you choose to. Small things such as walking away from a buffet or rushing to an exercise class increase your sense of dedication and commitment.

Often the act of doing something that a part of you doesn't want to do also frees up your inner energy. Committing yourself to action can shift you from a passive, helpless mindset to a motivated, enthusiastic one. This higher-energy mental state fuels future successful actions. Remember, no action is too small to help you move from despair.

Indecision can be more painful than actually choosing. Try this experiment when you have an urge that is filled with indecision: simply go with the clearest action. For example, if you are caught between a desire for a treat and what you should do on your health plan, simply take a deep breath and pick up the treat. Let it settle into your hand and see how you feel about it. Examine it, take a deep breath, and see how you feel. Don't rush to eat but experience it. Decide on your next action.

One of the most powerful will-builders is to do something you don't want to do and to do it every day. For example, if you don't feel like exercising, exercise. Set a reasonable goal, even if it means compromising your typical work-out, but get out there and see what happens. Use this technique next time you encounter a task that you dislike, one for which your automatic response is, "I'll do it later." Instead of feeling burdened or forced, feel free because you chose to do the activity.

Commit yourself to completing one chosen task every day. Note how you feel about yourself before and after you do it. Checking how you predict you'll feel and how you actually feel are important parts of gaining a more successful, confident you. You may find that your feelings are more positive and more energetic. For example: "Before the work-out I felt tired, run down, not interested, and could barely get up the four steps of the change room. Not short of breath, just short of enthusiasm." Afterwards: "I have a burst of energy. Great!" By acknowledging your achievements, you will also boost your self-confidence. The fastest, most effective way to overcome negative feelings is to commit yourself to doing something. Make it a reasonable goal. Don't wait to feel energized every day or to feel enthusiastic. Do something, and your enthusiasm and energy will follow.

The program in *Break the Weight-Loss Barrier* provides you with many choices. As you go through the program, decide what you can commit yourself to doing and make a 15-minute plan. Take the approach that any new action, any change in the way that you are, is a positive event. The accumulation of these small, realistic events will build your positive self-image and direct your successful journey to health and fitness.

Creating a Compassionate Inner Conversation

People often ask me what I believe is the essential ingredient for long-term success at your wellness and weight-loss goals. Without a doubt, the essential ingredient is beginning to speak to yourself with a compassionate voice. This first part of *Break the Weight-Loss Barrier* discussed how speaking to yourself in an attacking, perfectionist fashion leads to procrastination and quitting your latest diet or wellness plan. If you follow the steps we have outlined, compassion will begin to replace your harsh inner critic.

Compassion is not the same as positive thinking. Compassion demands that you understand deeply the situations, people, and feelings that trigger you to eat unhealthful foods, to not exercise, or to skip your daily vitamin commitments. By becoming aware of your inner conversations, a greater compassionate voice will develop. This voice will allow you to be less judgmental and better able to consider your deeper needs and desires.

Compassion will join forces with commitment to fuel this inner change. Your softer, less judgmental attitude will evolve into a voice that actively considers possibilities for realistic answers – a voice that accepts setbacks but always attempts to learn and be able to say "Next time I'll try this..." instead of simply berating or attacking. By having compassion we attain a level of deep acceptance of where we are really starting from.

This second aspect – the commitment to change – is the natural partner to compassion. Acceptance without a commitment to new goals quickly becomes resignation. To succeed in the long run, you need to achieve some sense of what we call a compassionate commitment. This requires that you understand and accept yourself while learning to set and re-evaluate your realistic health-promoting goals.

Some people have no difficulty committing themselves to restrictive programs but find it difficult to have compassion for their individual needs. They can set the goal of exercising six days a week but find it hard to deal with an injury or with those times when they feel sad or lonely or just tired. In the long run, simply committing yourself without compassion turns into resentment and eventual rebellion.

Others have compassion for their desires but little commitment to their bodies. They need to determine what benefits will fuel their renewed commitment to their body. In Part Two, James Meschino will introduce you to the concrete goals that will join with your growing compassion to create change. While reading the following section, ask yourself, "What will I gain by setting this goal?" Accept who you are and write down concrete, specific goals.

Carry your growing compassionate commitment into the next section of *Break the Weight-Loss Barrier*. Remember that who you are has all the potential for who you hope to grow into as long as you remain committed and compassionate to the full, authentic you. Good luck!

1. Feelings are not only the basis for setbacks and disappointments; they are also the source of your will to succeed. Some people believe that if they could just get rid of their feelings they'd be much better off. Nothing is further from the truth. Visualizing involves beginning a healing process, seeing your potential so you can move forward in your journey to better health and fitness.

2. The Big Squeeze
   There may be moments when you feel a general sense of tension. Deep breathing and the big breath are helpful but sometimes your body and muscles need a short extra exercise. To calm down, you can do a wilful squeeze.

(Not recommended for those with high or low blood pressure.)

- Take note of where the tension is in your body.
- If you find three or more locations, choose the two most tense areas.
- Tense one group of muscles in that part of your body all at once for 15 seconds. Deep-breathe during the hold.
- If that isn't enough, do a body squeeze. Start by curling your toes as hard as you can for 15 seconds. Keep breathing deeply. Relax that group of muscles. Move up your body, doing the same 15-second hold with your calves, thighs, lower back, stomach, upper back, chest, shoulders, and neck, face, and forehead.

3. Using Outside Reminders

- Choose your favourite reminder. You'll need lots of them, so make this reminder inexpensive.
- Make a list of your high-risk situations or locations by going through your typical daily schedule. Note when you eat or decide whether to exercise. Add to this list as you go through your day.
- Place your reminder in all of the places and situations you identified. Mark all high-risk situations.

4. The British poet Alfred Lord Tennyson wrote, "I must lose myself in action, lest I wither in despair."

5. It is not ability or intelligence that holds people back from working out or choosing a low-fat snack, it is how they feel.

James Meschino's
Plan

Let's get started

– the first steps to a healthier body

The promise of losing weight or, more accurately, of losing body fat, is a powerful incentive to change. Our program provides all the skills you will need to develop meal plans and a lifestyle that will keep you lean and healthy for a lifetime. When you begin, however, you may need a more structured approach and may want to start shedding some fat immediately. In this chapter, I outline a menu plan that can help you achieve this. Following an explanation of the Two-Staple System formula for healthy living, we describe our rapid weight-loss plan. Later in the book we also describe a more moderate weight-loss plan. Throughout Part II of *Break the Weight-Loss Barrier* you will find information about nutrition and metabolism that will help you understand how your body defends itself against cancer, heart attacks, stroke, osteoporosis, and diabetes, and how your body becomes a lean, fat-burning machine for life. So, let's get started on the road to success.

When you start the program, you may be absolutely certain that you will lose weight, tighten your tummy, firm your thighs, reduce your waistline, enhance your fitness level, lower your cholesterol level, and so on. However, as your daily activities and pressures – financial stress, family obligations, work deadlines, and social and recreational commitments – get in the way, your enthusiasm may wane. As those priorities take centre stage, it's easy to lose your focus and momentum. When you become tired, bored, burned out, depressed, or disappointed, your natural response is to return to your comfortable way of eating. We've seen this pattern repeated again and again with clients and other people.

It's not easy to succeed in the beginning, but it is important!

To help you take the first steps on your journey to better health and fitness, we have developed a user-friendly style of eating and living that you can follow to shed excess fat, possibly lower your cholesterol level, increase your fitness level and muscle tone, and lower your risk of heart disease, cancer, and other illnesses.

Our proven nutrition program can transform you into a slim, fit, well-toned, and healthy human being.

Most people would agree that it's worth the effort to implement a few basic strategies each day to help offset the risk of health problems, especially if these strategies are practical and reasonable. Some people don't care about issues of health and well-being, however. Twenty-six percent of North Americans continue to smoke, despite the fact that smoking causes cancer and heart disease. Similarly, some people who are overweight and out of shape lack the motivation or the will to change. But if you're tired of being overweight or flabby, or if you have recognized the importance of minimizing your risk of cancer, heart disease, and other diseases, then you're a good candidate for our program.

In addition to these physical benefits are emotional and psychological benefits: most people like themselves better when they're not fat and flabby. When people lose weight and become more fit and toned, they feel happier, more confident, and more willing to participate in activities. It feels good to look good, and it also reduces your health risks.

The Vegan Ideal

The optimal nutrition plan is most likely a strict vegan vegetarian lifestyle, which is limited to fruits, vegetables, grains, cereals, and legumes such as beans, peas, nuts, and seeds. Numerous studies suggest that a broad-based vegetarian diet is associated with significant reductions in the risk of heart attacks, strokes, all vascular diseases, and many cancers, including breast and colon cancer – two prevalent cancers in our society. Vegans also have a lower incidence of adult diabetes, osteoporosis, and obesity. In general, vegetarians who know how to combine food groups to ensure that they are getting the correct balance of nutrients demonstrate superior health to most people who live the typical North American lifestyle.

Although switching to a vegan vegetarian lifestyle may be the ultimate choice, most people are unlikely to adopt this lifestyle completely. At the spa in Florida where I lecture on these principles, clients often tell me that when they return home they won't be able to follow the vegetarian ways they've learned about. Regardless of how convinced they may be that it is the best choice, no matter how much better they feel or how much weight they lost during their stay, and no matter how tasty and enjoyable the cuisine, most people believe that it is extremely difficult to practise a vegan vegetarian lifestyle in today's world. Although aiming for this goal may be a worthwhile endeavour, many people will never achieve it in everyday practice. Instead, most people need a transitional program that is less restrictive, but is still a major step forward from the traditional North American lifestyle. If you ultimately succeed in adopting a vegan vegetarian lifestyle, congratulate yourself. But even if you don't restrict yourself to that degree, you can still enjoy good health, better fitness, and longevity by adopting some of these basic principles.

The Key Ingredients

Our experience as well as voluminous research tell us that the key ingredients for weight loss and disease prevention can be attained without depriving yourself of meat and dairy products. In fact, you can even have some sugary treats.

- Your success depends on having the *right proportion of nutrients*:
  - about 65 to 70 percent of your calories should come from carbohydrate foods,
  - about 15 percent should come from protein, and
  - no more than 20 to 25 percent should come from fat.
- Your body also needs the *essential protective nutrients* that ward off cancer, heart disease, diabetes, osteoporosis, and other degenerative problems such as cataracts and Alzheimer's disease. In general, these protective nutrients occur naturally in most carbohydrate foods. However, you should consider supplementing your diet with disease-fighting nutrients to enhance your health, condition your body for burning fat, and discourage the development of degenerative conditions.
- Finally, you must include at least a gentle endurance-exercise regime as part of your wellness program. Without a minimum level of gentle endurance exercise, it is impossible to attain a better-looking body that is truly healthy.

The Two-Staple System

In the mid-1980s, we created a nutrition program called the Two-Staple System, which we have taught successfully to numerous groups and clients. With this approach, you can consume some meat and dairy products, as well as many snacks and treats, and still attain your ideal weight and defend your body against degenerative diseases. As its name suggests, the program is based on two major food staples or groups — *carbohydrate* foods and *protein* foods.

CARBOHYDRATES

Carbohydrate foods are basically vegetarian foods — things that come from the Earth, such as fruits, vegetables, cereal products, grains, peas, and beans. These are classified as *complex-carbohydrate foods* because the simple sugars extracted from these foods by your body are complexed together or attached to each other like individual box cars linked on a railroad track. Your body secretes enzymes that release the box cars or individual sugars from their complex form, permitting them to be slowly and evenly absorbed into your bloodstream. A major function of carbohydrate foods is their ability to release carbohydrate sugars, which your cells use for energy. Carbohydrates are high-octane energy foods that provide the primary fuel that most body cells need to function. Carbohydrate foods also supply all of your dietary fibre and many protective nutrients that reduce the risk of heart disease, cancer, and most degenerative problems. These foods are the main staple for optimal health, weight control, and longevity.

Carbohydrate Foods

Fruit (fresh, canned, frozen)
Jams and jellies (made from fruit and pectin fibre)
Garden vegetables (cucumber, lettuce, tomato)
Starchy vegetables (potatoes, squash)
Cruciferous vegetables (cabbage, cauliflower, broccoli, Brussels sprouts, turnips)
Dark-green vegetables (spinach, asparagus, rapini)
Grains (rice, corn, oats, oatmeal, buckwheat)
Cereal products (bread, pasta, high-fibre cereal, bagels, low-fat biscuits, crackers)
Beans (kidney beans, white beans, navy beans)
Peas (chick peas, black-eyed peas, snow peas)
Soup with a broth base (no dairy) and noodles or rice
Vegetarian pizza (with no cheese or meat)

Because your body needs a continuous supply of energy, carbohydrate foods should supply 65 to 70 percent of your calories each day. Since the Two-Staple System ensures that this happens, you don't have to count calories with this program.

PROTEINS

Protein foods are derived mainly from meat products, dairy products, and legumes such as peas and beans. Grains and vegetables, however, also contain some protein. By combining grains and legumes with many vegetables, you can get all of the protein your body needs without ever eating meat, fish, poultry, or dairy products.

Essentially two sources of animal-based or non-vegetarian protein foods exist: meat or flesh protein foods and dairy protein foods. All meat or flesh protein foods and all dairy protein foods are classified as *complete proteins*. Complete protein foods contain all of the protein building blocks that your body needs to manufacture proteins for muscles, tissue, bone repair, and so on. Vegetarian foods, which are classified as *incomplete proteins*, do not contain all of the building blocks that your body needs to remain healthy. As a result, vegan vegetarians must combine foods such as grains and beans to satisfy their body's protein requirement. In terms of providing necessary protein, meat and dairy products appear to be superior to grains and beans.

Additionally, meat or flesh protein products are excellent sources of vitamin B-12 and iron, and dairy products are the richest food source of calcium and vitamin D. These four vitamins and minerals are key components of health and disease prevention.

Many meat and dairy products, however, are loaded with saturated fat and cholesterol, both of which promote weight gain, obesity, colon and reproductive organ cancers, high levels of blood cholesterol, heart attacks, and strokes. In other words, a diet that is high in saturated fat and cholesterol actually encourages the diseases and conditions you are trying to avoid. Fortunately, not all meat and dairy products are high in saturated fat and cho-

Protein foods from meat or flesh products and dairy products are acceptable as long as they're very low in saturated fat and cholesterol.

Low-Fat Flesh Protein Foods

(Fish-Poultry)
- chicken
- turkey
- Cornish game hen
- fish
- seafood
- egg whites

Low-Fat Dairy Protein Foods
- skim milk
- 1 percent milk
- non-fat yogurt
- 1 percent milk fat yogurt
- cheese (less than 6 percent milk fat)

lesterol. The Two-Staple System includes low-fat flesh protein foods and low-fat dairy protein foods.

Protein is the building block of muscle, bone, teeth, hair, and nails. Protein also serves other roles in the body, but for our purposes, when you think of protein, think of it in terms of rebuilding your structure. Because you don't lose a lot of muscle, bone, teeth, hair, and nails in a 24-hour period, only 12 to 15 percent of your calories need to come from protein to satisfy your protein requirement. To simplify this concept, you just need to remember that we recommend that you have one serving each day of a low-fat flesh protein food and one serving of a low-fat dairy protein food. Combined with the protein in grains, beans, peas, and vegetables, these two servings will easily satisfy your need for protein each day.

Since most red meat and pork products derive more than 25 percent of their calories from fat, much of which is saturated fat, we recommend that you exclude red meat or pork products and concentrate instead on the poultry-fish selections.

In addition to meeting certain nutritional needs, meat and dairy products provide a special kind of post-meal contentment that many of us seem to crave — a feeling that rice and vegetables fail to provide. Feeling contented after a meal helps you to succeed in this program. After all, if you don't feel deprived, you probably won't crave burgers and fries or chicken wings and ribs.

That's the basis of our program – the right balance of carbohydrates, proteins, and fat; an optimal intake of protective nutrients to neutralize cancer-causing agents, bolster your immune system, and preserve your genetic structure, and a gentle aerobic exercise program to burn body fat, strengthen your bones and heart, and discourage breast and colon cancer.

THE THREE MEALS OF THE TWO-STAPLE SYSTEM

On the Two-Staple System, you eat three meals each day. At each meal, you consume two or three carbohydrate foods. These carbohydrates provide energy to keep you going and facilitate the burning of body fat to help you shed excess weight.

- One meal each day is the *Carbo-Energy Meal*. This carbohydrate-only meal is vegetarian.
- The second meal is the *Dairy-Protein Meal*. You can

To be successful you must include at least 30 minutes per day of some form of endurance activity that burns calories and has other positive effects on your metabolism, muscle tissue, and cardiovascular system.

have a low-fat dairy protein food and two or three carbohydrate selections.

- The third meal is the *Fish-Poultry Meal*. You can choose skinless chicken, turkey, Cornish hen, or any fish, and two or three carbohydrate selections.

Although you can choose the order in which you consume these meals, in general the Carbo-Energy Meal and Dairy-Protein Meal can be breakfast, lunch, or dinner, and the Fish-Poultry Meal is usually lunch or dinner.

THE EXERCISE ADVANTAGE

One final reminder — it's not enough simply to change your eating habits or to follow our dietary menus. You *must* engage in some form of gentle endurance activity or exercise for at least 30 minutes each day. This activity can be any one or a combination of exercise machines such as a stationary bicycle, stairmaster, or treadmill. Remember that you do not need to push yourself to the limit. Although the intensity of the exercise should have you breathing a little harder, you should still be able to have a conversation with a person standing next to you.

When you start this program, you don't have to exercise for 30 consecutive minutes each day, but you do have to commit to 30 minutes of total exercise each day. For example, you may choose to break your activity into three 10-minute power walks or two 15-minute power walks each day.

Gentle Endurance Activity (Common Examples)

- Stationary bicycle
- Treadmill: fast walk or jog
- Stairmaster
- Rowing machine
- Jogging
- Stepmill
- Power walk — walking at a quick pace sufficient to elevate your heart rate into the fat-burning or aerobic zone (explained later)

Success Stories

The following stories represent typical examples in everyday life of how people struggle unnecessarily with the issues of weight loss.

If Carla Can Do It . . .

Carla, a middle-aged woman, came to see me in a desperate effort to lose weight. She had gained 100 pounds since she was married 25 years ago. After each of her three pregnancies, she had never lost the weight she had gained. She had tried various programs, weight-loss clinics and groups, and had received weight-loss counselling from eight doctors. She had also undergone hormone injections, acupuncture, and hypnosis. She had purchased exercise tapes and a line of multilevel nutrition products that provided weight-management advice. Needless to say, she was discouraged and frustrated.

Before we could proceed with the program, Carla and I had to address certain health and circumstantial factors in her lifestyle. We worked together to adapt the Two-Staple System to her life, her preferences, and her schedule. I also asked Carla to record everything she ate and her exercise program on a chart, which is reproduced below. Together we underlined the foods that were sabotaging her health and causing her weight problem. Note that every day she sabotaged herself in some way, and that even though she was exercising, her weight, measurements, and body fat remained the same. Each week I explained how nutrition interacts with her body to encourage or discourage fat accumulation and degenerative diseases. The second sheet is her

A Word from Dr. Simon

Watch your inner conversation during difficult moments. You might create a column on your daily food record for inner conversations you had with yourself.

Carla's Eating Chart Before the Two-Staple System

	1st Day	2nd Day	3rd Day	4th Day	5th Day	6th Day	7th Day
Morning Meal	1/2 c. Bran Buds 1/2 c. 1 percent milk 1 tsp. brown sugar	1/2 small diet yogurt 3 tbsp. Bran Buds 2 tbsp. blueberries	4 oz. one percent milk 2 slices flax bread with raspberry jam 4 oz. orange juice 1/3 c. blueberries	1/2 small diet yogurt 3 tbsp. blueberries 3 tbsp. Bran Buds Crystal Lite	1 egg 2 slices toast coffee jam	1 egg 2 slices toast coffee	1/2 small diet yogurt 1 peach 3 tbsp. Bran Buds
Noon Meal	1 egg-salad sandwich with lettuce regular soda	pasta tomato and meat sauce 1 tbsp. parmesan 1 peach	1 chicken-salad sandwich salad with Italian dressing 1 peach 1 glass Crystal Lite	Caesar salad onion soup 1 piece garlic bread 1 iced tea	1 turkey sandwich 1 roast beef sandwich with veggies 1 beer 2 glasses wine 1 peach	1 caraway-rye bun 1 peach peach juice	1 glass milk 2 tomato and light mayonnaise sandwiches coleslaw 1 slice apple cake lime soda
Evening Meal	3 glasses Crystal Lite 1 c. rice 3 oz. steak 1/2 tomato 1/2 small cucumber 1/2 stick celery 1 tbsp. oil	3 slices bread 1 small boneless, skinless, chicken breast 1/2 tomato low-fat mayonnaise pickled red cabbage Crystal Lite	1 plate spaghetti with tomatoes Crystal Lite watermelon 2 slices bread and jam 8 oz. one percent milk	grilled salmon baked potato 1 tbsp. sour cream 1 cob of corn 1 melba toast 1 scotch and soda	pork tenderloin mashed potatoes green beans squash cabbage soup 1 slice cheesecake	1 cob of corn 1 1/2 beef patties 1 large potato 1/2 tomato 1 small cucumber coleslaw peach	macaroni and cheese coleslaw 1/2 tomato celery cucumber 2 slices bread
Other Foods & Beverages Used	4 social tea cookies 1 peach 1/2 small diet yogurt	1 slice bread marmalade 8 oz. one percent milk 1/4 c. Bran Buds	2 slices bread with jam and peanut butter 4 oz. milk	1/2 bun 8 oz. one percent milk	2 scotch and sodas	2 slices bread and jam 8 oz. one percent milk	2 rice cakes 2 slices bread and jam
Exercise	40 min. treadmill @ 3.2 m.p.h.	40 min. treadmill @ 3.1 m.p.h.	40 min. treadmill @ 3.2 m.p.h.	10 min. bike, 20 min. treadmill, 10 min. steps, 20 min. weights & exercises (1 h)		20 min. treadmill	1 h workout

Carla's Eating Plan 10 Weeks into the Two-Staple System

	1st Day	2nd Day	3rd Day	4th Day	5th Day	6th Day	7th Day
Morning Meal	Bran Buds milk orange juice	Bran Buds milk orange juice	banana Bran Buds no-fat yogurt	rolled oats	Bran Buds milk banana 2 slices toast	1/2 grapefruit Bran Buds milk bagel jam	2 slices toast jam orange juice

Noon Meal	turkey broth
	pastina
	1 English
	  muffin
	5 percent
	  ricotta
		turkey sand-
		  wich
		salad
		oil and
		  vinegar
			pasta
			tomato sauce
			  and veggies
			salad
				pasta
				tomato sauce
				  and 5 per-
				  cent ricotta
				banana
					chicken breast
					bun
					biscotti
						chili
						roll
						salad
							turkey sand-
							  wich
							5 percent
							  ricotta
							lettuce
							no-fat mayon-
							  naise

Evening Meal	pasta
	tomato sauce
	  and veggies
	salad
	oil and vinegar
	no-fat yogurt
		chicken
		rice
		turnips
		no-fat yogurt
			chicken
			no-fat mayon-
			  naise
			2 slices bread
			cranberry relish
				rice
				chicken breast
				broccoli
				turnips
				2 slices bread
				  and jam
					pasta
					tomato sauce
					bread
					apple
						rice
						beans and peas
						turnip
						broccoli
						no-fat yogurt
							potato
							squash
							green beans
							chicken

Other Foods &
Beverages
Used
	1 percent milk
	angel cake
		English muffin
		  and jam
		milk
		low-fat
		  granola bar
			2 slices bread
			  and jam
				low-fat
				  granola bar
					pretzels	low-fat
						  granola bar
						2 slices bread
						  and jam
						milk
							6 melba toasts
							low-fat
							  granola bar
							2 slices bread
							  and jam

Exercise	40 min.
	  treadmill
		40 min.
		  treadmill
			40 min.
			  treadmill
				1 h workout	40 min.
					  treadmill
							1 h workout

diary of food intake and exercise after 10 weeks on the program.

Four months after starting the program, Carla had lost 10 percent of her body fat. By the fifth month, she had dropped four inches from her waist and hips. In the following weeks, she continued to make progress and her blood-sugar level dropped to a safer level — an important achievement considering that adult-onset diabetes runs in her family. If Carla can do it, so can you!

Fred – From Fat to Fit

Our second success story involves Fred, a man in his late thirties, who is self-employed and is raising a family with his wife in a suburb just outside a big city. During one of our weekly visits, he blurted out, "Being fat is not easy!" We had a good laugh, then examined the beliefs and feelings behind his statement. We concluded that life isn't easy, and that everyone experiences disappointments, boredom, frustration, and fatigue. However, people deal with these problems in different ways. For example, some of us turn to food for comfort in those moments. Over the course of several weeks Fred realized that you can minimize the damage you do in those moments of temptation.

The first chart shows what Fred ate when he first came to see me. The second chart shows his diet after 10 weeks on the program.

By simply following the Two-Staple System according to his food preferences and busy timetable, Fred lost 25 pounds in the first 10 weeks on the program, despite the fact that Christmas and New Year's fell during this period. Furthermore, his body fat dropped by nine percent. "I'm getting great results and I don't feel as if I'm dieting," he said. In fact, he wasn't dieting, but instead was living and feeding his body in a way that promoted the burning of fat, elevated his metabolism, and discouraged the development of degenerative diseases.

Fred's Eating Chart Before the Two-Staple System

	1st Day	2nd Day	3rd Day	4th Day	5th Day	6th Day	7th Day
Morning Meal	1 bagel with peanut butter 2 coffees	1 bagel with peanut butter and jam coffees	1 low-fat muffin coffee	1 large apple muffin coffee	1 bagel with peanut butter and jam	1 bagel with peanut butter and jam	1 large pancake 1 cappuccino
Noon Meal	1 egg and red pepper sandwich water	1 turkey sandwich with lettuce and tomato, no mayonnaise and cranberry 1 diet 7UP 1 cappuccino	split pea ham soup 1 slice of bread 1 diet coke	1 egg drop soup 1 tuna on bagel	sole with mashed potatoes salad 1 diet 7UP	1 salami sandwich with cheese 1 diet coke	1 plate of pasta 1 diet 7UP
Evening Meal	baked ham with rice and beans 1 glass Perrier		pasta with meatballs salad	pasta with chick peas bread salad	roast pork potatoes salad bread 1 cappuccino	roast chicken potatoes bread salad	1 rack of ribs 1 baked potato onion rings 1 diet coke 1/2 baked apple
Other Foods & Beverages Used	1 cappuccino 2 small chocolates 1 small chip 2 cookies small milk		1 cappuccino frozen yogurt 1 tea 4 biscuits	2 frozen yogurts 1 bag of popcorn	frozen yogurt 2 rugalas coffee	frozen yogurt 2 rugalas oatmeal bran 1/2 apple turnover	
Exercise	20 lengths			20 lengths		20 lengths	12 lengths

Fred's Eating Plan 10 Weeks into the Two-Staple System

	1st Day	2nd Day	3rd Day	4th Day	5th Day	6th Day	7th Day
Morning Meal	yogurt with Bran Buds apple juice	bagel with jam coffee	yogurt with Bran Buds coffee	yogurt with Bran Buds coffee	bagel with jam coffee	1/2 Bran Buds with yogurt (2 h later) bagel with jam	coffee
Noon Meal	pasta with tomato sauce and vegetables cappuccino	pasta with vegetables cappuccino	rotini with vegetables pasta sauce salad Diet Sprite	grilled chicken Diet A&W root beer	bowl of vegetable soup plate of pasta roll espresso	pasta primavera with lots of vegetables Perrier	pasta & vegetables Diet 7UP
Evening Meal	chicken grilled with vegetables	salmon with vegetables rice Perrier	chicken baked with vegetables potatoes salad Diet Coke	penne alle arrabiate with vegetables Diet Sprite	2 drumsticks, baked, no skin 3 small slices pizza, no cheese water	3 slices of pizza, no cheese large piece of cake 3 Rice Krispie squares coffee 5 finger sandwiches (egg & tuna)	stir fry, vegetables & chicken with rice 1 slice of pizza, no cheese Perrier
Other Foods & Beverages Used	1 bag of pretzels 4 arrowroot biscuits 3 apples	orange 2 pieces of cantaloupe 1 bag of popcorn	apple and grapes	fruit salad popcorn	fruit salad with large spoon of low-fat yogurt		fruit salad pretzels popcorn fruit
Exercise	30 lengths	40 min. treadmill	40 min. treadmill		35 min. treadmill	45 min. treadmill	40 min. treadmill

One of the most important aspects of our program involves converting your body into a fat-burning machine. Others have done it, and in the next chapter we help you undergo the same transformation.

A Rapid Weight-Loss Formula

If you want to get off to a quick start, follow our Super-Easy 14-Day Plan. We don't recommend that you follow this rapid weight-loss approach for an extended period, however. Over the longer term, a more realistic and less restrictive way of using the Two-Staple System for weight-loss purposes is available. We know that many of you want to get started and lose a few pounds of fat early in the program to gain some momentum. By using the Two-Staple System, you can succeed in doing this. Here are examples of some of our patients' success stories. The following chapters provide details of how the Two-Staple System works.

A Word from Dr. Simon

Starting a rapid weight-loss plan can lead to the damaging inner conversations associated with "going on a diet." If you are starting on this rapid weight-loss plan as a punishment or are driven by shame, perfectionism, or the need to succeed overnight, then either choose a slower beginning or consider it as an experiment to get to know your inner conversation. Watch for your inner conversations around deprivation, feeling angry, or not meeting your expectations. Since it is an experiment, you are simply watching both your weight results and inner dialogue. Be willing to change your plan if your inner conversation seems overwhelming or if it is heading you on a course to failure.

Breakfast	1 muffin (low-fat, high-fibre)
	black tea, herbal tea, or coffee, no dairy or sugar
Lunch	tuna (3 ounces water packed, no mayonnaise)
	sliced tomato (1 sliced tomato, no oil)
	1/2 bagel or 1 slice bread (nothing on it)
Snack	1 apple (plum, peach, nectarine, orange, grapefruit, or banana)
Dinner	pasta (1/2 cup, uncooked)
	tomato sauce (minimum amount of oil, add vegetables if desired – red peppers, onions, broccoli, mushrooms)
	1/2 cup chef's salad (1 tsp. of olive oil and vinegar of choice)
	lettuce, tomato, cucumber
	OR
	1/2 cup of cooked broccoli or cauliflower
At night	popcorn (2-3 cups low-fat or air-popped)

The First Steps to a Healthier Body

Exercise   30 minutes or more of endurance activity of your choice. This is critical to your success. If you're just beginning, walking is usually the best choice.

Supplementation On a low-calorie program, it's impossible to obtain all of the essential vitamins and minerals you need. Therefore, we recommend that you take a multiple vitamin and mineral each day, and, if the calcium in the supplement is less than 500 mg, that you also take an additional supplement of 500 mg of calcium citrate or calcium carbonate.

The Super-Easy 14-Day Plan

If an exact day-to-day meal plan will help you succeed, simply follow this plan for 14 days and then start again at Day 1. You can use the same day over and over again, if you find one that you prefer.

A Word from Dr. Simon

Get to know your inner conversation about certain foods. If your inner conversation is bored or tired with a food, then respect this and substitute another food. Use your new knowledge to guide your success. Be creative, not desperate! Find low-fat protein substitutes such as no-fat veggie hot dogs or veggie pepperoni. Read Rose's recipe section and see how an expert spices up food.

The Super-Easy 14-Day Plan

	Day 1	Day 2	Day 3	Day 4	Day 5	Day 6	Day 7
Morning Meal	*Dairy-Protein Breakfast* 8 oz. skim milk or low-fat yogurt 1/2 cup Kellogg's Bran Buds with psyllium	*Carbo-Energy Breakfast* 1/2 bagel with jam 1 fruit	*Dairy-Protein Breakfast* 8 oz. skim milk or low-fat yogurt 1/2 cup Nabisco 100 percent Bran	*Dairy-Protein Breakfast* 8 oz. skim milk or low-fat yogurt 1 fruit serving no-calorie beverage	*Dairy-Protein Breakfast* 8 oz. skim milk or low-fat yogurt	*Carbo-Energy Breakfast* 1/2 cup oatmeal uncooked with hot water	*Carbo-Energy Breakfast* 1 low-fat bran muffin 1 fruit
Noon Meal	*Fish-Poultry Lunch* 3-4 oz. water-packed tuna 1 cup mixed-green salad (oil and vinegar dressing) 1/2 bagel no-calorie beverage	*Dairy-Protein Lunch* 3 oz. low-fat cheese (1 or 2 percent milk fat) 2 slices whole-wheat bread 1 tomato	*Fish-Poultry Lunch* 3 oz. sliced turkey breast 1 cup mixed-green salad (oil and vinegar dressing) 1/2 bagel no-calorie beverage	*Carbo-Energy Lunch* 1 bowl minestrone soup 1/2 cup bean salad (see recipe) 1 slice whole-wheat bread	*Fish-Poultry Lunch* 3-4 oz. water-packed salmon 1/2 cup bean salad (see recipe) 1 slice whole-wheat bread no-calorie beverage	*Dairy-Protein Lunch* 8 oz. low-fat yogurt 2 fruits 1/2 bagel	*Fish-Poultry Lunch* 1/4 chicken and rice 1 roll no-calorie beverage
Evening Meal	*Carbo-Energy Dinner* 1/2 cup pasta with tomato sauce 1/2 cup fruit salad 1 slice bread no-calorie beverage	*Fish-Poultry Dinner* 1 medium chicken breast (no skin) 1 cup mixed-green salad (oil and vinegar dressing) 1 slice whole-wheat bread no-calorie beverage	*Carbo-Energy Dinner* basic stir-fry (see recipe) no-calorie beverage	*Fish-Poultry Dinner* 4 oz. swordfish 1/2 cup boiled rice 1 slice whole-wheat bread no-calorie beverage	*Carbo-Energy Dinner* 1/2 cup pasta with tomato sauce 1 cup mixed-green salad (oil and vinegar dressing) 1/2 bagel no-calorie beverage	*Fish-Poultry Dinner* 4 oz. grilled fish 1 baked potato plain low-fat yogurt or sour cream no-calorie beverage	*Dairy-Protein Dinner* 1 individual pizza (low-fat cheese and vegetable toppings) 1 cup mixed-green salad (oil and vinegar dressing) no-calorie beverage
Snack	popcorn	1 plum or nectarine	popcorn	2 apples	1 fruit	1/2 cup fruit cocktail	low-fat granola bar
Supplementation	multiple vitamin and mineral	multiple vitamin and mineral	multiple vitamin and mineral	multiple vitamin and mineral	multiple vitamin and mineral	multiple vitamin and mineral	multiple vitamin and mineral
Exercise	30 minutes of endurance activity	30 minutes of endurance activity	30 minutes of endurance activity	30 minutes of endurance activity	30 minutes of endurance activity	30 minutes of endurance activity	30 minutes of endurance activity

The Super-Easy 14-Day Plan

	Day 8	Day 9	Day 10	Day 11	Day 12	Day 13	Day 14
Morning Meal	*Carbo-Energy Breakfast* 1/2 cup oatmeal uncooked with hot water 1 slice whole-wheat toast with jam	*Dairy-Protein Breakfast* 8 oz. low-fat yogurt 1/2 cup Kellogg's Bran Buds with psyllium	*Dairy-Protein Breakfast* 1 pumpernickel bagel 3 oz. low-fat ricotta cheese black coffee	*Dairy-Protein Breakfast* 8 oz. low-fat yogurt 1 nectarine 1/2 cup high-fibre cereal herbal tea	*Carbo-Energy Breakfast* 1 pumpernickel bagel 1 tbsp jam 1/2 cup sliced cantaloupe	*Dairy-Protein Breakfast* 8 oz. low-fat plain yogurt 1/2 cup fresh fruit 1/2 cup high-fibre cerea	*Dairy-Protein Breakfast* 1 bagel 2 oz. low-fat cheese 1 grapefruit herbal tea
Noon Meal	*Dairy-Protein Lunch* 2 oz. low-fat cheese 1 bagel sliced tomato and cucumber	*Fish-Poultry Lunch* 4 oz. chicken breast (barbecue) 1 plain baked potato 1 cup mixed-green salad (oil and vinegar dressing) mineral water	*Carbo-Energy Lunch* chicken noodle soup 1 cup mixed-green salad (oil and vinegar dressing) 2 slices whole-wheat bread soda water	*Carbo-Energy Lunch* pasta with tomato sauce 1 cup mixed-green salad (oil and vinegar dressing) mineral water	*Fish-Poultry Lunch* 1 small tin salmon (water-packed) 2 slices whole-wheat bread 1 sliced tomato bowl vegetable soup	*Carbo-Energy Lunch* penne with tomato sauce mixed-green salad (oil and vinegar dressing) mineral water	*Fish-Poultry Lunch* 3 oz. sliced turkey breast 2 slices whole-wheat bread sliced tomato and lettuce mineral water
Evening Meal	*Fish-Poultry Dinner* 4 oz. white fish (broiled) 1/2 cup boiled rice with tomatoes 1 slice whole-wheat bread	*Carbo-Energy Dinner* 1/2 cup pasta with tomato sauce 1/2 cup bean salad 1 whole-wheat roll	*Fish-Poultry Dinner* 1/4 chicken breast 1 baked potato with low-fat plain yogurt 1/2 cup bean salad no-calorie beverage	*Fish-Poultry Dinner* 3-4 oz. halibut 1/2 cup brown rice (boiled) 1 slice whole-wheat bread	*Dairy-Protein Dinner* vegetarian lasagna with low-fat ricotta or tofu cheese 1 cup mixed-green salad (oil and vinegar dressing) soda water	*Fish-Poultry Dinner* 3-4 oz. poached salmon 1/2 cup steamed rice 1/2 cup cooked carrots 1 slice whole-wheat bread spring water	*Carbo-Energy Dinner* ratatouille (onions, green pepper, tomatoes, eggplant, zucchini) 1/2 cup boiled rice 2 cups fruit salad no-calorie beverage
Snack	popcorn	2 nectarines	1/2 cup fruit salad	2 plums	popcorn	1 apple	2 plums
Supplementation	multiple vitamin and mineral	multiple vitamin and mineral	multiple vitamin and mineral	multiple vitamin and mineral	multiple vitamin and mineral	multiple vitamin and mineral	multiple vitamin and mineral
Exercise	30 minutes of endurance activity	30 minutes of endurance activity	30 minutes of endurance activity	30 minutes of endurance activity	30 minutes of endurance activity	30 minutes of endurance activity	30 minutes of endurance activity

General Guidelines for Weight Management

DAIRY

- Use only skim or one percent milk.
- Use only yogurt that is less than one percent milk fat (mf). Read labels carefully. If you find plain yogurt is too bland, you can flavour or sweeten it.

CEREAL

- We recommend the following breakfast cereals:
  All Bran™
  Post Grape Nuts™
  Bran Flakes with Raisins™
  Nabisco 100 percent Bran™
  Bran Buds™ with psyllium husk fibre
  Puffed Wheat
Any other low-fat, not-too-sweet cereal with high fibre content. Check the fibre chart on the cereal box.

FRUIT

- Choose fresh fruits that are high in fibre where possible. Fruits such as apples, peaches, pears, plums, berries, papaya, and kiwi also help to decrease your cholesterol levels.

BREAD

- Do not butter bread: eat it dry, or spread some jam over the bread or toast. For sandwiches, moisten bread with tomatoes, lettuce, or a dab of olive oil.

Pasta

- Use light sauces such as tomato sauce seasoned with our list of allowable seasonings.
- To add variety, include some vegetables sautéed in a cooking spray, olive or peanut oil, or cook them in the sauce.
- Include clams (3 ounces), mussels (3 ounces), or scallops (3 ounces) in the tomato sauce as part of a Fish-Poultry Meal.
- Do not use any cream sauces.
- Due to their high fat content, do not use any meat sauces.

Rice

- Use boiled or steamed rice.
- Add mixed vegetables steamed or stir-fried using cooking spray, or olive or peanut oil.

Salads and Dressings

- You may use low-calorie oil dressings but not creamy dressings such as Thousand Islands, Ranch, or French.
- Make your own dressing from olive oil (1 to 2 teaspoons), vinegar, lemon, and seasonings.

Potatoes

- Serve potatoes without butter, margarine, or regular sour cream.
- Use flavourings such as pepper and salsa sauce.
- You can choose to top your potatoes with no-fat yogurt or sour cream.

COOKED VEGETABLES

- Bake, boil, steam, or stir-fry vegetables. Do not use butter.
- The closer to raw the vegetable is, the greater its fibre content and the fewer calories your body absorbs.

POULTRY AND FISH

- Grill, steam, barbecue, or broil meat and fish. Use seasonings from the allowed list.
- Use only water-packed canned tuna or salmon, not oil-packed.

DIURETIC FOODS

- Most fruits, especially ones with a high water content such as watermelon, act as a natural diuretic.
- Fruits are generally higher in potassium than sodium and prevent water retention.

BEVERAGES

- Drink water, distilled water, or low-sodium mineral or soda water.
- Try to choose decaffeinated coffee, which prevents blood-sugar rebounding and hunger response.
- Black or green teas are a better choice than coffee.
- Hot water with lemon is also a good choice.
- Drink beverages containing aspartame in moderation.

CHEESE

- Since most cheeses are high in fat and calories, eat them sparingly.

The First Steps to a Healthier Body

- Make sure that the amount of milk fat is five percent or lower, ideally two percent or lower. Cheddar and brick cheese are 31 percent or more. Skim-milk cheese, farmer's cheese, and cottage cheese are great choices.

VITAMIN SUPPLEMENTS

- To guard against nutrient deficiency, take a multiple vitamin each day. If the vitamin contains less than 500 mg of calcium, take an additional calcium supplement of 500 mg each day. Calcium citrate and calcium carbonate are your best choices. You may want to consider adding the antioxidants vitamin E, vitamin C, and beta carotene if your multiple vitamin contains only R.D.A. levels for these nutrients (i.e., vitamin C, 60 mg, vitamin E, 12 I. U.).

Bean Salad

1/4 cup chick peas
1/4 cup red kidney beans
1 tsp olive oil
salt and pepper, if desired

Mixed-Green Salad

Your choice of the following vegetables made into a one-cup salad
1 tsp. olive oil
vinegar of choice
salt and pepper, if desired

Vegetables

Asparagus

Bean sprouts

Beets

Broccoli

Brussels sprouts

Cabbage

Carrots

Cauliflower

Eggplant

Green pepper

Greens... beet tops, chard, collard
   dandelion, kale, mustard, spinach

Mushrooms

Okra

Radishes

Rhubarb

Sauerkraut

String beans, yellow
   or green

Tomatoes

Turnips

Zucchini

Stir-Fry

1/2 cup boiled or steamed rice

3/4 cup chopped vegetables sautéed and mixed with rice
(red peppers, snow peas, bean sprouts, bok choy, onions)

2 tsp. peanut oil

salt and pepper, if desired

Converting your body
into a fat-burning machine

For many people, being overweight is one of life's ongoing miseries. If being overweight bothers you, you're probably aware how much it can hold you back from doing certain things and how unhappy it can make you feel. It can affect many aspects of your life — from your confidence level to the way you shop for clothes.

If you are overweight, ask yourself the following questions. Do you want to lose the weight? And would you be happier with yourself if you did? If you answer "yes" to both of these questions, we can help. When it comes to health, nutrition, and exercise, most people have similar goals: they want to look fit, feel healthy, and reduce their risk of degenerative illnesses such as heart disease, cancer, osteoporosis, or diabetes. This chapter addresses the three principles to ensure your success. These principles are based on our experience with real people and all of the advice we provide is practical. We help you focus on the weight-loss component, teaching you how to convert your body into a fat-burning machine.

Weight or Fat Loss

When we say we want to lose weight, we really mean we want to lose fat. We don't want to lose our structural body proteins (lean body mass). We don't want to lose bone, muscle, our teeth, or our hair. We want to lose fat.

But can you actually *lose* fat? No, but you can shrink it. When you gain weight after the age of 20 or 25, you don't add any more fat cells. Instead, the fat cells that are already in your body increase in size. (From ages 0 to 19, our bodies can increase or decrease their number of fat cells. So, if you were overweight as an adolescent, you will have a greater number of fat cells for the rest of your life and you will have to be realistic about your weight-loss goals.)

Therefore, when we say we want to lose weight, we actually want to shrink our fat cells to a level that looks good, feels good, and is healthier for us. We want to reach our *ideal percentage body fat*. For women, that ideal percentage would be between 16 and 25 percent of their body composition. For men, between 12 and 15 percent of their body composition would be an ideal percentage body fat. If you're a male elite athlete, you may be aiming for nine percent body fat.

No Excuses

In all of the corporate programs that I teach and all of the nutritional counselling sessions that I provide to clients, I have never seen this program fail. Often, at the beginning of an initial consultation, patients will say to me, "I've tried everything but I have a special type of metabolism so I don't really think your program will work for me." It is surprising how many overweight people believe that they can't lose weight because somehow their metabolism won't co-operate. This belief sets them up for failure even before the program begins. I've also heard statements such as "My problem is food allergies. I don't have any control over the food allergy and I just don't think it's possible for me to succeed," or "Everything I eat turns to fat." These too are erroneous beliefs and my response to all of these excuses is the same: "That's nonsense."

The Three Principles

Long-term success in reducing body fat is based on three principles. We guarantee that if you combine these three principles, they will work for you (unless you have an undiagnosed medical condition). If you apply only one of the three principles, it won't work. If you apply two of the principles, they still may not work. But if you combine all three, you will be successful. When people say, "I tried the high-carbohydrate diet, it didn't work," or "I exercise all the time, I still can't lose weight. It must be my metabolism," they are applying these principles randomly. To achieve the results that you want, you must combine all three principles and build synergy for yourself.

PRINCIPLE #1: COMMIT YOURSELF TO AT LEAST 30 MINUTES OF DAILY ENDURANCE ACTIVITY.

The only way to eliminate fat is to release it from the fat cell and have it travel through the bloodstream. From there it primarily goes to the muscles, which burn it for energy. As you withdraw the fat, the fat cell becomes smaller. This is a normal physiological response that will occur regardless of what kind of metabolism you have.

Muscles love to burn fat. The more muscle mass you have and the better your muscles are toned, the more they burn fat just to keep themselves alive. As people age, they become less active and their muscles shrink. Therefore, they burn less fat per second and their metabolism slows down. This slowing down of the metabolism is not caused by aging but by the shrinking muscle mass. As soon as they start to do something with their muscles, the muscle tone comes back, the metabolic rate increases, and they become a better fat-burning machine.

So, how do you move the fat from the fat cell to the muscle cell? You do gentle, endurance activity for at least 30 minutes each day. Gentle endurance activity is any type of *ongoing, rhythmic activity* that you can sustain. For some people this might be jogging. For others it might be walking on a treadmill, using a stationary bike, using the stairmaster – any activity that is continuous and uses your endurance or aerobic energy system. All of these activities achieve the same goal. Once you reach your *fat-burning or aerobic zone*, the fat is released; it travels through the bloodstream, the muscles pick it up, and you start to burn fat very effectively.

There is no drug, surgery, magic pill, or supplement that can produce the same positive adaptations in your body as gentle aerobic activity.

What Is Your Fat-Burning or Aerobic Zone?

The fastest rate at which your heart can beat under maximum exercise exertion is called the *maximum attainable heart rate*. You can estimate your maximum attainable heart rate by subtracting your age from 220. Therefore, if you are 50 years of age, your maximum attainable heart rate would be 170 heartbeats per minute (220 - 50). You start to burn fat effectively at a level between 60 percent and 85 to 90 percent of your maximum attainable heart rate. This is referred to as your *target heart-rate zone, fat-burning zone,* or *aerobic zone*. In this case, the target heart rate is between 102 (170 x .6) and 153 (170 x .90). So, as soon as the heart rate of this patient reaches more than 102 heartbeats per minute, he or she will start to burn fat more efficiently and will shrink fat cells. The upper limit of fat burning in this range is 153 heartbeats (90 percent of your maximum). Do not exceed 85 to 90 percent of your maximum. You can determine the middle of the zone by subtracting your age from 180. In this case, 130 heartbeats per minute is the middle part of the zone, and is a good target to aim for.

For someone who is accustomed to regular aerobic activity, 30 minutes a day seems negligible. But if you are just beginning, 30 minutes a day may seem like a mountain of exercise. Don't panic. Studies have shown that in terms of burning fat, if you are not fit it is almost as good to do three 10-minute episodes of exercise as it is to do the full 30 minutes all at once. Then, when you have a little more endurance and are feeling healthier and more fit, you can do two 15-minute exercise episodes. Eventually you'll progress to one 20-minute episode with an additional 10 minutes later in the day, and then after a month or two you will be able to exercise for 30 minutes continuously. At some point you want to be able to do at least 30 minutes each day of continuous exercise for your overall fitness, to improve your cardiovascular system, and ultimately to become a great fat-burning machine.

A Word from Dr. Simon

If the term "aerobic exercise" intimidates you, call it aerobic movement instead. Be your own captain and "just do it."

How It Works

Let's look at what gentle endurance activity actually means and how it helps your body burn fat effectively. As you start to exercise, your heart starts to beat a little faster. If you exercise harder, your heart speeds up again. When your heart rate reaches 60 percent of your maximum, you start to burn fat. You do not need to go beyond the midpoint of the fat-burning zone — about 75 percent. As discussed in detail above, you can determine your midpoint by subtracting your age from 180.

If you find it difficult to calculate your heart rate, you can monitor your activity by how you feel. When you are in the lower part of the fat-burning zone, you will be breathing harder, but will still be able to hold a conversation. After 10 to 12 minutes of exercise, you should begin to perspire. Although you will be working a bit harder, and breathing harder, you will feel only mild discomfort. This is the feeling you should aim for.

Exercising below the fat-burning zone is not very effective for fat burning and fitness conditioning. Activities such as walking through a mall, shopping, vacuuming, doing household chores, and even some of the activities in fitness-club programs, will not provide the results you really want. Unless you are exercising within the fat-burning zone, you may be burning calories, but you're not effectively burning *fat calories*.

When you reach the fat-burning zone, your body releases adrenalin. The adrenalin targets the fat cells and releases fat into the bloodstream. The fat moves through the arteries until it passes the exercising muscle. At this point, the muscle picks up the fat and burns it as a source of energy. Therefore, the longer you exercise, the more fat you provide to your muscles.

Inside the muscles, other changes also occur. After many days of gentle endurance activity, the muscle responds by increasing its number of energy factories or *mitochondria*, the sites in which you burn fat. Your body can then produce more energy per second and burn more fat per second. Your body becomes a fat-burning machine. These changes explain why when you start a jogging program, you can run a mile in, say, 9 1/2 minutes, but a year later you can run it in less time but without increasing your heart rate. When you are fit, you can generate more energy per second. Your muscles do more work per second. They also respond by increasing the number of fat-burning enzymes that inject the fat into the energy furnace. Your muscles become better at picking up oxygen from the bloodstream and using the oxygen to burn fat as part of the combustion system inside your muscle.

If your muscles can pick up oxygen more effectively, your heart rate starts to slow down when you are at rest. Now you have a slower resting pulse rate, which also helps your heart. When your heart contracts, it forces blood to the periphery of the body. But during its relaxation phase, between heartbeats, your heart feeds its coronary blood vessels; that's when the heart sends oxygen-rich blood to the heart muscle to feed itself. With a slower pulse there's more time for the heart muscle itself, and the chances of cardiovascular problems occurring later are minimized.

What Doesn't Work

Many people exercise, but don't reap the full benefits. Let's look at some things that *don't* work and why:

- A low-fat diet alone is not enough. The changes caused by gentle aerobic exercise are the foundation of health and fitness, and of converting your body into an efficient fat-burning machine.
- If you want to lose weight, less than 30 minutes of endurance activity every day is not sufficient. At one time it was believed that doing endurance activity every other day was sufficient. However, most of us are so sedentary that we need to exercise more often than every other day. So, unless you have a job that is physically demanding, your body needs 30 minutes of endurance activity every day to get long-term results! Since you eat every day, you also need to withdraw fat every day.
- Committing to less frequent exercise than every day is not enough. Granted, there will be times when life gets in the way of your exercise plans – your car breaks down, your child is sick, you have to work late, and so on. Even if you plan to exercise seven days a week, you may only make it five or six times. But if you plan to exercise five days a week, you'll do it only three times. And if you plan to exercise three times a week, you'll do it only once. Therefore, by committing to exercise every day, you'll create momentum, and

will increase your chances of success. Plan this daily regime in the same way that you plan your business meetings and social activities. Decide on a time and a place to exercise. If you don't make exercise a part of your daily schedule, you won't do it.

- Not all activities burn fat. For example, many people mistakenly believe that swimming will burn calories. Unfortunately, people rarely lose weight by swimming for a number of reasons. First, they're too buoyant in the water because of their excess fat, and the work is too easy. Second, their body temperature is higher than the water temperature. Under these conditions, their body resists burning fat that might be needed as insulation. We are not suggesting, however, that you give up swimming. Rather, feel free to swim if you enjoy this activity, but do 30 minutes of some other kind of activity first. The same principle applies to most fitness classes at the beginner level. Each day, do 30 minutes of an endurance activity – a stairmaster, treadmill, stationary bicycle, step mill – in addition to the beginner-level fitness class and you will get better results and will burn fat more effectively. After all, fitness classes can help improve your flexibility and muscle tone. Once you are fit, some advanced classes can be a great workout.

Why Is Daily Exercise Important?

Only 22 percent of North Americans exercise for 30 minutes every day. Twenty-four percent of the population is completely sedentary; and 54 percent engages in activity sporadically – such as gardening, bowling, starting an exercise program – but not enough to reap the benefits that we're talking about.

PRINCIPLE #2: FOCUS YOUR DIET PRINCIPALLY ON CARBOHYDRATE FOODS.

To convert your body into a fat-burning machine, you must refuel your body each day with carbohydrate foods – cereals, grains, rice, pasta, whole-wheat bread. If you do 30 minutes of endurance activity each day to get your heart rate into the fat-burning, aerobic zone, you burn fat as a source of energy. However, this is not the only thing that is happening. Your muscles also store carbohydrates, and they become part of the carbohydrate fuel tank inside the muscle.

In fact, two fuel tanks feed the muscles — the fat fuel tank and the carbohydrate fuel tank, and you burn both at the same time. Each day as you exercise, you burn fat and carbohydrates. People who don't exercise, and are overweight, complain that everything they eat turns to fat — even the carbohydrate foods — "I eat good food. I eat rice, organic carrots, lots of vegetables, and no red meat." When we eat those carbohydrate foods, after they get broken down, they go to the liver. The liver stores some carbohydrates, so that between meals it can release blood sugar to the cells of the body; it then tries to send the rest to the muscles' carbohydrate tank. If you haven't done any exercise and the carbohydrate fuel tank is still full, your body converts the carbohydrates mainly into saturated fat and sends the saturated fat to your fat cells. So, if you're on a high-carbohydrate diet, but you're not exercising enough, even the good carbohydrates you eat may be converted into saturated fat.

On the other hand, by doing gentle endurance activity, you burn down your carbohydrate fuel tank each day. Then, when you eat carbohydrates, they refuel your muscles. You spend your day reloading the carbohydrate fuel tank, which allows you to eat more calories, and even cheat a little with other refined sugary carbohydrate foods such as jujubes, jelly beans, low-fat granola bars, muffins, or white sugar in your coffee.

One of the advantages of our program is that you can consume a lot more calories (between 1500 and 2500) throughout the day and still lose weight. On traditional diets, you are often restricted to 700 calories a day, or you must weigh your food, eat artificial food, join a weight-loss service that provides all of your meals, and so on. Obviously it would be impossible to continue doing this for the rest of your life.

Furthermore, when you eat only 700 calories a day, you lose both fat and muscle mass. About 60 percent of the weight you lose is fat, and 40 percent is muscle. In essence, your body eats its own muscle mass and uses it as a fuel. Your metabolic rate is determined by how much muscle mass you have. *The more muscle tone you have, the faster your metabolic rate.* As a result, people who lose weight on a low-calorie diet decrease their body fat and their muscle mass, and their metabolic rate declines. As long as they eat only 700 calories a day for the rest of their lives, they'll be fine. People who deprive themselves on this type of punishing, gruelling program are often proud of the compliments they receive for losing weight. But eventually they succumb to their hunger and have one, two, four, or eight cookies. Then they feel like losers who can't control their eating impulses and start to binge until they're totally out of control. Then they gain the weight back and more, and restart the cycle. We have all seen this pattern, either in ourselves or in people we know. We know it doesn't work.

The U.S. weight-loss industry is a $30-billion-a-year industry, compared to cardiovascular disease, the number-one killer, at $50 billion a year, osteoporosis at $10 billion, or breast cancer at $6 billion. And dieting doesn't work – 95 percent of people who lose weight by dieting regain all the weight within a two-year period, and usually end up at a weight that is higher than when they started.

When you exercise every day and eat carbohydrates as your principal fuel, the rewards are immense. Not only do you lose weight and reduce your body fat, but your muscle tone actually increases – you become more toned because you are exercising your muscles. As a result, you increase your metabolic rate and can eat 1500 to 2500 calories a day without regaining the weight. You can continue this weight-loss program and never feel hungry. This program works for us and for every person we have introduced it to.

PRINCIPLE #3: EAT FEWER THAN 15 TO 20 GRAMS OF SATURATED FAT DAILY.

Our program requires that you eat no more than 20 grams of saturated fat per day; in fact, fewer than 15 grams is even better. Saturated fat is found in red meat products such as ground beef, pork chops, hot dogs, pastrami, corn beef, salami, pepperoni, and in heavy dairy products such as whipped cream, sour cream, ice cream, and cream cheese. Homogenized milk, two percent milk, and butter are loaded with saturated fat. Foods baked with palm and coconut oil are also high in saturated fat. For example, a three-ounce chocolate bar typically contains 12 to 18 grams of saturated fat.

On our program, instead of choosing red meats, ground meats, and luncheon meats, you can choose chicken, turkey, and fish, which are low in saturated fat. Low-fat dairy products are also acceptable. Few people can taste the difference between two percent milk or yogurt and one percent milk or yogurt, but the difference in fat content is significant. Although two percent milk may sound as if it is low in fat, its "two percent" designation means that only two percent of the milk's total volume or weight is fat. But 36 percent of its calories actually come from fat. In one percent milk, however, only 14 percent of its calories come from fat. So, the difference in calories from fat between the two kinds of milk is quite dramatic. With our Two-Staple System, your total number of fat grams and saturated-fat intake will remain in the ideal range, so you will not need to count fat grams.

A Word from Dr. Simon

The *solution substitution* is the most important step you can take in your daily eating and exercise habits. To find the best solution substitution, ask yourself the following questions:

- Do I know what I really need at this moment?
- Is there an underlying painful feeling or way of being that I want to soothe or get rid of at this moment?
- Do I know three alternative ways I could begin to satisfy it?
- Is there a way that is not damaging to my health?

Then, you think of an action to satisfy that need. Be creative. List as many alternatives as you can. Think of what you need or what feeling you're trying to soothe. Think of what taste experience you're looking for. After you've generated the list, evaluate it. Once you understand that it doesn't need to be deprivation or guilt, you can celebrate your ability to find a suitable choice.

How to Cheat

We are all tempted to cheat now and again, especially when we are stressed, upset, or tired. In this regard, people fit into two categories — those who eat to soothe themselves when they're stressed, nervous, and upset, and those who can't eat anything when they are experiencing these emotions. It's unrealistic to think that you can go on a program and deny that this relationship of emotions and eating exists. You can make a mental commitment to eat carrot sticks, and then you experience an emotional upset. You face a choice – either carrot cake or carrot sticks. An activator makes you behave in a particular way when it comes to food.

When you're stressed, upset, or tired, food is the stimulus, and you respond. In between the stimulus and the response, there's a gap – a chance to make a better decision that you can live with. For example, imagine that you are walking down a cafeteria line selecting good food – a stir-fry and a decaffeinated drink. At the end of the line you see a slice of raspberry cheesecake. You're having a tough day. Suddenly, you're immobilized, and you feel anxiety building up. Your inner voice says, "Wait a minute now. You're on this wellness program, eating only low-fat food. You're exercising every day. That's not who you are." And the other part says, "So what, you're not going to live forever anyway. You've had a tough day. Enjoy yourself. It's only a little piece of cake." Anxiety, conflict, and tension may make you choose the cheesecake. You say, "I'm going to hate myself later for this," but you do it anyway. Afterwards, you beat yourself up – "I can't believe I just did this. I was supposed to be so good, and now I'm so bad."

It doesn't have to be like that. Here are some ways to deal with moments of temptation:
- Step back and visualize the saturated fat going into your fat cells and making them larger, raising your blood cholesterol levels and clogging your heart and vascular system.
- Step back and take a deep breath. Breathing defuses the anxiety and your craving.
- Play the game "Let's Make a Deal." In any moment of temptation, there's a gap between the temptation and the action. Use that gap to say, "I know I'm tempted,

but I'm going to do something less harmful than I was about to do. Maybe it's not the most health-promoting thing, but it's less harmful. And then, if I still want the raspberry cheesecake, I'll go back and have it." Don't tell yourself you will never have the food again.

Instead, compromise by having something that is less damaging to get you through the moment. Call it a *solution substitution food.* The chart below offers some solution substitutions that can get you through that moment.

When You're About to Cheat . . .

High-Fat Treats	Have a Solution Substitution
Instead of	*Have*
Pastries: doughnuts, cake, pie, croissants, and most pastries	low-fat muffin (i.e., oat bran, blue berry), top of muffin only, biscotti, bagel (plain or with jam), low-fat granola bar
Instead of	*Have*
Chippy-dippy: potato chips, nacho chips, tortilla chips, cheesies, any fried chip	popcorn (light variety, air popped), pretzels, fibre biscuits with salsa dip, flavoured rice crackers, low-fat crackers with salsa dip
Instead of	*Have*
Dairy desserts: ice cream, banana split, sundae	low-fat frozen yogurt, sherbet, frozen fruit ice
Instead of	*Have*
Other: chocolate bars, twinkies, ding dongs	licorice, jujubes, wine gums, gummy bears, low-fat granola bars
	* Fruit is always an excellent choice!

Joey's Story

About a year ago, Joey broke up with a girl he was living with. He was sad and didn't have any place to turn. So I asked him to move in with me for a few months. I was actually looking forward to the companionship. I set three rules: there would be no smoking, we would eat good food, and we would go to the gym and exercise every day. Joey agreed to these conditions and moved in.

Joey was 30 to 40 pounds overweight when we started our arrangement. He began to follow a gentle aerobic program and to eat the same way I did. Since we both love to eat we were eating all the time. We ate volumes of food, but mostly carbohydrate ones. We spent many late nights together, eating low-fat, air-popped popcorn while watching reruns of *Perry Mason*. Every day Joey would get on the stairmaster for an average of 30 minutes. Since he didn't like to push himself too hard, he would remain in the lower end of his aerobic training zone. Three months passed, and he continued at the gym. At the end of this period, Joey found that he had lost 36 pounds. What had he changed? He stopped eating high-fat foods — sausages, meatballs, chicken wings and fingers, and butter on his bagels. He eliminated saturated fat from his diet and exercised for at least 30 minutes every day. He focused his diet on complex carbohydrates. He ate some of the bad carbohydrates too — jujubes, licorice, and the late-night popcorn snacks — and he did exceptionally well. Joey didn't completely deprive himself by struggling to follow an unrealistic diet plan. Instead, he slowly changed his relationship with food and exercise. As he progressed, he felt healthy, not hungry. He found solutions that worked for him.

MAKE IT WORK FOR YOU

You can't go on someone else's program. You must personalize or internalize it so it becomes an extension of who you are. Let our three principles — to exercise 30 minutes a day, focus your program primarily on carbohydrate foods, keep your intake of saturated fat below 15 to 20 grams a day — become a natural, automatic extension of your life. Your program must reflect your approach to life and health. You must find a style and an approach that suits you. In the same way that you have a style of dressing, of speaking, or a business manner that you feel comfortable with, your style of how you feed yourself must fit you in the same way. One person may love pasta with tomato sauce and some vegetables; another may like stir-fried vegetables with chicken or shrimp. Ultimately, you must determine your game plan for the long term. And your relationship with food and exercise will continue to evolve throughout your lifetime. Just keep thinking your way through it each day. Do your best and you'll be amazed at how far you can go.

Your Body, The Fat-burning Machine

TIPS

- There will inevitably be days when you're tired, emotionally upset, bored or down, or there's some kind of disappointment or time urgency, and you just can't get around to everything. Even on those days, say to yourself, "I'm going to look after my body anyway." If you can't do the full 30 minutes of exercise, do 10 or 15 minutes. Do *something* so you don't lose momentum. Even people who exercise regularly and have incredible energy still have tough days, major stresses, and emotional upsets. The difference is that they continue to look after their body.

A Word from Dr. Simon

Watch how your inner conversation, your feelings, and your body tensions shift from before you exercise to afterwards. You'll see that exercise not only gets your body moving but also your mind.

- With time, you'll realize that motion changes emotion. Even on your tired and glum days, plan to do 15 minutes of exercise. Within five minutes of starting, your body will begin to feel rejuvenated and, believe it or not, you'll probably end up doing all 30 minutes. You'll feel better and it will be easier to choose healthful foods. You'll feel recharged and better able to deal with the stress of the day or face the stress of tomorrow.

- Each day, say to yourself "Another day and another chance to shrink my fat cells further by:
  1. Doing at least 30 minutes of gentle endurance activity.
  2. Eating mostly carbohydrates.
  3. Eating fewer than 15 grams of saturated fat as formulated in the Two-Staple System."

Building your
nutrition plan

In this chapter, we will look at the three main foods that provide energy and structure to your body – carbohydrates, fats, and proteins – and the role they play in weight gain and loss and in health.

Carbohydrates

Carbohydrate foods can help you burn fat, reduce cholesterol, enhance athletic performance, and reduce the risk of cancer. Vegetarians who eat mainly, or often exclusively, carbohydrate foods, have less heart disease and are generally healthier than people who follow the typical North American diet.

The best carbohydrate foods to eat are the ones that are closest to the form in which they grew. All fruits, vegetables, grains, cereals, beans, and peas are considered naturally occurring *complex-carbohydrate foods*. Naturally occurring complex-carbohydrate foods are the fruits, vegetables, legumes, and grains that nature provides for us to use in their original unprocessed form. Other complex carbohydrates processed by the food industry provide similar benefits – bagels, whole-grain breads, many breakfast cereals, minestrone and vegetable soups, low-fat crackers, jams and jellies, popcorn, pretzels, pasta, and flavoured rice cakes. Less healthy, but more fun are the more refined sugary carbohydrates such as licorice, jujubes, wine gums, jelly beans, sherbet, frozen fruit ices, low-fat frozen yogurt, angel food cake, and low-fat muffins. Even these somewhat unhealthful foods are mainly carbohydrate in nature and are less damaging than high-fat alternatives such as chocolate bars, cheesecake, and ice cream.

Obviously it is better to eat the more naturally occurring carbohydrates such as fruit, vegetables, whole-grain breads, pasta, and high-fibre breakfast cereals than it is to eat jujubes and licorice. Experience tells us, however, that people do better if they can consume some fun foods during moments of vulnerability. Even so, the more you can eliminate these refined carbohydrates and focus on complex carbohydrates, the better.

Although the primary role of carbohydrates is to provide energy, many naturally occurring carbohydrate foods also contain nutrients that defend us against cancer and cardiovascular disease. We will discuss this issue in more detail in Chapter 8. For example, orange, yellow, red, and green vegetables are loaded with protective carotenes. Citrus fruits contain vitamin C and bioflavonoids that defend our tissue from disease. Other compounds, known as *micronutrients*, defend the body against disease and premature aging.

Therefore, as you select your daily carbohydrates, choose the ones that will provide maximum benefits for you. Since all carbohydrate foods provide energy, consider which ones also provide disease-fighting micronutrients.

DO CARBOHYDRATES MAKE YOU FAT?

Although carbohydrates can make you fat, they are not usually responsible for weight gain. As we discussed in Chapter 6, your body is designed to draw energy from the carbohydrate foods you eat to power its moment-to-moment energy needs. Your liver also stores some carbohydrate fuel, which it releases to your bloodstream between meals, so that your tissues can continually extract carbohydrate sugars and burn them for energy. Your muscles can also store considerable amounts of carbohydrate fuel. When you exercise, your muscles burn that carbohydrate fuel. When all of the carbohydrate fuel stored in the muscle is burned, the muscle reaches a state of complete exhaustion and no further muscle work occurs. When you exercise regularly, however, the carbohydrate "fuel tank" in your trained muscles doubles in size, and you can store twice as much carbohydrate fuel.

If you eat more carbohydrate food than your body burns, your liver and muscles store the excess. Most vegetarians are not overweight because the body generally resists converting carbohydrates into fat. Eventually, however, if you eat too many carbohydrates, the liver will convert some of them into fat. Consequently, following a big meal with a whole bag of jelly beans is asking for trouble.

Another troubling issue arises from the fact that many people are tempted to smother a good, healthful carbohydrate food with fat. Consider, for example, the following common examples: pasta with cream sauce; a baked potato with butter or sour cream; broccoli or cauliflower with melted cheese; popcorn with butter; bread with butter; and a salad with a creamy dressing such as French, blue cheese, or Thousand Islands. In each of these dishes, the fat makes you fat, not the carbohydrate underneath.

Consequently, it is unfair to blame carbohydrate foods

Carbohydrate Foods Without a Great Deal of Fat

To	Add
Breads and bagels	• jam or jelly, but no butter or margarine.
Pasta	• a tomato-based sauce and add vegetables. A little olive oil is fine.
Baked potato	• add black pepper, salsa sauce, or low- or no-fat sour cream or yogurt.
Popcorn	• air-popped with no butter, or microwave popcorn with no more than two grams of fat per three cups. Low-salt variety is also a good idea.
Vegetables	• herbs and spices.
Salads	• olive oil and vinegar dressing (lightly dressed) or just squeeze lemon juice over vegetables for a no-fat version.

110

for weight gain. By learning to eat carbohydrate foods without adding a lot of fat and by relying on carbohydrates for at least 65 percent of your daily calories, you'll start to break the weight-loss barrier and improve your health status.

CARBOHYDRATES AND DIETARY FIBRE

In addition to providing energy and protective nutrients, carbohydrate foods also contain the only source of dietary fibre. Dietary fibre is defined as the part of a carbohydrate food that the body cannot digest. As a result, it is not absorbed into the bloodstream, but rather travels through the intestinal tract and is expelled from the body in fecal matter. As it travels through the intestinal tract, however, dietary fibre provides various powerful disease-fighting functions.

From a functional standpoint, two types of dietary fibre are found in carbohydrate foods. One type of fibre helps to lower blood cholesterol and is therefore an *anti-cholesterol fibre*. The other type reduces the risk of colon cancer and possibly breast cancer, and is therefore an *anti-cancer fibre*.

Anti-Cholesterol Fibre

Anti-cholesterol fibre binds to cholesterol like a magnet and prevents it from being absorbed into the bloodstream. Instead, the fibre drags the cholesterol through the intestinal tract, and is eventually excreted in fecal matter. Anti-cholesterol fibre also clings to a building block of cholesterol in the body, known as a bile acid, and reduces its absorption into the bloodstream. As a result,

If your cholesterol is above 200 mg%, we suggest that you eat a fibre-rich oatmeal cereal for breakfast at least four times a week and half a cup of red kidney beans every day. In addition, eat at least two anti-cholesterol fruits such as apples, peaches, pears, and plums daily. You may also want to sprinkle one to two tablespoons of flaxseed powder on your cereal or take two teaspoons of Metamucil per day. Of course, reducing your intake of saturated fat is another necessary component of lowering your cholesterol level.

A Word from Dr. Simon

As you eat anti-cholesterol fibre, imagine the benefits to your body. One woman used to enjoy her morning Bran Buds while visualizing cholesterol being sucked into her bowels. She would smile to herself as she focused on this image. It was only a 10-second visualization, but many brief moments will change how you perceive certain foods.

anti-cholesterol fibre can lower blood cholesterol level by 10 to 25 percent — an extremely significant drop since one of every two people dies from heart disease or related cardiovascular problems, partly due to cholesterol clogging their arteries. For example, the average North American has a blood cholesterol level of 215 to 225 mg% (5.4 to 5.7 mmol/L). Although a safe level of cholesterol is considered to be under 200 mg%, an ideal level of cholesterol would be 150 to 160 mg% (3.9 mmol/L).

> **Carbohydrate Foods with Anti-cholesterol Fibre**
>
> Oat bran: oatmeal breakfast cereals
> Beans and peas: especially red kidney beans
> Fruits: especially apples, peaches, pears, plums
> Berries: strawberries, blueberries, blackberries, raspberries, boysenberries
> White rind of citrus fruits: oranges, grapefruit, tangerines, clementines
> Carrots and potatoes
> Psyllium husk fibre (the active ingredient in Metamucil)
> Flaxseed powder

If a person with a blood cholesterol of 225 mg% lowers his or her level by 15 percent, it would become 192 mg%. Similarly, a person with a blood cholesterol of 240 mg% who would have double the risk of a heart attack than the average person, would experience a drop to 204 mg%. This significant drop would reduce the risk for a heart attack by at least 50 percent. The studies that yielded the best results for lowering cholesterol used oat bran and red kidney beans as the anti-cholesterol fibre. To replicate these results, you must eat about four ounces of oat bran or half a cup of red kidney beans each day.

Anti-Cancer Fibre

Certain carbohydrates found in whole wheat, corn, and rice contain a type of fibre that promotes the health of the large bowel and may also reduce the risk of breast cancer and other hormone-dependent cancers. Wheat bran, corn bran, and rice bran act like sponges in the intestinal tract, attracting water to the developing fecal matter. This process creates a bulking effect, which puts pressure on the walls of the intestinal tract. The muscular layer of the intestinal wall responds by contracting rhythmically, pushing the fecal matter through the large bowel faster than usual. The result is better regularity and softer stools.

Colon cancer is the second-leading cause of cancer deaths in North America. Lung cancer, the leading death-causing cancer, is linked in 87 percent of the cases to cigarette smoking. And up to 80 percent of all cases of colon cancer are estimated to result from faulty dietary habits. Furthermore, inadequate consumption of anti-cancer fibre appears to be a significant contributing factor to the incidence of this devastating disease. Both the American and Canadian Cancer Associations recommend that we consume 25 to 35 grams of dietary fibre daily, at least half of which should come from anti-cancer fibre sources. Yet, the average North American currently eats only 12 to 15 grams of fibre — one-third to one-half the recommended amount.

Eating fat also contributes to increased risk for colon cancer. When we eat fat, both the gall bladder and liver release bile acids into the intestinal tract. As these bile acids travel through the large bowel, bacteria can convert them into cancer-causing sterols. We should also avoid eating smoked meats and fish since the smoking process releases polycyclic aromatic hydrocarbons into the food. These products are classified as carcinogens because they are believed to produce cancerous changes. The same principle applies to heterocyclic amines formed when we eat charred meat. When anaerobic bacteria die in the intestinal tract, they release agents called fecapentaenes that are also believed to damage colon cells.

Colon cancer is also linked with the consumption of more than one alcoholic drink per day (either one five-ounce glass of wine, 12 ounces of beer, or one ounce of hard liquor). Alcohol accelerates the delivery of cancer-causing

Carbohydrate Foods Containing Anti-Cancer Fibre

High wheat-fibre breakfast cereals
Whole-wheat bread and pastas
Pure wheat bran
Brown rice
Puffed rice cereals
Whole rice crackers
Corn
Popcorn
Cornmeal
Corn bran
Corn flakes
Peas and beans, especially chickpeas and red kidney beans
Psyllium husk fibre (Metamucil-R)

agents to the cells and produces damaging free radicals that are linked to genetic damage and cancer. Two large studies, the Nurses' Health Study and the Health Professionals' Follow-Up Study, which tracked the dietary behaviour and health histories of almost 200,000 U.S. health care professionals, showed a very strong association between alcohol and colon cancer.

Despite these grim statistics, the good news is that you can play an active role in preventing colon cancer. First, avoid or minimize exposure to foods that generate carcinogens in the body. Second, increase your consumption of the protective nutrients that help to minimize the damage, such as anti-cancer fibre. Anti-cancer fibre is an important nutrient that dilutes cancer-causing agents due to its high water volume, and, in turn, dilutes the concentration and power of any carcinogens present in the bowel. It also moves the developing fecal matter through the body faster, decreasing the time during which cancer-causing agents are in contact with the bowel wall. Many researchers believe that anti-cancer fibre also helps to prevent appendicitis, irritable bowel syndrome, diverticular disease, gall-bladder disease, varicose veins, hemorrhoids, and constipation.

Furthermore, recent studies suggest that wheat bran may also help to reduce the risk of breast cancer and other estrogen-dependent cancers such as breast, ovarian, endometrial, and cervical cancers. Here's how it works. Besides its other functions, the liver acts continuously as a filter for the bloodstream, and filters out various estrogen hormones. When we eat a meal, the liver dumps some of these estrogens into the intestinal tract, where they are reabsorbed into the bloodstream. Wheat bran can bind to these estrogens in the intestinal tract and prevent their reabsorption into the body. In turn, this lowering of the background levels of cancer-promoting estrogens may reduce the risk of cancer, especially of breast cancer.

As a result, you should choose wheat bran as your main anti-cancer fibre, with others as complementary sources. The easiest way to consume 10 to 15 grams of wheat bran fibre daily is to eat a high-fibre wheat bran breakfast cereal with low-fat (1% or skim) milk or yogurt. Read the label on the cereal box to ensure that one serving contains at least 10 grams of fibre. You can also sprinkle pure wheat bran on other cereals or add it to other foods. Whole-wheat, pumpernickel, and seven-grain breads are other good sources of wheat bran.

Dietary Fat

The typical North American diet provides 20 percent of its calories from the good carbohydrates and another 20 percent from sugary carbohydrates like the white sugar used in coffee, tea, soft drinks, doughnuts and pastries, chocolate bars, and other sweets. About 15 to 20 percent of calories come from protein and about 35 to 40 percent from fat. Not only do we have an inadequate intake of good carbohydrates, but our intake of fat is also ridiculously high. To improve our health, prevent degenerative illnesses, and make our bodies fitter and leaner, we need to eat low-fat foods and focus on good carbohydrates at every meal.

Studies clearly show that vegan vegetarians, who eat no animal fat, have very little heart disease and cancer, and tend to be at or near their ideal body weight. A strict vegetarian program of this type usually provides only 10 percent of its calories from fat. As a result, die-hard health evangelists believe that everyone should convert to a strict vegan vegetarian program. We agree that this would be an ideal solution. However, as discussed earlier, very few people will stop eating meat, chicken, fish, cheese, milk, eggs, and ice cream for the rest of their lives.

Consequently, our Two-Staple System offers a more reasonable and practical way to lower your fat intake, while still having some meat and dairy products, and snack and dessert foods.

Total fat intake is composed of four types of fat – saturated fat, polyunsaturated fat, mono-saturated fat, and Omega 3 fats. Studies conducted by the National Cholesterol Program in the United States indicate that we should not consume more than 15 to 20 grams of saturated fat per day. Despite this recommendation, the average North American consumes 60 to 70 grams of saturated fat per day.

Following our discussion of how too much saturated fat encourages weight gain, colon cancer, breast cancer, prostate cancer, and heart attacks, you can decide how much saturated fat you will allow into your body each day. Once you understand how saturated fat interacts with your body's metabolism, you'll be able to visualize the consequence of eating a hamburger, milkshake, bacon and eggs, sausages, a steak or veal sandwich, or a plate of nachos covered with melted cheese, sour cream, and guacamole.

COMMON SOURCES OF SATURATED FAT

Let's first examine some common foods that are high in saturated fat.

- High-fat meats include most pork and beef products – steaks, ground beef, burgers, hot dogs, luncheon meats, corned beef, pastrami, salami, spare ribs, and bacon.
- Many dairy products, including homogenized milk, cream, whipped cream, regular sour cream, and most cheeses, derive between 50 and 90 percent of their calories from fat, mostly saturated fat. A low-fat cheese is one that is no more than two percent milk fat, as listed on the label.
- Most cheeses, from cheddar cheese to cheese spreads to ricotta cheese, are all 50 to 90 percent fat, mostly saturated fat. Many low-fat and no-fat cheeses are available on the marketplace today. Read the labels

carefully. Although many labels will claim that a cheese is "light" or lower in fat, the label will indicate that the product actually contains 15 to 17 percent milk fat. For example, regular cream cheese is about 29 percent milk fat, providing 90 percent of its calories from fat. The light variety is 17 to 19 percent milk fat but still derives 75 percent of its calories from fat or five grams of fat in just one ounce. Use cheeses that indicate that they are no higher than two percent milk fat.

- Regular ice cream is high in total fat and saturated fat, containing 40 to 77 percent calories from fat and usually about five to seven grams of saturated fat in just half a cup.
- One whole egg provides 68 percent calories from fat (two grams of saturated fat) and about 213 mg of cholesterol. All of the fat and cholesterol in the egg are found in the yolk. Egg white, an excellent source of protein, contains no fat or cholesterol.
- Most chocolate bars contain 12 to 17 grams of saturated fat and about 50 percent calories from fat.
- Pastries made with palm or coconut oil are high in saturated fat.
- Butter, with seven grams of saturated fat in one tablespoon, has 99 percent calories from fat in total.
- The typical glazed doughnut has 61 percent of calories from fat and five grams of saturated fat.

You get the idea!

THE CASE AGAINST SATURATED FAT

In recent years the Surgeon General of the United States has stated that eating too much saturated fat is the primary nutritional problem related to obesity and other degenerative problems. We couldn't agree more! The following section explains how saturated fat is linked to disproportionately high levels of colon cancer, breast cancer, and heart disease – not to mention weight gain – in this part of the world.

Saturated Fat and Colon Cancer

As we discussed earlier, fat contributes to colon cancer. Even if you're thin and your blood cholesterol is at a safe level, a diet high in saturated fat increases bile-acid secretion and leads to more cancer-causing sterols in the colon. In fact, the evidence shows strongly that a diet high in fat, especially saturated fat, is linked to a high incidence of colon cancer, which will affect one in 20 people in their lifetime. Eating a high-fat, low-fibre diet is believed to significantly encourage the development of this devastating illness.

Saturated Fat, Obesity, and Reproductive Organ Cancers

Eating foods that are high in saturated fat can cause reactions in the body that could encourage cancers of the breast, ovaries, endometrium, and prostate. After the small intestine digests saturated fat, the fat is absorbed into the body and travels to the liver. There, it is packaged with cholesterol and other ingredients and is shipped to the bloodstream. Once in the bloodstream, the saturated fat is picked up by fat cells, which then increase in size. Our bodies are programmed to absorb saturated fat and store it efficiently in fat cells.

Consequently, eating saturated fat is one of the main causes of weight gain and obesity. As fat cells become larger, they are more likely to pick up cholesterol from the bloodstream in the form of a hormone called *androstenadione,* which is composed of cholesterol in the adrenal glands. Inside the fat cell, androstenadione is converted into an estrogen hormone called *estrone hormone.* The fat cells then secrete the estrone hormone into the bloodstream, where it will eventually exert its effects on the breast, ovaries, and uterus. The estrone hormone is considered to be the most cancer-permissive estrogen that the body produces. The larger the fat cells, the more estrone hormone they tend to produce.

Breast cancer now afflicts one in nine women during their lifetime. Any breast-cancer study has suggested that being overweight is a risk for developing breast cancer. For example, a five-year follow-up study to the New York University Women's Health Study noted that overweight women, who also had the highest blood levels of estrone hormone, were three times more likely to develop breast cancer over the next five years of their life than women of normal weight who had lower levels of the hormone in their blood. Similarly, two prominent cancer researchers, Drs. Doll and Peto, who have extensively investigated environmental causes of breast cancer, recently suggested that it may be possible to avoid up to 50 percent of breast cancer simply by altering dietary patterns. This finding was reported by P.T. Strickland and J.D. Groupman in the March 1995 supplement edition of *The American Journal of Clinical Nutrition*. Furthermore, since the ovaries and endometrium are also affected by the estrone hormone and other estrogens made in fat cells, cancers of these organs are also linked to a high-fat diet and weight gain.

This is not to suggest, however, that only women are susceptible to the effects of estrogen hormones. Men's prostate glands also contain estrogen receptors. Similar to the increased likelihood of overweight women developing breast cancer, overweight men have a greater risk of developing prostate cancer than leaner men. For example, Dr. Edward Giovanucci of Harvard University recently studied the relationship between the incidence of prostate cancer and the environment. In his review, he indicated that there is a 120-fold variation in the incidence of prostate cancer between the countries with the lowest incidence of this disease, and the countries, such as Canada and the United States, with the highest incidence. He states that only nine percent of the cases of prostate cancer have a genetic component and that environmental exposures probably produce the overwhelming majority of cases. Interestingly, the primary promoter of prostate cancer from the environment is considered to be too much dietary fat, especially saturated fat. As stated earlier, saturated fat is strongly linked to colon cancer, is the strongest dietary promoter of weight gain and obesity, and elevates blood cholesterol levels that become the building block of the estrone hormone and other cancer-permissive reproductive hormones.

Saturated Fat and Heart Attacks

Besides its link to colon, prostate, and breast cancers, saturated fat also promotes heart attacks, strokes, and related vascular problems. In fact, approximately 50 percent of North Americans die from heart attacks and other cardiovascular diseases. Tragically, these problems begin prematurely in our society. For example, from the age of 35 for men and 45 for women, the chance of dying from heart disease increases progressively and dramatically. All of the evidence shows that by eating less saturated fat, increasing our exercise, quitting smoking, and remaining at a more ideal weight, many cardiovascular problems would never occur or could be postponed for 20 years.

The way in which saturated fat contributes to heart disease and other vascular problems is fairly straightforward. Not only do fat cells pick up saturated fat from the bloodstream, but muscles also pick up that fat and burn it in their resting metabolism just to sustain themselves. Consequently, the more muscle composition you have, the more quickly your metabolism will extract fat from the bloodstream and burn it, even while you're resting. Each pound of muscle consumes up to 35 calories per day in its resting state. So, if you begin to exercise and gain five pounds of muscle, you actually increase your resting metabolism by up to 175 calories per day – 10 to 15 percent.

Your muscles will then pick up more of the fat in your blood-stream and less will be stored by fat cells.

Cholesterol

As saturated fat is picked up by muscles, fat cells, and other tis-sues to be stored or immediately used for energy, the remaining component is primarily cholesterol. Cholesterol serves many important functions: it is the building block of the outer skin of all the cells, of the steroid and reproductive hormones, and of bile acids required for fat digestion. Exposure to direct sun-light converts cholesterol stored beneath the skin into vitamin D, which is required for calcium absorption and other impor-tant functions. However, once the cells have all the cholesterol they need, they stop drawing cholesterol from the bloodstream.

If more cholesterol is produced than the body needs, it remains in the bloodstream for up to three to five days. As it travels through the bloodstream, cholesterol is inclined to stick to the artery walls, causing a progressive narrowing of the arteries. Over your lifetime, this progressive cholesterol nar-rowing, called plaque, can eventually block blood flow to your heart muscle, brain, toes, kidneys, and so on. If this narrowing occurs in the heart, it can cause a heart attack, angina, or heart failure. In the brain, it can cause a stroke or transient ischemic attack. In the fingers or toes, it can lead to gangrene and requires amputation. And, in the kidneys, it can lead to kidney failure and the need for dialysis treatments.

Luckily, we know both the safe and unsafe levels of choles-terol in the bloodstream as well as the safe and unsafe levels of saturated fat in a diet. As discussed earlier, in North America, the average blood cholesterol level is between 210 and 225 mg% or between 5.4 and 5.7 mmol/L on the Canadian scale. To reduce the risk of heart disease by 50 percent, blood choles-terol must be below 200 mg% or 5.2 mmol/L on the Canadian scale. If blood cholesterol rises to 240 mg% or 6.2 mmol/L on the Canadian scale, there is double the risk of heart disease. In terms of cardiovascular risk, the safest point is at 150 mg% or 3.9 mmol/L on the Canadian scale.

The primary reason for unsafe levels of cholesterol in our society is that North Americans eat too much saturated fat. Granted, some people have a genetic problem that results in excessively high cholesterol problems even when they eat a low-fat diet, and these people need drug treatment to control their cholesterol. In a review of this subject, Dr. William Castelli, the scientific director of the prestigious heart study, "The Framingham Heart Study," found that 55 percent of Americans have unsafe levels of blood cholesterol. However, he also stated that only 10 percent of these people require drug intervention to reduce their cholesterol levels to a safe range. This means that 90 percent of North Americans with high cholesterol can attain safe levels of cholesterol by adopting different lifestyle patterns, including eating less saturated fat. Dr. Castelli's findings support those of the National Cholesterol Education Program, which suggest that a person should consume no more than 15 grams of saturated fat per day. Our Two-Staple System includes this guideline as one of the essential components of the program.

How Much Cholesterol Is Too Much?

Researchers of cardiovascular disease tell us that we should eat no more than 150 to 200 mg of cholesterol each day. Yet just one egg yolk contains more than that amount! Other significant sources of cholesterol include organ meats such as liver, kidneys, and brains. For example, three ounces of liver contain 366 mg of cholesterol, three ounces of kidney contain 625 mg, and three ounces of brains have 1,680 mg. Some controversy concerns shellfish such as crab, lobster, and shrimp, which are low in fat, but have a moderate amount of cholesterol. For example, three ounces of crab or lobster contain about 78 mg of cholesterol and three ounces of shrimp have about 128 mg. According to recent findings, these levels of cholesterol may be too high by 30 percent. If your cholesterol is already low enough, however, you can probably include these foods in your diet two or three times per month.

Obviously, eating a high-fat food presents no immediate threat to your life. In fact, you probably won't have a heart attack in the five minutes following after a high-fat binge. But eventually a day of reckoning will arrive, and those people whose daily diet is filled with high-fat foods will desperately seek ways to avoid the inevitable by-pass heart surgery. Although it can be somewhat lonely to choose fruit salad while your friends are indulging in more decadent desserts, the rewards speak for themselves. From a dietary standpoint, the most important thing you can do to avoid degenerative disease and weight gain is to monitor your saturated-fat intake.

UNSATURATED FATS

Saturated fat is not the only fat you should be aware of. You should also consider two types of oily fats: oils that have as their principal fat *polyunsaturated fats*, and oils that have as their principal fat *mono-unsaturated fats*. The common polyunsaturated oils are corn oil, sunflower seed oil, safflower oil, and mixed vegetable oils. Until recently, these oils were considered to be the answer to many health problems because they tend to lower blood cholesterol when they are substituted for saturated fat.

Recent studies, however, suggest being cautious about these oils for several reasons. First, many polyunsaturated fats in the body are converted into a type of hormone called Prostaglandin-Series 2. Prostaglandin-Series 2 tends to promote stickiness of the platelets or clotting cells in the blood. This stickiness can result in a clumping together of platelets, which obstructs blood flow. Second, Prostaglandin-Series 2 encourages spasms of the artery wall, which can further restrict blood flow. Prostaglandin also promotes inflammatory reactions in the blood vessel wall, and may even aggravate arthritic conditions, premenstrual syndrome, fibrocystic breast disease, and other inflammatory conditions. Finally, several animal and laboratory studies suggest that polyunsaturated fats more easily allow cancer-causing agents to damage body tissues, thereby producing tumours.

For these reasons, you should use oils that are dominated by the mono-unsaturated fats such as olive oil, peanut oil, and canola oil. The mono-unsaturated fats in these oils are just as effective in lowering cholesterol as are the polyunsaturated fats. However, mono-unsaturated fats do not make the blood platelets sticky and are not converted into Prostaglandin-Series

2 hormones. Moreover, several studies link the use of olive oil and peanut oil with a decreased risk of certain cancers. Breast cancer is one such example: this cancer is less prevalent among Asian and Mediterranean people who use peanut oil and olive oil respectively as their main source of fat.

With the Two-Staple System, however, we suggest that you use as little total fat as possible. Granted, a little oil can add a lot to a meal. To dress a salad, we suggest using a little olive oil. To stir-fry vegetables, chicken, or shrimp, use a little peanut oil or canola oil. To sauté vegetables, use peanut oil or canola oil. And to make a tomato-based pasta sauce, add a small amount of olive oil. In summary, feel free to use small amounts of the mono-unsaturated fats from olive oil, peanut oil, and canola oil on the Two-Staple System. We discourage the use of corn oil, sunflower oil, and mixed vegetable oils, however.

HYDROGENATED FATS

Hydrogenated fats are found in margarine, shortenings, and commercially made salad dressings and are often included in many commercial baked goods. Hydrogenated fats tend to elevate cholesterol in a similar way to saturated fat, and to encourage the production of the Prostaglandin-Series 2 hormone. Some of the solution-substitution foods such as jujubes and licorice on the Two-Staple System contain small amounts of hydrogenated fats, trans-fatty acids, or partially hydrogenated fats. Although you can eat small amounts of these foods, do not add them to foods you are preparing. For example, do not spread margarine on a slice of toast or a baked potato. And don't assume that it is better to use shortening instead of butter if you decide to bake cookies. Instead, spread jam on your toast or bagel. Make your own salad dressing from olive oil and vinegar. Eat a low-fat diet, and don't be overly concerned that a low-fat granola bar, low-fat popcorn, or jujube contains a little hydrogenated fat.

Omega 3 Fats

All of the news about fat is not necessarily bad. For example, the Omega 3 fats found in fish appear to be helpful in reducing the risk of heart attack and other vascular problems. The early evidence that fatty fish could reduce heart disease came from studies involving Eskimos in Greenland. Their traditional diet, which is primarily fatty fish, seal, and whale meat, looked like a prescription for heart disease: it was high in fat, high in protein, and low in fruit, fibre, and leafy green vegetables. Surprisingly, however, researchers found little evidence of heart disease. Similarly, in Japanese fishing villages where the consumption of fatty fish is also a main staple of the diet, heart disease is extremely rare.

Fatty fish are a rich source of a special type of fat called Omega 3 fats. In the body these fats can be converted into a hormone known as Prostaglandin-Series 3. Prostaglandin-Series 3 has the opposite effect of Prostaglandin-Series 2; it tends to reduce the stickiness of the blood by making blood platelets less likely to clump together inside the arteries. These hormones relax the blood vessel wall, allowing better blood flow to each tissue, and discourage inflammatory reactions inside the blood vessel and in the body in general. Some studies suggest that Omega 3 fats may also discourage cancer development by their impact on the fluidity of the cell's outer skin or membrane.

From a health perspective, it is likely optimal to eat the fattest selections of fish because they contain the highest amounts of Omega 3 fats. The best selections include salmon, tuna, sardines, sablefish, mackerel, anchovies, and herring. Your next best choices are turbot, shark, bluefish, bass, smelt, oysters, swordfish, rainbow trout, and pompano. Even shellfish such as shrimp, crab, and lobster contain Omega 3 fats and are low in saturated fat. However, as discussed earlier, since they contain the equivalent amount of cholesterol per serving as lean beef, include them infrequently in your diet. Omega 3 fats are also found in vegetarian sources such as whole grains, beans, seaweed, and soy products such as tofu and soy milk. Flaxseed oil capsules have gained popularity in the wellness movement because of their high Omega 3 fat composition. However, once in the body, Omega 3 fats from vegetarian sources must undergo a lengthening of their fatty acid chain before they can be transformed into the disease-preventing Prostaglandin-Series 3. The attractive feature of deriving Omega 3 fats from fish is that these fats are immediately available for conversion to Prostaglandin-Series 3 hormone and they provide a wide variety of flesh foods to include in your daily meal plans.

Protein

As a result of aggressive marketing campaigns and much misquoted evidence, many people mistakenly believe that protein provides an excellent source of energy. Yet protein actually plays a minimal role in the body's energy production. Its primary role is to build and rebuild body structure. It is used to form muscle, bone, teeth, hair, and structural tissue in the body as well as to serve myriad other functions.

Unless you are an athlete who is doing heavy training in a 24-hour period, your body doesn't use much protein. Therefore, your body needs protein for only 15 percent of its total daily calories. More specifically, daily protein need is based on body weight. To maintain lean mass – muscle, bone, connective tissues – and remain in good health, the average person needs about one gram of protein daily for every kilogram (2.2 pounds) of body weight.

A person who does 30 minutes or more of aerobic activity more than four times per week or who is on a strength-training program, however, can increase protein intake up to 1.5 grams of protein for every kilogram of body weight. This increased protein will replace the protein breakdown that accompanies regular aerobic training and will provide an anabolic effect for strength-training athletes. The term "anabolic" infers an increase in muscle size.

The Two-Staple System provides two primary sources of protein: low-fat flesh sources including poultry and fish selections, and low-fat dairy products. Additional protein is also found in some carbohydrate foods such as beans, peas, grains, starchy vegetables, and cereal products. As an added benefit, poultry-fish selections also provide iron and vitamin B-12, which are often lacking in a strict vegetarian program. Low-fat dairy protein foods provide a rich source of calcium and vitamin D, which can also be difficult to attain at optimal levels when following a strict vegan vegetarian program.

Many meat and dairy products that are high in protein are also high in saturated fat and are often high in cholesterol. Examples include ground beef, bacon, most luncheon meats, most cheeses, ice cream, whole eggs, spare ribs, and veal chops. The Two-Staple System is designed to meet your protein needs through the use of low-fat flesh protein foods, low-fat dairy protein foods, and complementary protein from many complex-carbohydrate foods.

Low-fat flesh and dairy protein foods included on the Two-Staple System:

- Skinless chicken breast
- Skinless turkey breast
- Cornish hen
- Fish – salmon, tuna, mackerel, sablefish, herring, sardines, anchovies, turbot, shark, bluefish, bass, smelt, oysters, swordfish, rainbow trout, pompano
- Shellfish (1 to 2 times per month) – shrimp, crab lobster
- No-fat milk (skim)
- No-fat yogurt
- 1% milk
- 1% yogurt
- Cheese – no fat or 1% or 2%
- Egg whites

Putting it
all together: the Two-Staple System

In this chapter, we help you use your knowledge of carbohydrates, fibre, fat, and protein to develop a nutrition plan that will minimize your risk of degenerative diseases and transform you into a fitter, leaner, healthier person.

A Breakdown of Calories on the Two-Staple System

Here's a review of how your food choices should be divided:

Carbohydrates 60 to 75 percent, with emphasis on complex carbohydrates and 25 to 35 grams of dietary fibre daily

Protein 12 to 15 percent, from low-fat flesh and dairy sources and additional protein found in some complex carbohydrate foods — legumes, grains, starchy vegetables

Fat no more than 20 percent, limiting saturated fat to fewer than 15 grams, with the major contribution of fat coming from mono-unsaturated fats — olive oil, peanut oil, canola oil — and the Omega 3 fats from fish

If you can reach these targets every day and maintain your fitness goal of at least 30 minutes of gentle endurance activity daily, you'll see results. Remember that it is not enough to reach these targets partway. For example, to reduce your risk of colon cancer, it is not enough just to have a high wheat-bran-fibre breakfast — you must also lower your fat intake.

The Three Meals

Let's review the three meals of the Two-Staple System.

1. One meal includes a low-fat dairy protein food such as low-fat milk, yogurt, cheese, or egg whites with two or three good carbohydrate selections. This is your low-fat Dairy-Protein meal.
2. One meal includes a poultry-fish selection such as chicken breast, sliced turkey, tuna, or salmon with two or three good carbohydrate selections. This is your low-fat Fish-Poultry meal.
3. One meal is composed of two or three good carbohydrate selections only. This is your Carbo-Energy meal.

Your plan should also take into account the following elements:

- Cheating — If you are going to cheat between meals or have a dessert, choose foods from our solution-substitution list (see page 104).
- Oils — If you are making a salad, use a small amount of olive oil and a vinegar of your choice. If you are making a stir-fry or vegetable sauté, use peanut or canola oil.
- Drink fluids that don't add calories to your diet such as
  - Water: filtered water, spring water, soda water, mineral water, or distilled water. Distilled water is your

best choice. Use tap water sparingly unless you have a home-filtration system.

— Coffee and tea: black with no sugar. Your next best choice is to add low-fat milk and/or an artificial sweetener. Tea is a better choice than coffee. Chinese green tea and regular black teas contain antioxidants that appear to reduce risk of heart disease.

— Diet sodas: sugar-free varieties. Limit your intake to one or two per day.

— Juices: It is better to eat the whole fruit than it is to drink the juice. Pure fruit juice or carrot juice is a concentrated form of sugar and calories. Since the fruit's fibre has usually been removed, you lose the cholesterol-lowering benefit. Dilute juice with 50 percent water to reduce the calories and sugar.

A Word from Dr. Simon

Take two slow deep breaths and focus on your wellness image to remind yourself that this program is for you. If you become anxious or your inner conversation is confused or unsure, reread the information. Listen to your inner dialogue.

A Summary of the Two-Staple System

Rule #1 Eat one of each type of meal daily – a Dairy-Protein Meal, Fish-Poultry Meal, and Carbo-Energy Meal. You can have them in any order you choose.

Rule #2 Use mono-unsaturated fat oils such as olive oil, peanut oil, or canola oil.

Rule #3 Keep your salt intake low, especially if you have high blood pressure. Salt can also increase water retention, and its caustic properties are linked to stomach cancer.

Rule #4 Choose carbohydrate foods that are high in anti-cholesterol or anti-cancer fibre.

Rule #5 Select snack foods from the list of solution-substitution foods.

Rule #6 Do at least 30 minutes of gentle endurance exercise daily.

The Vegetarian Alternative

The Two-Staple System can become a complete vegetarian program by substituting soybean products for the dairy and meat products and by focusing on carbohydrates that contain the most protein such as beans, peas, grains (rice, barley, oats, corn), bread, and on starchy vegetables such as potatoes, sweet potatoes, and squash. Soybean products are also a good source of protein and are available in many forms. For example, soy milk can substitute for regular milk; low-fat tofu cheese for regular cheese; tofu for chicken or shrimp in a stir-fry. Tofu hot dogs, sausages, and a variety of tofu and textured vegetable-protein meat substitutes are also available. Make sure that you choose low-fat varieties. As well, there are fermented soy products such as miso and tempeh, some of which contain vitamin B-12 from the fermentation process.

Although a vegetarian lifestyle is a healthy approach to living, if you choose to adopt this lifestyle, you must be careful to provide your body with sufficient protein, iron, vitamin B-12, calcium, and vitamin D. To safeguard against a deficiency of these vital protective nutrients, you should take a broad-spectrum multiple vitamin and mineral. We will discuss supplementation in more detail in Chapter 9.

The Daily Success Journal

The Daily Success Journal is a powerful, self-monitoring tool that we recommend for each of our nutrition clients to use. This journal provides an opportunity for you to track your nutrition and exercise performance. Each day, you record the food you eat and the exercise program you complete. As you follow the Two-Staple System, identify which meal during the day represents your Dairy-Protein Meal, Fish-Poultry Meal, and Carbo-Energy Meal. Don't skip this step. Recording your dietary intake will keep you on track.

Combination Foods

Dishes that are prepared with more than one main ingredient are referred to as *combination foods*. Examples of combination foods include pizza, lasagna, cabbage rolls, and stuffed peppers, all of which contain both protein and complex carbohydrates. When you record these foods in your journal, count them as both protein and complex carbohydrates.

In general, try to avoid eating a dairy protein and a flesh protein during the same meal. Instead, divide your daily consumption of protein between two meals. That way,

Example of a Daily Success Journal

Date: February 26

Breakfast   Type: Dairy-Protein Meal
1/3 cup bran cereal with 8 oz. no-fat yogurt
1 slice brown toast with jam
black tea

Lunch   Type: Carbo-Energy Meal
penne primavera (pasta with tomato sauce, red peppers, onions, broccoli, snow peas)
whole-wheat roll
mineral water

Dinner   Type: Fish-Poultry Meal
1/4 chicken (skinless broiled breast)
3/4 cup brown rice
sliced tomatoes

Snacks
3 cups popcorn
small fruit salad

Supplementation
multiple vitamin with extra vitamin E and C and calcium

Physical Activity/Exercise
30 minutes on treadmill at 3.5 m.p.h.
30 minutes weight training

Daily Success Journal

Date:

Breakfast   Type: Dairy-Protein Meal

Lunch   Type: Carbo-Energy Meal

Dinner   Type: Fish-Poultry Meal

Snacks

Supplementation

Physical Activity/Exercise

your body will be better able to use the protein as it needs it. If you eat too much protein at one time, you could overload your body's capacity to use it efficiently. As a result, some of the excess protein could be converted into fats and carbohydrates, leaving damaging by-products in your system.

The following examples of healthful foods combine protein and complex carbohydrates. Because all of these foods contain one low-fat dairy or flesh protein and at least two complex carbohydrates, they meet the requirements for a protein meal.

- Italian manicotti: tubular pasta noodles stuffed with low-fat ricotta cheese and cooked spinach, covered with seasoned tomato sauce and baked
- Vegetarian pizza: pizza dough, covered with low-fat cheese and tomato sauce. Additional toppings can include green peppers, mushrooms, onions, sliced tomatoes, and red peppers
- Vegetarian lasagna: pasta noodles baked with low-fat ricotta cheese, tomato sauce, and additional vegetables such as spinach and mushrooms
- Stuffed tomatoes: baked tomatoes stuffed with low-fat cheese and spinach

- Cabbage rolls: boiled cabbage stuffed with rice, tomatoes, and optional lean ground veal or turkey
- Stuffed green peppers: baked green peppers stuffed with rice, tomatoes, and optional lean ground turkey or chicken
- Stir-fry: small chunks of chicken or seafood and assorted vegetables – broccoli, peppers, onions, green beans, zucchini, and cabbage – stir-fried in peanut oil and served on steamed rice
- Seafood and pasta salad: cooked pasta served cold with crab or shrimp, lightly seasoned with an olive oil or vinegar dressing
- Soup: vegetable, minestrone, cabbage borscht, chicken noodle, and other broth- or tomato-based soups are fantastic complex-carbohydrate foods. These foods help fill your stomach and provide a pleasant alternative to salads. Be careful of commercially prepared soups; they usually have a very high sodium content. Cream-based soups are very high in fat.
- Pasta fagioli: pasta and beans
- Ratatouille served with rice
- Tuna and vegetable salad: chunks of water-packed tuna served on a bed of mixed vegetables and dressed with olive oil and vinegar.

Samples of Easy-to-Prepare Meals

Vegetarian Breakfast Meals

Meal One
- 8 to 12 ounces hot oatmeal
- 1 slice of toast with 2 tsp. jam
  OR
  1 fruit serving
- no-calorie beverage

Meal Two
- 1 bagel with up to 4 tsp. jam
  OR
  2 slices toast with up to 4 tsp. jam
- one fruit serving
  OR
  8 oz. diluted juice
- no-calorie beverage

Meal Three
- low-fat bran muffin (maximum: 2 grams fat)
- one fruit serving
  OR
  8 oz. diluted juice
- no-calorie beverage

VEGETARIAN LUNCH AND DINNER MEALS

Meal One
- 1/2 cup pasta (measure prior to cooking)
- tomato sauce
- bean salad or mixed-green salad
- 1 slice bread (optional)

Meal Two
- 1 cup steamed or boiled rice (uncooked)
- 1 cup stir-fried vegetables (broccoli, green beans, Swiss chard, onions, green peppers). Use 1 tsp. peanut or canola oil in cooking.

Meal Three
- 1 mini or individual pizza made without cheese
- vegetable toppings
- bean salad or mixed-green salad

Meal Four
- 1 bowl minestrone, vegetable, or chicken noodle soup
- bean salad
- 2 slices bread or 1 bagel

DAIRY-PROTEIN BREAKFAST MEALS

Meal One
- 8 oz. skim milk
- up to 1/2 cup high-fibre cereal
- 1 slice toast with 2 tsp. jam
  OR
  1 fruit serving or 8 oz. diluted juice

Meal Two
- 8 oz. low-fat yogurt
- up to 1/2 cup high-fibre cereal
- 1 slice toast with 2 tsp. jam
  OR
  1 fruit serving or 8 oz. diluted juice
- no-calorie beverage

Meal Three
- egg-substitute breakfast
- 1 slice toast with 2 tsp. jam

Meal Four
- 3 to 4 oz. low-fat cheese (0-2 percent milk fat)
- 1 bagel or 2 slices toast
- 1 fruit serving or 8 oz. diluted juice

DAIRY-PROTEIN LUNCH AND DINNER MEALS

Meal One

- 3 to 4 oz. low-fat cheese (0-2 percent milk fat)
- 2 slices toast or 1 bagel
- 1 fruit serving or 8 oz. diluted juice
- no-calorie beverage

Meal Two

- low-fat manicotti with cheese and bean salad
- low-fat cheese and vegetable lasagna and mixed-green salad

FISH-POULTRY LUNCH AND DINNER MEALS

Meal One

- 3 to 4 oz. fish, unskinned chicken, or turkey breast
- 1 vegetable serving
- 1 bread serving (optional)
- no-calorie beverage

Meal Two

- 3 to 4 oz. sliced chicken or turkey breast
- 2 slices bread
- mixed-green salad

Meal Three

- 1/2 cup pasta
- 3 to 4 oz seafood or fish cooked with a tomato sauce of your choice
- mixed-green salad
- 1 bread serving (optional)

Complex-Carbohydrate Snacks

fresh fruit
dried fruit
crackers
raw vegetable sticks
low-fat or no-fat popcorn
low-fat or no-fat muffins
rice crackers
low-fat granola bars

A Shopping List for Your Program

Shopping for the foods to include in your program can be easy and enjoyable if you follow a few basic steps.

- Prepare a list of foods that are included on the Two-Staple System and ensure that they are always readily available.
- Do not buy tempting foods such as potato chips, cakes, pies, pastries, ice cream, candy, cookies, and chocolate. If junk food is not available, you won't be tempted by it. Furthermore, don't buy these high-fat treats for your friends or family members. Like you, they will also benefit from the healthful alternatives outlined in the solution-substitutions list on page 104.

To get started, here's a sample shopping list from which you can choose the foods you like the best.

BEVERAGES

- Pure fruit and/or vegetable juices, with no added sugar.
- Distilled water, spring water, low-sodium mineral water, and soda water.
- Bottled water should be ozone-treated to help prevent bacterial growth. The best choice is either distilled water or water that has undergone reverse osmosis and de-ionization.

The Emergency Snack

Even the most dedicated of us may give in to urges when we are hungry. After all, all of us face situations that test our willpower. For example, how do you deal with meetings or seminars where doughnuts and pastries are provided as the mid-morning or mid-afternoon snack? Or what happens if you are driving all over town with a hundred errands to do and only have time for a quick bite?

The solution is to prepare for those moments of weakness. Always carry an emergency snack with you in case hunger strikes in a situation where a Two-Staple System meal is impractical. Any easily transportable complex-carbohydrate food will do. By snacking in this manner, you can restore your blood sugar to a normal level at vulnerable moments during the day, and stave off hunger until you have time for a proper meal.

In addition to choosing raw fruits and vegetables as an emergency snack, you will find other nutritional snacks on the market. For example, nutrition bars have a lower fat content than traditional snack foods and are enriched with health-promoting nutrients such as fibre, calcium, and iron. This new type of snack offers a healthful alternative to traditional chocolate bars. Preparing an emergency snack takes only a few minutes each day. Advance planning can help to ensure your success on the wellness track.

- Low-sodium mineral water and/or low-sodium soda water.
- Diet drinks.
- Other no-calorie beverages, such as herbal tea.

FRUITS AND VEGETABLES

- Fresh fruits that are high in vitamin C, beta carotene, and/or anti-cholesterol fibre. The best cholesterol-lowering fruits are apples, peaches, pears, plums, nectarines, the white rind of citrus fruits, blueberries, strawberries, raspberries, mangoes, and papaya. Anti-cancer fruits are those with lots of vitamin C or beta carotene. Citrus fruits and kiwis contain the most vitamin C. Orange fruits, including cantaloupe, apricots, peaches, nectarines, oranges, mangoes, and watermelon are highest in beta carotene.
- Fresh vegetables that are high in fibre and anti-cancer nutrients. Cruciferous vegetables such as Brussels sprouts, cabbage, turnips, cauliflower, and broccoli, are good anti-cancer foods. Vegetables that are high in beta carotene are also good anti-cancer foods. Carrots, squash, eggplant, and other orange/yellow vegetables, broccoli, spinach, and dark-green, leafy vegetables are all high in beta carotene. Carrots, potatoes, and peas are also high in fibre, so they are especially good for your heart.
- Canned or frozen fruit packed in its own juice, without added sugar
- Dried fruits, including raisins, for between-meal snacks
- Salad vegetables
- Vegetables, such as carrots, that can be eaten raw for snacks
- Potatoes

- Canned tomatoes
- Frozen vegetables, without added sodium

BREAD PRODUCTS

- Whole-grain breads and rolls, including wheat, rye, pumpernickel, whole-wheat bagels, pita; products that are high in fibre and low in fat
- High-fibre, low-fat biscuits
- Bagels
- Melba toast, rice crackers, bread sticks, soda crackers, and matzoth
- Pizza dough
- Low-fat muffins
- Pita bread
- Fibre cookies (available at drugstores)
- Baked pita and bagel chips

CEREALS AND GRAINS

- High-fibre breakfast cereals
- Oat bran and wheat bran
- Wheat germ
- Rice and other grains
- Pasta and noodles; all noodles are acceptable, but egg noodles are higher in cholesterol. Whole-wheat noodles and spinach noodles are especially good choices. Gnocchi, made from potatoes and flour, is another good option. It is a good source of protein that is low in fat and high in complex carbohydrates.

LEGUMES

- Peas and beans, fresh, dried, or canned, especially chickpeas and red kidney beans. Peas and beans are perfectly

balanced foods. Most are 60 percent complex carbohydrates, 15 percent protein, and 25 percent fat — perfectly in tune with your genetic dietary requirements.

LOW-FAT FLESH PROTEINS

- Chicken breasts
- Cooked, sliced chicken, or turkey breast for sandwiches
- Turkey — white meat
- Cornish game hens
- Fresh or frozen fish, preferably varieties high in Omega 3 fats such as salmon, mackerel, herring, trout, sardines, shad, anchovies, and albacore tune. Clams, crab, and mussels also contain Omega 3 fats.
- Canned water-packed salmon and tuna
- Seafood, such as clams, crabs, mussels, and shrimp

LOW-FAT DAIRY PROTEIN

- Plain yogurt with no more than one percent milk fat
- Skim milk or 1% milk
- Buttermilk made from skim milk
- Low-fat cheese (under five percent milk fat)

MISCELLANEOUS

- Popcorn
- Tomato sauce
- Extra virgin olive oil
- Peanut oil
- Vegetable-oil sprays
- Herbs and spices
- Vinegar
- Whole-fruit or dietetic jam, low in added sugar
- Salsa sauce

- Low-sodium clear broth and legume soups
- Vegetarian alternatives such as miso, tofu, soy milk, and tempeh

OCCASIONAL FOODS

- Avocados
- Diet soda drinks
- Frozen fruit ices or sherbets
- Low-fat frozen yogurt
- Pretzels — low sodium
- Lean beef or veal
- Margarine

Food Preparation

How you prepare food can affect its health-fixing qualities and taste. Here are some suggestions on how to prepare interesting and healthful meals for the food types used in the Two-Staple System.

"Give a man a fish and feed him for a day, or teach him how to fish and feed him for a lifetime."

GENERAL TIPS

- When you are shopping, read labels and choose foods with 2.5 or fewer grams of fat per 100 calories. Since each gram of fat contains nine calories, the calories you get from fat from these foods would be almost ideal — about 22.5 percent or less of the total.
- Nonstick pans enable you to cook without adding extra fat. Use a vegetable oil spray on ordinary pans instead of using oil, butter, or shortening.
- Prepare foods in ways that don't require added oil. Try broiling, baking, microwaving, or steaming.
- Sauté in wine or broth instead of oil.

Low-Fat Flesh Protein Foods

- Broil, grill, or steam poultry and fish.
- Cook poultry and fish in a fondue pot using consommé broth or a clear broth instead of oil.
- Poach poultry and fish in clear broth, vegetable juices, or water seasoned with lemon.
- Barbecue chicken or, occasionally, low-fat ground beef.
- Remove the skin from chicken, preferably before cooking it. Choose white rather than dark meat.
- When roasting chicken or turkey, baste with broth instead of fatty drippings.
- If you occasionally eat red meat, buy lean cuts and remove all excess fat.
- Add seafood, such as clams or mussels, to pasta dishes.
- Choose water-packed, not oil-packed, canned fish. Rinse to remove the salt.
- Mix tuna or salmon with yogurt instead of mayonnaise.
- Frozen dinners that are labelled "light" or "low-calorie" are not necessarily low in fat. Read the label carefully and choose only those with fewer than 7.5 grams of fat per 300-calorie serving.

Low-Fat Dairy Protein

- Drink milk with no more than one percent milk fat.
- Buy a pizza shell or plain frozen pizza and add vegetable toppings.
- Spread low-fat cheese thinly on bread as a substitute for butter or margarine.
- Use low-fat milk instead of cream or non-dairy creamer in coffee.

BREAKFAST CEREALS

- Choose breakfast cereals that provide at least six grams of fibre, but ideally 10 grams or more per serving. Use skim milk, 1% milk, or no-fat or 1% yogurt with dry cereals. You can also choose to add fruit.

BREAD

- Toasting bread increases its fibre content.
- Don't butter the bread. Butter is 80 percent fat. Also try to avoid margarine.
- Whole-fruit jam is a good alternative to butter. Read the label to ensure that it is high in fruit and low in sugar. Jam that is spread thinly on bread counts as one serving of complex carbohydrates.

CRACKERS AND BISCUITS

- Avoid all fried biscuits, chips, nachos, and tortillas, regardless of what type of oil they were fried in. Not only are these foods high in total fat, but the oil in which they were fried may also have been heated to high temperatures and left exposed to light and air, causing it to become carcinogenic.
- For snacks, try baked, crispy bread products such as pita chips or baked chips that are low in fat.

FRUIT

- Fruit salad makes a wonderful dessert.

VEGETABLES

- Try vegetables raw, steamed, broiled, microwaved,

marinated, or stir-fried. Serve them with rice.

- Bake or boil potatoes. Do not add butter; instead, use low-fat yogurt (one percent milk fat) or ultra low-fat sour cream (three to five percent milk fat). Try eating baked potatoes plain or with black pepper or salsa sauce.

- Avocados are high in mono-unsaturated fat. They are also high in vitamins and minerals, so you may eat small amounts occasionally. Try two small slices in a sandwich along with tomatoes, cucumbers, and alfalfa sprouts. A little avocado is a good substitute for cheese and other animal-based foods.

- Salads are a healthful way to eat vegetables. Spinach salad, chef's salad, and mixed-green salads, tossed with a light olive oil and vinegar dressing, are your best options. Shredded cabbage, seasoned with a light dressing of olive oil and vinegar is a tasty alternative to lettuce. Avoid Greek salads — feta cheese is loaded with both fat and salt, and hard-boiled eggs are high in cholesterol. Caesar salads are also very high in fat.

- To add variety to salads, try flavoured vinegars. Make your own by placing fresh herbs or garlic in wine vinegar and allowing the mixture to sit for a week.

GRAINS

- Rice is best steamed or boiled.
- Brown rice is better than white rice because of its higher fibre content.

PEAS AND BEANS

- Rinse canned peas and beans with water to remove excess salt and oil.
- Completely cover dried beans with cold water

overnight. Drain and cook them in fresh water until they are tender.

- Use light (low-fat) tomato sauces. Sauté vegetables in water or olive oil to add to the sauce. Green peppers, red peppers, mushrooms, onions, and zucchini are all excellent choices. Add clams, mussels, scallops, or chicken to your tomato sauce.
- Do not use cream or meat sauces since both are very high in fat.
- Canned tomato sauces with meat are very high in fat. Buy a fresh marinara sauce and add your own fresh vegetables. The vegetables improve the taste, add vitamins, and dilute the fat content.

OILS

- Use olive oil for salad dressings or sautéing vegetables.
- Use peanut oil for stir-frying.
- Vegetable oil sprays are acceptable substitutes for vegetable oils.

SNACK FOODS AND DESSERTS

- The urge to eat dessert often results from a delayed sense of fullness following a meal. Since it takes more than 30 minutes for your brain's appetite centre to shut off, wait 10 to 15 minutes after a meal before deciding to indulge in a dessert. You will probably find you are satisfied and no longer crave a treat.
- Get up from the table before dessert is served and go for a walk. This will curb your appetite and help you digest your meal.
- If you are a dessert-lover, plan to have dessert once a week so you don't feel deprived or unrewarded for your day-to-day efforts. Choose your moments

carefully and don't overindulge. Eating dessert once or twice a week is a good strategy. Sherbets, fruit ices, and frozen tofu desserts are all good options. You can also eat low-fat frozen yogurt occasionally. Your best everyday choice of dessert is fresh fruit.

- Unbuttered popcorn is a good snack food. Popcorn that is made in an air popper contains the least amount of fat. Most microwave popcorn is high in fat, but some low-fat varieties contain less than one gram of fat per three cups. Try using a salt substitute, too.
- Snacks such as potato chips and nacho chips are very high in fat. For healthful munchies, eat melba toast with salsa, rice crackers, raisins, baked bagel slices, or low-fat biscuits.
- Low-fat bran, oatmeal, or blueberry muffins are better options than doughnuts.
- Make your own chips. Cut corn tortillas into pieces, lightly coat a baking dish with nonstick spray, and bake at 375 degrees Fahrenheit (200 degrees Celsius) until they are light brown and crunchy.

BEVERAGES

- Drink six to eight glasses of water every day.
- As one of your complex-carbohydrate selections, you can dilute 1/4 glass of unsweetened juice with 3/4 glass of water or soda water.
- Limit your intake of caffeine beverages. Drink no more than two cups of black coffee a day.
- Try herbal teas or hot water and lemon as an alternative to coffee or regular tea.
- Diet drinks that contain aspartame are the most acceptable soft drinks, but don't overdo them. Diet soft drinks contain no nutritional value whatsoever.
- Avoid all beverages sweetened with sugar.

- Tap water is always an unknown commodity. Attach a water purifier to the water tap or reduce the amount of tap water you drink.
- An occasional alcoholic beverage is acceptable, but moderation is the key.

Dining Out

When you are dining away from home, it is often difficult to keep on track. The following suggestions will allow you to enjoy the dining-out experience without feeling guilty.

- Ask that your meal be prepared with less fat than the chef would typically use. For example, ask the chef to reduce the amount of oil used for stir-frying.
- When travelling by plane, request a low-fat meal or vegetarian option in advance.
- Salad bars are filled with high-fat extras, such as bacon bits, egg yolks, olives, and potato salads. Avoid these foods, and concentrate on fresh vegetables instead.
- Ask for sauces and dressings to be served on the side. This way you can control how much you use.
- Order baked potatoes, rice, or pasta instead of French fries.
- Order plain bean tostadas or bean burritos. Order fish or chicken sandwiches without the sauce. Make sure they are grilled, not fried.

The following examples are good food selections at different types of restaurants:

CHINESE RESTAURANTS

- Our favourite is Moo Goo Gai Pan — a bed of steamed rice covered with stir-fried vegetables — broccoli, onions, Swiss chard, Chinese vegetables, carrots, and shrimp or chicken.

- You might also want to try:
  - vegetable chow mein or chop suey
  - orange chicken
  - shrimp in garlic or tomato sauce
- Avoid fried dishes, especially foods in batter such as chicken balls or lemon chicken. Avoid any pork selections.

ITALIAN RESTAURANTS

- As an appetizer, try
  - minestrone soup
  - radicchio salad, dressing on the side
  - mixed-green salad, dressing on the side
  - calamari salad, oil dressing on the side
- For the main course, consider
  - pasta primavera
  - pasta in red sauce
  - pasta with seafood in a red sauce
  - penne with spicy tomato sauce
  - any grilled fish or chicken
  - pizza, with half the normal amount of cheese or no cheese. Ask what percentage of milk fat is listed for the cheese they are using. Add vegetarian toppings of your choice except olives, which are high in fat. A cheeseless vegetarian pizza is your best option.
  - avoid high-fat toppings such as bacon, sausage, pepperoni, and olives.

MEXICAN RESTAURANTS

- Our favourites are chicken fajitas, made with stir-fried chicken and onion. Make it into a sandwich by rolling chicken, onions, and other vegetables with salsa sauce in a soft tortilla bread.

- Leave out the sour cream and guacamole, which are both high in fat.
- Bean burritos are also quite low in fat, if you leave out the cheese.

CHICKEN RESTAURANTS

Good choices include

- chicken breast – grilled or barbecued with skin removed
- baked potato or rice, no French fries. Eat the potato without butter or margarine
- whole-wheat roll, no butter.

DELI DINING

Sandwiches and deli meal options include

- turkey sandwich on whole-wheat, pumpernickel, or rye bread with tomato, lettuce, and mustard for moisture, but no butter, margarine, or mayonnaise
- chicken breast sandwich
- single serving of canned salmon or tuna on a plate, no mayonnaise
- toasted bagel or bread, no butter or margarine
- mixed salad, dressing on the side
- vegetable, pea, or minestrone soup
- pancakes occasionally, instead of waffles or bacon and eggs. Use just a little syrup, but no butter. Buckwheat pancakes are the healthiest choice.

FAST-FOOD RESTAURANTS

- Try the salad bar or grilled or barbecued chicken

Recipes

Now that you understand the rules, you can decide whether a recipe meets the requirements of your program. If the recipe doesn't meet your needs, you may be able to adapt it.

Here are some tips for adapting recipes to fit your program:

- Cut back, by as much as half, the amount of fat that a recipe calls for — especially the amount of oil needed to sauté vegetables.
- Thicken sauces and soups with mashed potatoes, pureed beans, or cornstarch dissolved in water.
- Instead of sautéing onions before adding them to food, chop and cook them in the microwave for about 30 seconds.
- Replace all butter with olive or peanut oil.
- Substitute yogurt for sour cream or mayonnaise.
- Substitute skinned chicken for beef or pork.
- For muffins or quick breads, substitute apple sauce for the same amount of oil or butter. They will still be moist and delicious.
- Substitute two egg whites for each whole egg in a recipe.
- Use evaporated skim milk instead of cream in sauces and desserts.

Starting Right Now ...

These basic steps will get you started without delay.

1. Review Rose Reisman's recipes at the end of this book for healthful, delicious meal ideas.
2. Review your own recipes to see which ones you can adapt to your new wellness lifestyle.
3. Look through some wellness-oriented cookbooks and find other new recipes to try.

4. Make a shopping list of staples from pages 137 to 141 and the ingredients in the recipes you have chosen.

A Typical Day

We are often asked what we eat and how we make the program work for *us*. Here's how we stay on track.

- Breakfast is a low-fat, high-fibre meal. We start with six to 10 ounces of low-fat yogurt and add about 1/2 cup of bran cereal and two tablespoons of oat bran. We might add some slices of honeydew melon, peaches, or other fruit for flavour, and a glass of fruit juice diluted with pure spring water. The yogurt is an excellent source of protein, calcium, and vitamin D. The bran cereal contains colon-cleaner fibre and enough complex carbohydrates to kick-start our day. The oat bran also helps to keep our cholesterol levels low.

- For lunch, we might choose a low-fat flesh protein meal such as steamed rice with stir-fried vegetables and pieces of chicken or shrimp. We try to choose vegetables that are rich in anti-cancer nutrients such as broccoli or carrots.

- For our complex-carbohydrate-only dinner, we often eat a plate of fresh pasta with lightly seasoned tomato sauce, a salad with olive oil and vinegar dressing, and a whole-wheat roll.

- We usually have fresh fruit for a snack, but low-fat granola bars, popcorn, and low-fat muffins sometimes appear in our food diaries.

Protective
Nutrients

If your general health is good enough, we advise that you undertake a strength-training program two to three times per week. Increasing your muscle tone and strength helps to speed up your metabolism, improve your body shape, and prevent osteoporosis. If you feel you're ready, speak to a personal trainer or fitness instructor at a health club.

Our program offers many benefits. First, it will help you lose weight and improve your level of fitness. Second, you will become more fit and toned. Third, you will reduce your risk of degenerative illnesses such as heart disease, adult-onset diabetes, and osteoporosis. By attaining a more ideal weight and becoming more fit, you will automatically reduce the risk of a heart attack and related vascular diseases, reproductive organ cancers, gall-bladder disease, and other problems.

In this chapter we will look at the many protective micronutrients occurring naturally in food that defend our bodies against other degenerative problems. Protective micronutrients are vitamins and minerals that help to fight against degenerative diseases. Although we may not notice these vitamins and minerals in our food because in general they are tasteless, they affect our bodies' ability to maintain optimal health. These micronutrients also discourage processes that lead to cancer, heart attacks, and other diseases linked to deterioration. Various phytochemicals and phytoestrogens also play a critical role in protecting our tissues from damaging carcinogens, oxidation, cigarette smoke, environmental pollutants, and other factors that can cause premature disease and aging.

Rather than simply listing each micronutrient, in this chapter we will explain how the body defends itself against disease. By understanding these processes, we can more readily appreciate the individual micronutrients that perform these functions.

Calcium for Optimal Bone Mineralization and the Prevention of Osteoporosis

Despite the availability of a vast and varied supply of foods required for optimal development and health, North Americans experience an extremely alarming incidence of osteoporosis — a condition that arises when calcium leaks out of the bone during the aging process. Osteoporosis literally means lack of bone minerals — the minerals in bone that make it strong. Although bone contains minerals such as fluoride, magnesium, zinc, and sodium, calcium is the main mineral. In 1994, the National Institute of Health reported in *The Journal of the American Medical Association* that osteoporosis affects more than 25 million people in the United States and is the major cause of bone fractures in post-menopausal women and the elderly. Previous surveys also revealed that Americans experience more than 1.5 million fractures annually at an annual cost to the health care system in excess of $10 billion. Unfortunately, over the next 10 years, as baby boomers age, the incidence of osteoporosis will increase.

Two main factors determine whether a person will develop osteoporosis — calcium accumulation in bone, which occurs most effectively up to the ages of 24 to 30, and the rate at which bone is lost in later life. This age-related bone loss results from a decrease in estrogen levels in women that, in turn, allows calcium to leak out of the bones into the bloodstream. From there it is filtered by the kidney and passed in urine.

Degenerative and Vascular Illnesses

Heart Disease
Cancer
Adult-Onset Diabetes
Osteoporosis
Cataracts
Immune System Decline
Deterioration of the Brain and Nervous System

Simply stated, a woman who failed to consume 1200 to 1500 mg of calcium per day between the ages of 11 and 24 will have bone-mineral density that is already suboptimal. Studies from the National Health and Nutrition Examination Surveys I, II, and III show that, since 1971, pubescent women have not ingested the recommended amounts of calcium to increase their resistance to osteoporosis later in life. Today, an average young woman consumes fewer than 900 mg of calcium per day. Similarly, the National Institute of Health recommends that adult men and women consume 1,000 mg of calcium per day. Yet, 75 percent of women over the age of 35 do not consume even the minimum recommended daily allowance level of 800 mg per day. According to the National Health and Nutrition Examination Survey II, on average, adult women consume only 474 mg and adult men consume only 733 mg of calcium per day. Women over age 50 who are on estrogen-replacement therapy can remain at 1,000 mg per day. Those who are not on estrogen-replacement therapy and who are between 50 and 64 years of age should aim to consume 1,500 mg per day. Both men and women over age 65 should aim for 1,500 mg of calcium per day.

How to Get Enough Calcium

With the Two-Staple System, the low-fat dairy products selections provide the main source of calcium. For example, eight ounces of low-fat milk or yogurt provide 300 to 400 mg of calcium, 1/2 cup of low-fat cottage cheese provides 75 mg, and most low-fat cheeses provide up to 200 mg per ounce. Fortunately, other foods can also supplement your calcium intake. Many fruits and vegetables, particularly dark-green, leafy veg-

Recent recommendations from The National Institute of Health Consensus Panel

Age Group	Optimal Daily Intake of Calcium (mg)
Infant	
birth–6 months	400
6 months–1 year	600
Children	
1–5 years	800
6–10 years	800–1,000
Adolescents/Young Adults	
11–24	1,200–1,500
Men	
25–65 years	1,000
over 65 years	1,500
Women	
25–50 years	1,000
over 50 (post-menopausal)	
– on estrogen	1,000
– not on estrogen	1,500
over 65 years	1,500
pregnant and nursing	1,200–1,500

etables, are a good source of dietary calcium. Canned salmon, shrimp, and sardines with bones are other excellent sources. Tofu products, lentils, and most beans are also good sources.

A brief look at the calcium level in common foods reveals why osteoporosis is such an enormous health problem. Evidently it is quite difficult to consume 1,000 to 1,500 mg of calcium per day from food without eating an inflated number of calories. Even on the Two-Staple System, reaching the optimum level is not easy. The dairy protein selection for each day contains 300 to 400 mg of calcium, and you can easily get 200 mg from fruits, vegetables, peas, beans, pasta, rice, and other carbohydrate foods. But, depending on your age and gender, you will still fall short of your calcium goal by 500 to 1,000 mg.

As a result, we recommend that you use a calcium supplement to make up the difference. Calcium citrate and calcium carbonate tablets are the best choices and come in strengths of 300 to 1,000 mg of elemental calcium. Some well-designed multiple vitamin and minerals also contain up to 500 mg of calcium. Check your local drugstore or health-food store, or consult a supplier of health-food products to find a suitable calcium supplement.

Vitamin D and Exercise for Better Bone Calcium

In addition to ensuring an adequate intake of calcium, you must also consider other nutritional factors that encourage the absorption of calcium for bone mineralization and stronger bones. The two main factors that help the absorption of calcium are

Calcium Levels in Food		
Product	Amount	Calcium (mg)
Low-fat yogurt	1 cup	415 mg
Low-fat milk	1 cup	300 mg
Low-fat cottage cheese	1/2 cup	75 mg
Sardines with bones	3 oz	370 mg
Salmon with bones (canned)	3 oz	165 mg
Processed tofu with calcium sulfate	4 oz	145 mg
Canned shrimp	3 oz	100 mg
Cooked lentils	1 cup	75 mg
Chicken	3 oz	10 mg
Tuna	3 oz	5 mg
Collard greens	1/2 cup	180 mg
Spinach	1/2 cup	85 mg
Stalk of broccoli	1/2 cup	70 mg
Orange	1 medium	55 mg
Green beans	1/2 cup	30 mg
Lettuce	1/4 head	15 mg
Orange juice	1/2 cup	10 mg
Apple	1 medium	10 mg
Whole-wheat bread	1 slice	20 mg
Cooked spaghetti	1 cup	15 mg
Cooked rice	1/2 cup	10 mg

lactose and vitamin D, both of which are found in almost all dairy products. Several studies have also linked optimal intakes of vitamin D and calcium to reduced risk of cancers of the colon, breast, and even prostate.

Vitamin D is synthesized under the skin when cholesterol is exposed to direct sunlight. In northern climates such as in Canada and parts of the United States, people tend to have lower blood levels of vitamin D, due to reduced sunlight exposure during the winter months. As with calcium, it is difficult to consume the recommended daily 400 I.U. of vitamin D from food. However, virtually all multiple vitamin and mineral supplements provide the recommended 400 I.U. of vitamin D.

Exercise also plays a critical role in retaining calcium in bone. Thirty minutes per day of gentle aerobic exercise greatly reduces the chances of bone loss. A recent study at Tuft's University demonstrated that post-menopausal women who participated twice per week in a five-exercise strength-training program for 30 minutes per session demonstrated an increase of one to two percent in bone calcium (bone-mineral density) in the hips and lower back after one year of training. None of these 40 women received estrogen-replacement therapy, but they did receive a calcium supplement if their dietary calcium was determined to be suboptimal. This study showed that a moderate amount of weight training can actually help to increase bone strength, muscle mass, and strength, and improve balance. All of these factors help to reduce the risk of osteoporosis.

FACTORS THAT DRAW CALCIUM OUT OF BONE

Various nutritional factors tend to leach calcium from bones and accelerate the onset of osteoporosis. The main offenders are nicotine (cigarette smoking), alcohol, caffeine, and a high-protein diet. Furthermore, many women who consume too little calcium and vitamin D worsen the situation by also drinking more than two cups of coffee per day and by consuming too much alcohol. And those among the 26 percent of the population who still smoke are much more likely to develop osteoporosis.

The following keys to success will offset osteoporosis:
- Follow the Two-Staple System and choose foods that contain high levels of calcium.
- Supplement your diet with additional calcium from calcium citrate or calcium carbonate (500-1,000 mg), depending on your age and gender.
- Exercise regularly.
- Limit caffeine intake to less than two cups of coffee or tea per day. Choose decaffeinated selections.
- Limit alcohol consumption to one drink per day; no alcoholic drinks is even better on most days.
- Consider taking a multiple vitamin and mineral supplement providing 400 I.U. of vitamin D.
- Stop smoking.

Calcium and Vitamin D for Cancer Prevention

In recent years, studies have suggested that calcium and vitamin D may work together to help prevent colon, breast, and possibly prostate cancer. Researchers have recognized that these nutrients decrease the turnover rate of cells. A turnover of cells in the body is constantly occurring — old cells die and new cells replace them. Certain factors accelerate this turnover rate, and a faster turnover rate is often associated with an increased risk of cancer because of the increased likelihood that a cell will make a genetic mistake that carries cancerous properties. For example, a person with ill-fitting dentures is more likely to develop mouth cancer because as the dentures irritate the gums, they produce inflammation and a faster division and turnover rate of cells in the inflamed area. Some chemicals also promote cancer in the same way. For example, bile acids secreted from the liver and gall bladder in response to consuming a great deal of fat have been shown to increase the turnover rate of cells in the large intestine. The same principle applies to the secondary sterols formed from bile acids by colonic bacteria – one way in which a high-fat diet is linked to colon cancer. Certain hormones such as estrogen, which increase the mitotic activity (turnover rate) of breast cells, are linked to breast cancer and other reproductive organ cancers.

Colon cancer is the second-leading cause of cancer deaths in North America. Many of the good observational studies are colon-cancer studies such as the Western Electric Study by Dr. C.F. Garland, which followed 1,954 men for 19 years. Dr. Garland demonstrated that men who eat fewer than 1,200 mg per day of calcium, on average, have a 75 percent greater incidence of colon cancer than men who consumed this amount or more. Other studies, including the Washington County, Maryland study by Dr. Garland and fellow researchers, demonstrated that lower blood levels of vitamin D were also associated with a much higher subsequent risk of colon cancers. A higher intake of vitamin D (more than 3.8 micrograms per day) was associated with a 50 percent reduction in the risk of colon cancer compared to the men who ingested lower amounts in the Western Electric Study. Recent studies on high-risk colon-cancer subjects and previously afflicted colon-cancer patients have yielded promising results in deterring this disease by adding up to 1,500 mg of calcium and 400 I.U. of vitamin D through supplements. Calcium and vitamin D exhibit the property of *down regulation*; that is, they slow down the pace at which cells divide, thereby decreasing cancer risk. This is a very desirable effect. Many researchers now believe that lowering fat intake, increasing the amount of anti-cancer fibre in diet, and elevating calcium intake to 1,500 mg per day and vitamin D intake to 400 I.U. (from about 170 I.U., which is the average intake in Canada, and 189 I.U. in the

United States) will greatly minimize the risk of colon cancer, which now affects one in 20 people in their lifetime.

Evidence is also slowly mounting that suggests that calcium and vitamin D may help to reduce the risk of breast cancer. In the 1980s, Dr. Garland and his associates noted that in areas in which there is less sunlight intensity, a higher incidence of breast cancer occurs, just as there is for colon cancer. In one study, researchers examined the rates of breast and colon cancer in 29 U.S. cities and 20 Canadian cities and reported that the greater the amount of sunlight-blocking air pollution, the higher the rates of breast and colon cancer. Once again, the belief is that less sunlight intensity translates into lower blood levels of vitamin D for people in these areas. These lower levels are then linked to higher rates of cancer. The researchers also reported a threefold increase in the incidence of breast cancer in the former Soviet Union, where there was less sunlight intensity. Another striking trend is that the incidence of colon and breast cancer declines further as you move toward the equator. In fact, Dr. Garland and his associates reported in *The American Journal of Clinical Nutrition* (July 1991) that colon cancer virtually vanishes within 10 degrees of the equator.

Recent preliminary studies indicate that vitamin D may be an important nutrient to discourage the formation of prostate cancer. We have learned that the human prostate gland has vitamin D receptors, and animal studies have demonstrated that vitamin D can inhibit the growth of prostate cancer cells under experimental conditions.

More research about the anti-cancer influences of calcium and vitamin D is required before we will know how effective they may be in the war against cancer. At present, the best advice for most healthy adults is to enhance their intake of calcium to between 1,000 and 1,500 mg per day and vitamin D to between 400 and 600 I.U. daily.

Vitamin A for Full Maturation of Cells

The foods with beta carotene are orange and yellow, red and green.

Micronutrients can also help to defend against cancer development by promoting the full development of a cell to its mature, adult form. The more mature and fully developed a cell becomes in its evolution from an immature newborn to an adult cell, the more resistant it seems to be to the influence of cancer-causing agents and the less likely it is to become a cancer cell.

Certain micronutrients, the most important of which is vitamin A, are actively involved in the full maturation process of cells. A deficiency of vitamin A results in very immature, irregular cells, which are prone to infection and cancer. In fact, vitamin A is considered to be one of the strongest naturally occurring anti-cancer nutrients. Some water-soluble vitamin A look-alike drugs have been developed and their success in treating various cancers is reported regularly. This is especially true for head and neck cancers and cervical dysplasia – a precancerous conviction on the cervix. As well as containing anti-cancer properties, vitamin A is also required for optimal immune function, to fight off germs that can infect the surface lining tissues of the body – the respiratory tract, urinary tract, intestinal tract, bladder, cervix, and so on.

From a prevention perspective, you should consume 5,000 I.U. per day of vitamin A. On the Two-Staple System, the low-fat dairy products and fish provide most of the vitamin A requirements. Most of the other sources of vitamin A are too high in fat for us to recommend – beef liver, egg yolk, butter, and margarine are examples. However, many fruits and vegetables provide good sources of vitamin A. Virtually all of the fruits and vegetables that are orange, yellow, red, and green are loaded with beta carotene, which the body converts into vitamin A. As an anti-cancer agent on its own, beta carotene acts as an antioxidant. In several trials, beta carotene in daily doses of 50,000 I.U. has been shown to reverse a pre-cancerous mouth condition called leukoplakia and to reduce the further degeneration of these lesions to a malignant cancer. Beta-carotene supplementation has also reversed cervical dysplasia, as reported in the antioxidant update symposium in *The American Journal of Clinical Nutrition*.

Furthermore, according to head researcher Dr. Walter Willett of Harvard University, who conducted the Nurses Health Study, of the 87,245 female registered nurses participating in the study, nurses with the highest intake of vitamin A and/or beta carotene demonstrated a 20 to 30 percent reduction in breast cancer. Dr. Willett reported that nurses who had the lowest 20 percent intake of vitamin A and beta carotene from food experienced a 50 percent reduction in the risk of breast cancer by taking a supplement of vitamin A or beta carotene. Dr. Willett concluded that these data provide evidence that the protective effect in relation to breast cancer is due to vitamin A itself and not to some other yet unidentified nutrient in these foods, as was previously argued.

Vitamin A and beta carotene are known to possess various anti-cancer properties. We should eat enough of the foods that contain these nutrients to ensure that every cell in our bodies can fully develop into adult, mature cells that are less prone to become cancer cells.

As a result, we recommend that you take a multiple vitamin and mineral supplement that provides 5,000 I.U. of vitamin A and some additional beta carotene. In addition to a low-fat dairy serving and a low-fat fish-poultry serving each day, choose carbohydrate foods that are a rich source of beta carotene in order to ingest at least 15 mg of

Fruits/Vegetables Containing Beta Carotene	(mg)
Sweet potato – 1 medium	10.0
Apricots, dried – 10 halves	6.2
Chicory, raw – 1 cup	6.2
Carrot, raw – 1 medium	5.7
Spinach, cooked – 1/2 cup	4.9
Cantaloupe – 1/8	4.0
Turnip greens, cooked – 1/2 cup	3.9
Pumpkin, cooked – 1/2 cup	3.7
Collard greens, cooked – 1/2 cup	3.4
Swiss chard, cooked – 1/2 cup	3.2
Kale, cooked – 1/2 cup	3.0
Winter squash, cooked – 1/2 cup	2.9
Apricots, fresh – 2 whole	2.5
Spinach, raw – 1 cup	2.3
Spaghetti squash, cooked – 1/2 cup	1.9
Mustard greens, cooked – 1/2 cup	1.9
Beet greens, cooked – 1/2 cup	1.8
Grapefruit, pink or red – 1/2	1.6
Mango – 1/2	1.4
Dandelion greens, cooked – 1/2 cup	1.4
Bell peppers, sweet red, raw – 1/2 cup	1.1
Romaine lettuce, raw – 1/2 cup	1.1
Watermelon – 1 slice	1.1
Broccoli, cooked 1/2 cup	1.0

beta carotene (25,000 I.U.). Beta carotene is non-toxic, even at very high levels. However, vitamin A supplements containing 10,000 I.U. or more can be toxic over a long period.

Folic Acid, Vitamin B12, and Vitamin C for Normal DNA Replication

Body cells undergo normal division to duplicate themselves from one generation of cells to the next. A critical step in this process involves the ability of genetic material to pass along a perfect template of genetic material or DNA to the new developing cell. An accumulation of genetic mistakes and damage can easily trigger formation of an aggressive cancer cell. For example, too much radiation can damage the DNA of the immature cells in bone marrow and can trigger cancers such as leukemia and lymphomas. Similarly, cigarette smoke can damage the DNA in the lungs and respiratory tract.

However, three micronutrients – folic acid, vitamin B12, and vitamin C – play a key role in ensuring that genetic material is strong and can replicate itself without any weak links. In an interview published in *The Journal of the American Medical Association* (April 1995), Dr. Ames stated, "The gold in disease prevention, particularly cancer prevention, is in diet and nutrition." He discussed the fact that low intakes of folic acid (a B-vitamin) result in DNA damage, where chromosomes break and increase the risk of cancer. Because folic acid activity depends on the presence of vitamin C, Dr. Ames contends that if you lack sufficient vitamin C, you are doing the equivalent of stepping unprotected in front of an x-ray machine.

In recent years, a low intake of folic acid has been linked to a number of cancers, namely cervical cancer, colon cancer, and cancer of the air passages (bronchial tissues). Incredibly, in several preliminary intervention trials, the introduction of a folic acid and vitamin B12 supplement has reversed pre-cancerous lesions on the cervix and in bronchial tissues. In the Health Professionals follow-up study and the Nurses Health Study, a low intake of folic acid was associated with twice the risk of colon cancer compared to subjects who consumed the highest levels of folic acid. Vitamin C supplementation has reversed a pre-cancerous stomach lesion known as *atrophic gastritis*. The current belief is simply that folic acid, vitamin B12, and vitamin C can correct genetic errors provided they are not irreversible. In turn, the next generation of cells becomes healthier and appears normal again.

More recently, women have been advised to increase their folic acid intake to 400 micrograms per day before they become pregnant to significantly reduce the chances of having a child with spina bifida or other spinal defects. As the fetus develops, it requires a great deal of folic acid to keep pace with the rapid cell division that is occurring. This is no time to be deficient in the nutrient that's required to form DNA – the blueprint of life!

The recommended amount of folic acid is 400 micrograms per day. Unfortunately, the average intake is less than 200 micrograms per day. The best food sources of folic acid are romaine lettuce, broccoli, asparagus, spinach, beans, and peas. Whole-wheat flour and wheat bran, each of which provides 130 micrograms of folic acid in just 3.5 ounces, also contain a generous amount of folic acid. Wheat germ and brewers' yeast have the most folic acid of any foods listed, providing 257 and 175 micrograms respectively in 3.5 ounces. Complex carbohydrates are a storehouse of protective micronutrients. As a result, when you're selecting carbohydrate foods during the day, remember that many vegetables, legumes, and whole grains contain folic acid.

VITAMIN C CONTENT OF SELECTED FOODS

The following is a list of carbohydrate foods that contain vitamin C and also provide beta carotene and/or folic acid.

Vitamin C levels in Food

Food	Amount	Vitamin C (mg)	Food	Amount	Vitamin C (mg)
Kiwi	1	265	Papaya	1/2 cup	39
Broccoli			Lemon	1	39
fresh	1 whole stalk	162	Grapefruit	1/2	37
frozen, chopped	1/2 cup	52	Honeydew melon	1/10 melon	35
Brussels sprouts	8	146	Cauliflower, cooked	1/2 cup	35
Peppers, sweet green	1	94	Mustard greens, cooked	1/2 cup	34
Cantaloupe	1/2 melon	90	Potato		
Collards (cooked)	1/2 cup	72	baked, then peeled	1 medium	31
Peppers,			boiled, then peeled	1 medium	22
sweet	1	70	peeled, then boiled	1 medium	18
immature, green			mashed	1/2 cup	11
chili sauce (canned)	1/2 cup	83	French fries	10	7
mature, red chili			chips	10	3
sauce (canned)	1/2 cup	37	Watermelon	1 slice	30
Orange	1	66	Sweet potato, baked or boiled	1 medium	25
Orange Juice			Spinach		
fresh	1/2 cup	62	fresh	1/2 cup	25
frozen, diluted	1/2 cup	60	frozen	1/2 cup	25
canned	1/2 cup	50	canned	1/2 cup	16
Kale, cooked	1/2 cup	51	Cabbage		
Turnip greens	1/2 cup	50	cooked	1/2 cup	24
Strawberries	1/2 cup	44	shredded	1/2 cup	21
Grapefruit juice,			Tangerine	1	22
canned, unsweetened	1/2 cup	42	Okra, cooked	10 3-in. pods	21
Tomatoes			Cranberry juice cocktail		
fresh	1	42*	(Vitamin C added)	1/2 cup	20
canned	1/2 cup	21			
juice	1/2 cup	20	* Vitamin C content depends on type of cultivation and		
Mango	1/2 cup	40	harvest and time of year.		

To be safe, take a multiple vitamin that contains 400 micrograms of folic acid, 5 micrograms of vitamin B12, and is enriched with the antioxidants vitamin C at 750 mg and vitamin E at 400 I. U.

Dr. Ames concludes, "I'm not sold on mega-doses of vitamins, but moderate doses are probably helpful. For example, a pill containing the recommended daily allowance (RDA) of each vitamin. It's inexpensive insurance, and telling people to take a multi-vitamin is pretty conservative advice. A little extra vitamin E and C is more likely to help than harm, in my view — perhaps in the range of 400 units of vitamin E and 250 mg of vitamin C, but this is still somewhat controversial."

Many doctors, researchers, and scientists faithfully take vitamin supplements each day and, based upon the body of evidence that now exists, most of them believe that folic acid, vitamin B12, and vitamin C are key micronutrients in the war against cancer. As a result, it's important to include these micronutrients in your diet.

Folic Acid for the Prevention of Heart Disease

Folic acid also helps to prevent heart disease. Researchers recently recognized that high blood levels of a substance called *homocysteine* were related to an increased risk of heart disease. Under normal conditions, folic acid, as well as vitamins B6 and B12, help to metabolize homocysteine and remove it from the bloodstream. Left unchecked, homocysteine encourages cholesterol to stick more aggressively to the artery walls, causing accelerated narrowing. The artery eventually becomes blocked and a heart attack often results.

Most people don't receive the recommended 400 micrograms of folic acid per day, thereby permitting high levels of homocysteine to build up and do its damage. In the United States, the national data estimate that 88 percent of adults consume less than the recommended daily amount each day. A review in *The Journal of the American Medical Association* (October 1995) suggested that 10 percent of all heart disease problems result from high homocysteine blood levels due to insufficient intake of folic acid. In the *Physician's Health Study*, doctors with high homocysteine levels had a threefold increase in the risk of heart attack compared with male doctors with normal levels. More research is necessary to establish how effective folic acid will be in preventing cardiovascular disease, but it seems prudent to ensure that we consume at least 400 micrograms each day. A multiple vitamin and mineral supplement provides good added insurance.

Vitamins C and E for Blocking the Formation of Nitrosamines

A group of nitrogen-containing agents called *nitrosamines* is classified as carcinogens because, in experimental trials, they cause cancer in many animal species and the similarities in their actions on animal and human cells in other experiments make it unlikely that humans are exempt from their cancer-causing effects. A high intake of nitrates and nitrate-containing foods, alcoholic beverages, cigarette smoke, and other agents is strongly linked to increased risk of cancer in humans.

Studies have shown that our bodies will readily form nitrosamine carcinogens in the stomach, mouth, colon, and infected urinary bladder. In fact, it is widely suspected that our greatest exposure to these damaging nitrosamines comes from the nitrosamines that are formed within our bodies. In other words, our bodies actually produce this cancer-causing agent under certain conditions. Therefore, our goal is to discourage these conditions, so that our bodies will not form any nitrosamines that could initiate genetic damage and cancer development.

The building blocks of nitrosamines are extremely prevalent in our environment today. For example, the nitric oxide from air pollution is in contact with our lungs. The widespread use of nitrogen fertilizer has greatly increased our background exposure to nitrogen compounds in drinking water, plant foods, and in the air we breathe. Many luncheon meats contain nitrate and nitrite salts to preserve their colour and ward off bacterial growth. Nitrates derived from alcoholic beverages and nitrogen oxides from cigarette smoke are other sources of nitrosamines. Even prolonged exercise can elevate urine nitrate levels. Studies have clearly shown that when we eat or inhale these compounds, the levels of nitrosamines rise in our bodies. Nitrosamines have been measured in stomach juices, urine, and the bloodstream. The average person in the United States is estimated to ingest about 74 mg of nitrates each day from all of these sources.

The good news, however, is that two main micronutrients can block the formation of nitrosamines in our bodies – vitamin C and vitamin E. The role of vitamin E in preventing nitrosamine development is still unfolding. Experimental evidence is very strong, and conclusive evidence now shows that vitamin E blocks the formation of nitrosamines in the stomachs of humans. This finding was reported by Dr. Lester Packer in *The American Journal of Clinical Nutrition* (April 1991). In Linxian, China, an area of north-central China in which more than 85 percent of cancers occur in the esophagus and stomach, a vitamin supplementation trial was undertaken using various vitamin combinations. After 5.25 years, subjects who had received a daily supplement of 30 I.U. of vitamin E, 50 micrograms of selenium, and 15 mg of beta carotene demonstrated a nine percent lower overall death rate, a 21 percent reduction in stomach cancer rate, a four percent reduction in cancer of the esophagus, and an overall reduction in cancer mortality of 13 percent compared to subjects who had received a placebo. Other vitamin formulas were less effective than the combination of vitamin E, selenium, and beta carotene in preventing these cancers.

Other studies have correlated higher intakes of vitamin E with a reduction of colon cancer. Whether vitamin E discourages cancer throughout the intestinal tract via its nitrosamine blocking action is still open to debate. However, it is worth being aware that vitamin C and vitamin E can reduce concentrations of nitrosamines in the body. Both of these micronutrients play a key role in disease prevention.

Antioxidant Function

One of the main ways in which micronutrients can help defend us against heart attacks, certain cancers, cataracts, possibly Parkinson's disease, and other diseases, is believed to be through their antioxidant function. The major nutritional antioxidants are vitamin A, beta carotene, vitamin C, and vitamin E. Minerals such as selenium, zinc, manganese, and copper are also required to activate other antioxidant enzymes that the body produces. These minerals hook up with certain enzymes that the body makes naturally, bolting them into action.

Antioxidants quench or neutralize some very harmful substances called *free radicals*, which we are exposed to every day. In fact, your body forms free radicals from oxygen every minute of your life. Free radicals are very reactive, unstable agents that contain what is known as an *unpaired electron*. To explain this process, we will use an analogy. A free radical can be viewed as a compound with a hand waving freely, wanting to hold hands with a partner. The free radical pulls away a hand (an electron) from another element that was sitting quietly holding another hand (electron). Now, the free radical is happy and satisfied (stable) and no longer seeks another hand to hold (electron to steal from another molecule). However, when a free radical pulls away a hand (electron) from the other element, the other radical is left with a free hand. This element becomes a free radical and seeks to steal a hand (electron) from another element. This cycle continues until an antioxidant compound steps in and stops the process. Antioxidants offer a hand (electron) to the free radical, quench its aggressive behaviour, and yet cannot themselves be converted into free-radicals. Antioxidants sacrifice themselves to stop free-radical propagation.

Many researchers are convinced that the regular consumption of soybean products – tofu, soy milk, tempeh, miso, and so on – by the Japanese largely accounts for the fact that their breast cancer death rate is 25 percent of the North American rate and their prostate cancer death rate is 20 percent.

Free radicals have been shown to damage and alter the genetic material of cells (DNA), creating mutations that lead to cancer development. In fact, many carcinogens such as nitrosamines and cigarette smoke do their damage by a free-radical attack on genetic material, leading to cancer initiation. Free radicals can also damage the outer membrane of cells and disrupt the cell's integrity and function. They can damage and destroy proteins and enzymes within the body. They cause cross-linking of structural proteins that can lead to wrinkles and premature aging. This damage explains why a long-term heavy smoker or drinker's face often looks more wrinkled and older than the person's actual years. Ultraviolet light from the sun also creates free-radical skin damage that accelerates the aging process and elevates risk of skin cancer.

By not smoking, drinking, or exposing ourselves to the sun, we certainly help reduce our exposure to some common and dangerous carcinogens. But even if we're careful, up to five percent of all of the oxygen our bodies process to produce energy becomes transformed into oxygen-free radicals, which are very reactive and known to cause significant damage over a lifetime. Optimal levels of antioxidant vitamins and enzymes can quench most of these oxygen-free radicals. To demonstrate this, cut an apple in half and expose it to the air. After a few minutes, the flesh of the apple turns brown due to the corrosive, free-radical effects of oxygen. We refer to this process as oxidation. However, by squeezing lemon juice on to the flesh of the apple immediately after cutting it, the apple doesn't turn brown as readily because the vitamin C in the lemon juice can interrupt the free-radical attack by quenching the oxygen-free radicals and stabilizing them so they don't attack the apple. In this process, the vitamin C sacrifices itself to protect the apple's structural integrity. Eventually, all of the vitamin C will be consumed and the apple will oxidize. Similarly, we want to coat our cells with vitamin C so it can help defend against free radicals in our bodies.

Researchers have been conducting studies on antioxidant vitamins for more than 45 years. Thousands of published papers illustrate their potential role in disease prevention and strongly implicate antioxidant vitamins as preventors of heart disease and cancer. The available research on antioxidants suggests that consuming foods each day that contain generous amounts of naturally occurring antioxidants is a key strategy for disease prevention. Many fruits and vegetables also contain thousands of other disease-fighting compounds. Some are antioxidants, like some of the sister compounds of beta carotene such as *lycopene*, found in tomatoes, strawberries, and red-looking fruits and vegetables, while *bioflavanoids*, vitamin C's sister compounds, contain antioxidant properties and enhance the effectiveness of vitamin C itself. Over and above consuming five fruit servings per day and at least three antioxidant-rich vegetable servings, it is wise to take supplement products that provide antioxidants.

These levels of intake result in a rise in blood levels of these antioxidants into a range that is strongly associated with reduced risk of many cancers and heart disease, although further research is required before we fully understand exactly how much of a protective effect we can expect from antioxidants.

Suggested Daily Antioxidant Supplement Doses

Vitamin C – 1,000 mg
Vitamin E – 400 I. U.
Beta carotene – 10,000 to 20,000 I.U.
Selenium – 100 to 150 micrograms

ANTIOXIDANTS AND HEART DISEASE

Higher blood levels of antioxidants have been found to be related to a dramatic reduction in heart attacks and other vascular problems. Vitamin E appears to be especially outstanding in this role. Antioxidants apparently reduce heart disease by protecting the cholesterol in the bloodstream from free radicals generated from oxygen and/or air pollutants and cigarette smoke. Cholesterol that has been damaged by free radicals is much more likely to stick to the walls of the arteries and cause accelerated narrowing, leading to a heart attack or angina. Vitamin E and beta carotene actually travel with cholesterol through the bloodstream and, therefore, can protect it throughout its journey. Vitamin C is also carried in the bloodstream and can quench nearby free radicals.

Food alone doesn't supply sufficient vitamin E (100 to 400 I.U. daily) to get the full, protective effects. In fact, in Canada the average intake of vitamin E per day from food is only 9 I.U. In the United States, the average intake is 12 I.U.

ANTIOXIDANTS, CATARACTS, AND AGE-RELATED MACULAR DEGENERATION OF THE EYE

A number of impressive studies have demonstrated that higher intake and/or blood levels of vitamin C, vitamin E, beta carotene, and its sister compounds, lutein and zeaxanthin, are associated with a lower incidence of cataracts. The hypothesis is that these antioxidants protect the lens of the eye from the sun's damaging ultraviolet light, which generates free radicals. Free-radical damage to the lens can lead to a cloudiness

The French Paradox

In France, people eat high-fat meats and heavy meals smothered with creamy cheese sauces and butter, and yet they don't die of heart attacks and cardiovascular problems to the same extent as North Americans. Researchers believe that because the French drink a lot of red wine and eat a lot of fruit, they benefit from the antioxidant protection from these sources. Red wine is known to contain many antioxidants, such as *quercitin* and *catechins*, that may protect blood cholesterol from free radicals. Furthermore, alcohol tends to make blood cells less sticky so platelets are less inclined to stick together and form a clot inside the artery wall. However, alcohol is a powerful carcinogen and, as a result, the French have a cancer rate that is much higher than for North Americans. Longevity statistics indicate that more of the French die of cancers and fewer die of heart attacks.

in vision known as a cataract. Similar findings are now emerging for a serious condition of the retina called *age-related macular degeneration*. The belief is that the oxidation damage (free radical) initiated by light hitting the retina can lead to degeneration of this part of the eye. Observational studies suggest that higher intakes of vitamin C, vitamin E, and the carotenoids (lutein and zeaxanthin) are associated with a much lower risk of developing this condition. Spinach appears to help prevent this disease, probably because of its high levels of lutein.

ANTIOXIDANTS AND THE IMMUNE SYSTEM

As reported by Dr. Meydani and fellow researchers in *The American Journal of Clinical Nutrition* (December 1995), several studies have shown that supplementing vitamin E, beta carotene, and vitamin C can increase immune-system function, even in elderly subjects who are most likely to have a compromised immune system. More studies with human subjects are being carried out in this field to better understand the impact of antioxidants on improved immunity. It is important to remember that a better-functioning immune system and cancer prevention go hand in hand — one more reason to supplement our intake of antioxidant vitamins.

Toning Down Cancer-Permissive Estrogens

Estrogen hormones encourage the development of breast cancer and other reproductive organ cancers, although medical researchers are unsure exactly how certain estrogens exert their cancer-permissive effects.

Overweight post-menopausal women have a two to three times greater risk of developing breast cancer than women who are less fat. Fat cells and their supporting tissues produce cancer-permissive estrogens, such as estrone and 17-beta-estradiol, which are then secreted into the bloodstream. In the bloodstream, the estrogens attach to estrogen receptors near the surface of breast cells, cells on the cervix, the endometrium, and other cells that are influenced by these hormones.

The male prostate gland also has estrogen receptors, and overweight men, especially those with more abdominal fat, are at higher risk for prostate cancer than leaner men. Just like breast cancer,

prostate cancer development is strongly influenced by reproductive hormones such as estrone, testosterone, and possibly others.

Cancers of the breast, ovaries, cervix, endometrium, and prostate are all classified as *hormone-dependent cancers*. Reducing body fat to a safer level and performing at least 30 minutes per day of gentle aerobic exercise ensures that the background secretion rate of these cancer-permissive estrogens will be less pronounced.

Some complex carbohydrate foods contain natural ingredients that can lessen or tone down the impact of your body's cancer-permissive estrogens. The main food products that contain these estrogen competitors are cruciferous vegetables such as broccoli, Brussels sprouts, cabbage, cauliflower, and turnips, as well as flaxseed and soybeans. The estrogen look-alike compounds in these foods can attach themselves to the estrogen receptors on breast cells, cervical cells, endometrial cells, or prostate cells and thereby minimize the number of sites where the body's estrogen can bind to these same cells.

These food-based look-alike estrogens do not encourage cancer development. Conversely, they tend to decrease the risk of reproductive organ cancers.

Detoxifying and Deactivating Dangerous Toxins and Other Substances

Complex-carbohydrate foods contain thousands of *phytochemicals* – agents found in many fruits, vegetables, and legumes that help the body defend itself against degenerative diseases. These agents switch on detoxification centres inside the cells. In turn, these detoxification centres neutralize environmental toxins that may otherwise initiate cancer or cause other problems. Some phytochemicals help defend against disease by deactivating cancer-permissive hormones or deactivating the enzymes that make cancer-permissive hormones. It would be impossible to discuss all of these natural detoxifiers and deactivators in this chapter, but by targeting the really important ones we can show how powerful daily complex-carbohydrate choices can be in preventing cancer and other diseases.

FOODS CONTAINING PROTECTIVE PHYTONUTRIENTS

Soybean Products and Genistein

In addition to the estrogen look-alike compounds that they contain, soy products also contain a premiere cancer-fighting isoflavonoid called *genistein*. This phytonutrient has been shown to deactivate cancer cells from forming the blood vessels they need to invade adjacent tissues and metastasize. Under experimental conditions, genestein directly blocks the growth of breast, colon, lung, prostate, and skin cancers, and some forms of leukemia. Although genistein and other isoflavonoids found in soy products appear to have multiple anti-cancer properties, the influence of genistein on inhibiting blood vessel growth around cancer cells is considered to be unique in preventing cancer. If cancer cells can't form blood vessels, not only can't they spread, but they also suffocate themselves from lack of oxygen and other nutrients.

Broccoli and Sulforaphane

Broccoli contains an estrogen look-alike compound, is a rich source of two antioxidants — vitamin C and beta carotene — contains other carotenoids, and is a good source of fibre. This cruciferous vegetable is truly one of nature's carbohydrate wonder foods. Another phytonutrient found in broccoli is *sulforaphane*. Sulforaphane boosts the activity of the cell enzymes that neutralize many cancer-causing agents. Under the influence of sulforaphane, carcinogens are detoxified and are then ushered out of cells to be removed from the body.

Garlic and Allylic Sulfides

Allylic sulfides found in garlic also activate the detoxification enzymes within cells, enabling the body to more effectively detoxify cancer-causing chemicals. Garlic seems to be a storehouse of disease-preventing phytochemicals and is one of nature's most potent disease-prevention foods. It contains natural phytochemicals that reduce blood cholesterol, lessen the clotting tendency of platelets, help to dissolve blockages in arteries, lower blood pressure, strengthen the immune system, and exhibit antibacterial and antiviral activity. Deodorized garlic capsules such as *kyolic* or *kwai* preserve the active ingredients in garlic and have been tested and shown in clinical trials to lower blood pressure and cholesterol, and exhibit anticoagulant and antioxidant properties. The equivalent of two cloves of garlic can be found in one teaspoon of garlic powder, four 1,000 mg kwai tablets, four gel caps of kyolic garlic, or one teaspoon of liquid kyolic garlic.

Tomatoes and Phytochemicals

Tomatoes are estimated to contain about 10,000 different phytochemicals. Two of their carcinogen-detoxifying compounds include p-coumaric acid and chorogenic acid, both of which work much like vitamin C and vitamin E to block the formation of cancer-causing nitrosamines in the body. These compounds are found in green peppers, pineapples, strawberries, and carrots. They survive the cooking process without being destroyed. A recent study suggests that tomatoes are associated with a significantly lower risk of prostate cancer. It is also likely that an antioxidant called *lycopene* gives the tomato its ability to inhibit prostate cancer. Studies have shown that the male prostate gland picks up lycopene from the bloodstream and that lycopene is the major antioxidant that protects this gland from attacks by free radicals. Higher intakes of tomato sauces and other tomato products result in higher blood levels of lycopene and higher concentrations of lycopene found in the prostate gland. In one study, tomato from sauces and other sources where some fat was present significantly lowered prostate cancer rates.

Fruits, Vegetables, and Their Protective Agents

Fruits and vegetables are loaded with countless numbers of micronutrients and phytochemicals — many of which have yet to be discovered. In our society of quick fixes and miracle drugs, the trend is sometimes to forego the protective nutrients from complex-carbohydrate foods and rely instead on various vitamin supplements and other supplement products to fortify the body with disease-fighting protective nutrients. This is not a good strategy for increasing resistance to degenerative diseases.

For thousands of years, our bodies evolved to use nutrients from complex carbohydrate foods as a means to quench free radicals, detoxify carcinogens, and compete with our body's cancer-permissive estrogens. A vitamin supplement product should be used as an added layer of insurance in conjunction with a health-promoting diet that includes at least five daily servings of fruits and vegetables.

Supplements can also be used to attain higher levels of nutrients that diet alone cannot provide. In the recent *National Health and Nutrition Examination Survey* in the United States, it was noted that more than half of Americans do not eat a single serving of fruit, vegetable, or fruit juice on any given day. Less than 10 percent of Americans eat five or more servings of fruit and vegetables a day. This pattern is prevalent across North America. With the Two-Staple System, each day you will have ample opportunities to include fruits and vegetables as a main part of the carbohydrate selections.

Burning Fat

One of the micronutrients that has received attention in recent years is chromium, which is an essential mineral for health. Chromium works with insulin to enhance the ability of cells to pick up carbohydrate sugars and amino acids from the bloodstream. For this reason, the right amount of chromium in a diet tends to improve blood sugar regulation, often helping to correct low blood sugar (hypoglycemia) or borderline diabetes (hyperglycemia). However, it is estimated that 90 percent of Americans consume less than one-quarter of the recommended 200 micrograms a day of chromium. Due to the depletion of chromium in the soil as a result of nitrogen fertilizers and other agricultural practices, the amount of chromium in our everyday food supply is presently suboptimal.

Chromium also assists the processes of losing body fat and becoming more fit in two important ways. Because chromium increases the effectiveness of insulin, carbohydrate sugars are more efficiently picked up by cells and used as a carbohydrate fuel, resulting in fewer carbohydrates being converted into fat and stored in fat cells. The second benefit of extra chromium is that it improves the uptake of protein building blocks (amino acids) by muscles. Protein building blocks are used to build a more toned and better-defined muscle. Studies performed on subjects involved in weight training showed that the group that received 200 micrograms of chromium per day increased their muscle size by more than the placebo group. This is an important consideration for those who want to shed body fat, increase muscle tone, or both.

Each pound of muscle gained can increase resting metabolism by up to 35 calories per day. So, if a person gains six pounds of muscle while losing fat, he or she would increase the resting metabolic rate by 210 calories per day, permitting him or her to eat an extra 210 calories per day without gaining any fat.

Other substances that help burn fat more effectively are often packaged with chromium in fat conditioner supplements. They include L-carnitine, L-methionine, L-lysine, and hydroxy citric acid.

BUILDING MORE EFFICIENT ENERGY FACTORIES

Coenzyme Q-10 is a micronutrient that is normally synthesized by the body and occurs naturally in a few foods, most abundantly in seafood. The body begins making less and less coenzyme Q-10 once it reaches the age of 20. By middle age, this can result in a deficiency state that affects heart muscle energy production and causes a decline in the antioxidant nutritional status. Coenzyme Q-10 is a component of the energy factories inside muscle cells, including the heart muscle. With a decline in coenzyme Q-10, the ability of muscles to convert fat and carbohydrates into energy is impaired to some degree. For this reason, a decline in coenzyme Q-10 has been strongly linked to the development of heart failure. If the heart muscle cannot generate the energy it needs to pump blood adequately, it weakens and a backup that can result in grave consequences occurs in the entire circulatory system.

Dr. Folkers from the University of Texas at Austin has been one of the pioneer researchers of coenzyme Q-10. He has shown that a large percentage of patients with heart failure (cardiomyopathy) and other heart problems have lower blood levels of coenzyme Q-10. He has also shown that by supplementing these patients with coenzyme Q-10, they often improve and their heart failure problems can be reversed. The treatment dose for heart disease patients is usually between 100 and 200 mg of coenzyme Q-10 per day. For otherwise healthy individuals, most experts suggest a supplement of 30 to 60 mg per day to re-establish more youthful blood levels of coenzyme Q-10.

The health-promoting benefits of coenzyme Q-10 extend beyond simply the prevention and treatment of heart failure. Coenzyme Q-10 is a powerful antioxidant that appears to work with vitamin E. Supplementation studies have also shown that it can reduce high blood pressure and strengthen the immune system. Many cancer researchers now claim that coenzyme Q-10 is an effective agent in cancer prevention and as part of cancer treatment. In light of the research and in conjunction with some first-hand experience that we have had with certain patients taking coenzyme Q-10 for therapeutic reasons, we are convinced that it is a supplement worth including in the quest for better health and the prevention of many conditions.

Our Protective Nutrient Game Plan

We take vitamin and mineral supplements to add an extra layer of protection to our already healthy style of eating. We recommend the following doses. Check with a doctor to ensure that you don't have a medical condition that would prevent you from following a supplementation program.

Vitamin/Mineral Supplementation

Vitamin E: 200 to 400 I.U.
Vitamin C: 500 to 1,000 mg
Beta carotene: 10,000 to 20,000 I.U.
Calcium: 500 mg (more under certain conditions)
Chromium: 50 to 200 mg

- A multiple vitamin and mineral, ideally antioxidant-enriched (higher levels than the R.D.A. for vitamin C, vitamin E) and containing extra calcium (500 mg). It should have no more than 7,500 I.U. pre-formed vitamin A and should contain as much as 10,000 to 20,000 I.U. beta carotene and 50 to 200 micrograms chromium.
- Coenzyme Q-10: 30 to 60 mg per day
- Alyllic Sulfides: Four deodorized garlic capsules per day.
  Remember that the absorption of vitamin A, beta carotene, vitamin E, vitamin D, vitamin K and coenzyme Q-10 requires the presence of fat in the intestinal tract. So, take these supplements right after a meal for optimal absorption.

Key Nutrition Strategies in Disease Prevention

- Have all the estrogen look-alikes daily:
  - cruciferous vegetables
  - two tablespoons of flaxseed powder
  - soy product.
- Eat three to five fruit servings per day as part of the carbohydrate portion of the Two-Staple System.
- Eat at least three orange, yellow, red, or dark-green vegetables each day as part of the carbohydrate portion of the Two-Staple System.

- Include anti-cholesterol and anti-cancer fibre foods for disease prevention.

The following sample meal plans show how easy it is to reach these nutrition targets:

Meal	Food	Nutrient
Breakfast		
Dairy protein meal	High-fibre cereal	anti-cancer fibre
	2 tbs. flaxseed powder on cereal	flaxseed powder
	Low-fat yogurt	
	1 nectarine	orange fruit
Lunch		
Vegetarian meal	Pasta, tomato sauce, broccoli, green peppers, red peppers, red, green, and cruciferous vegetables	
	High-fibre roll	anti-cancer fibre
Mid-afternoon	Large fruit salad with pear, apple, orange, grapefruit, red grapes	2 anti-cholesterol fibre 2 citrus fruit and
	1 red fruit	anti-cholesterol fibre
Dinner		
Soy or flesh protein meal	Two soy-based vege-burgers with tomatoes (lettuce)	soy product red vegetable
	Baked squash or sweet potato	orange vegetable
	Brown rice	anti-cancer fibre
Late night	3 cups of low-fat popcorn	anti-cancer fibre

* 30 minutes of aerobic exercise and vitamin supplements.

Over and above a supplementation program, the complex-carbohydrate selections decide how much and how many protective micronutrients, phytochemicals, and fibre the body will have to help defend against cancer, heart disease, diabetes, osteoporosis, and other degenerative ailments. Losing weight and becoming fit are worthy goals, but we should also fortify our resistance to disease with nature's protective nutrients. They are an essential part of a wellness journey.

A Refresher Course with Dr. Simon

By now, you have most of the information and tools to succeed at your long-term wellness plan. Ultimately it will be a moment-to-moment, day-to-day experience that will lead to long-term success. Let's reflect on some of the considerations and techniques we've suggested to help you on your journey to better health and fitness.

Inner Conversation and Dialogue

The new knowledge you have gained by reading *Break the Weight-Loss Barrier*, like any of life's experiences, awakens many inner feelings, thoughts, and conversations. For example, during moments when you are tired, your inner conversation might crave sweets or high-fat foods to soothe or comfort your fatigue, while at other times, a high-fibre apple may be just as satisfying.

Remember how Barb would find herself eating cookies when she was unable to express her anger? After we helped her look at her inner conversation, she was able to take a deep breath and examine her dialogue. She began to explore other ways to express her anger or to reduce the angry feeling. By simply becoming aware of this situation, she was able to stand back and begin the process of change. Barb's desire for those high-fat cookies shifted completely once she addressed her inner conversation. The same principles can apply to you. Helpless and hopeless feelings can overwhelm you when what was easy to do yesterday becomes difficult today. If you were able to choose the salad or the fruit yesterday, it can be very frustrating to feel drawn to the high-fat food today. Try not to focus on where you *should* be now, but where you *are*. Your inner conversation has shifted how you feel. This doesn't mean you have to act on your feelings or that you have done something wrong. Remember: your commitment to the Two-Staple

System will vary. And that's what living in the moment is all about. The most devastating conversation you can have is to be angry with yourself about what you are thinking and feeling. Helplessness is an inevitable result. Recognize the anger and begin to develop solutions to deal with it. In Barb's case, she substituted well-toasted, high-fibre bread with double fruit jam for cookies. Not only was she giving up saturated-fat calories, but she was also able to get seven grams of fibre with this solution substitution. Just as important as the change in behaviour was her shift out of the devastating hopeless position. Flexibility, solution seeking, and acceptance of her inner conversation kept her on the road to success.

Let's look at the process that Barb underwent during her inner search for understanding in this overwhelming moment.

- She took a few deep breaths but was unable to smile and stand back. She had a temporary opportunity to change. It was temporary because, although we might expect this moment to last for several minutes or longer, it lasts for only a second or two. She took another few deep breaths and was then able to pause and look at her inner conversation.

- She then identified her inner conversation – the feelings, thoughts, desires, and needs. Barb considered how angry she was with her mother but how she was unable to express this anger, so she did nothing. She recognized that she felt trapped and frustrated and wanted a treat just to soothe her need to be direct.

- After Barb identified what had activated this moment, she began to develop alternatives. She found a safe way to express her rage that helped relieve her anger with her mother. In the future, the assertiveness techniques she discovered would free her of the need to protect people by suppressing her feelings.

Many times, reading a self-help book, speaking with a therapist, or talking a friend will relieve inner conversations or thoughts. At other times, acceptance and allowing the feeling or thoughts to pass is the only course of action. Experiment with options. If one option doesn't work, try something else. There is always a solution, maybe not a perfect or permanent solution, but one that allows a difficult moment to pass and lets you move on to the next moment.

Bring your new knowledge to mind and see if you can find an alternative action when you are faced with a challenging moment on your journey to better health and fitness. Flip through *Break the Weight-Loss Barrier*, looking for suggestions that might be useful or appealing during the moment. For example, Barb saw our suggestion about speaking to the fast-food store and modified it slightly for her purposes. Instead, she spoke to a picture of her mother, releasing all of her negative thoughts and feelings. By following this formula of stop, listen, and create a playful response, you will change your success story. Rather than being devastated by your needs and desires, become aware of them by saying "I am aware of _____" and experiment to find a solution that works. Whether it is a food substitute, a few deep breaths, your wellness image, or your own idea, real living is solving a problem with a better solution.

ACTIONS FOR CHANGE

Let's consider Bob's situation. He came to me with a problem — he hated himself for snacking continuously. Once home from work, he would feed his youngest child dinner, eat something, make and eat dinner, and then have a few evening snacks. He ran 45 miles a week. He ate mostly carbohydrate treats such as jujubes, low-fat ice cream, and crackers with jam. His cholesterol level was fine.

By examining his inner conversation, we found that he was anxious and lonely while waiting for his wife to come home. During the evening, after his children were in bed, he also felt let down. In addition, as a teenager he was a big snacker and had always turned to food to fill him up. By recognizing his lonely feelings, he could identify how his inner conversation affected his eating. Since he was a runner and ate the right foods, we worked hard on developing alternative ways to overcome his lonely feelings. A new hobby and a late-night dinner with his wife were part of the solution. Just recognizing the feeling was very powerful for him. To quell his late-afternoon hunger, he ate a serving of high-fibre cereal at work, so he didn't come home starving. A small step, but by changing his inner feelings and desires he felt less vulnerable and at risk of eating. By drinking eight glasses of water before he came home, he eliminated his desire for food. As a fun step, he did push-ups instead of reaching for snacks. This was right for him because he used his ability to "just do it" when it comes to exercise to override his helpless snacking style.

Techniques for Change

Acting or behaving in a new way is probably the most convincing proof that you can change. If it happens during a moment you previously failed at, it is even more convincing. The first few times the shift occurs you'll need to accept the unsteadiness and unfamiliarity of the new course. Deep breathing, your wellness image, and reviewing the health benefits outlined in our book all provide a stabilizing effect.

Earlier in *Break the Weight-Loss Barrier*, we discussed how meditation and deep breathing can be helpful in overwhelming moments. People in stressful or high-pressure jobs, such as salespeople and people with children, are particularly at risk of feeling tense and overwhelmed by their day. Many diminish this feeling with food. By simply practising daily meditation, you can reduce the entire cycle of feeling tense, developing an uncomfortable feeling, beginning to salivate, giving in to eating, feeling a reduction of tension followed by regret and guilt. Think of ways you could use these techniques, not reasons why you can't. For example, if you don't have time to meditate, find time to take a few deep breaths every hour as a calorie-free break.

CHARTING YOUR WELLNESS JOURNEY

People sometimes challenge me. One of my favourite examples is of a man who didn't have a great deal of commitment to changing his lifestyle. He admitted, "I don't want to give up pizza at night, I love ice cream, my cholesterol is high, and my family doctor told me to come to see you." This situation wasn't a challenge – it was impossible. To successfully change, he must decide that the pain of continuing in his present lifestyle is worse than the pain of changing. If you feel on the edge as to whether change is worth the effort to achieve your health and fitness goals, ask yourself "What are the concrete benefits of losing weight? What are the benefits of less fat, more fibre, more protective nutrients in my diet?" When you create your list of benefits, be clear about the fact that health is at the centre of your life. Besides better fitness, reduced fat, a shapelier body, higher energy, and disease prevention, you will enjoy added benefits such as feeling better and having more self-confidence. Read Chapters 5 to 9 and personalize the benefits of following our program. For example, if you have a family history of heart disease or colon cancer, don't just read the facts about the benefits of the health-promoting foods – apply them to your life.

When people ask how to do the psychological exercises, they are really asking, "How do I know I'm doing them right and how should I feel while I'm doing them?" By following the instructions outlined in Chapter 3, you will have enough information to apply these techniques as you need them. What we cannot achieve in a book is to take you through the period of uncertainty and hesitation that you will experience as you begin to use these techniques. Remember that your uncertainty and concerns about doing these exercises properly are examples of your inner conversation. Recognize this, smile when you hear your conversation, and move forward.

If you feel tense and unsure about which technique to choose, simply take a few deep breaths or a couple of stress-breakers to calm yourself. At that moment, it will be up to you. The wellness image that you bring to mind at that moment might help, but so might a little self-talk. Experiment with a technique five times and if you're getting nowhere, it isn't for you. Combine it with another technique or try a new one. Don't become attached to any of them, simply make your own choice. Like all of life's experiences, these exercises will be easier or more difficult at different times. The secret is that the act of "doing it" will change you over time.

Setting your health goals and
staying on track

Now that you understand the principles of nutrition and exercise and know how to apply them every day, your next step is to determine which aspects of our program are best suited to you and to create a program that is uniquely your own.

First, you will need to complete the following Goal-Setting Wellness Planner. This Planner enables you to identify the goals you want to set for your body and health as well as any obstacles that may stand in your way. It also provides sensible strategies for overcoming those barriers. Finally, the Planner highlights the efforts required to make this transition a reality. After all, you must feel strongly about the rewards you will experience when you reach your goals. You must believe that your efforts will significantly change your quality of life so that will remain motivated to resist temptations along the way. The Goal-Setting Wellness Planner is a tool to harness your new-found convictions for a healthier lifestyle and a fitter body. When you write down your goals and identify your strategies to achieve success, you enhance the promise of your success. Get a pen and put your commitment on record!

The Goal-Setting Wellness Planner

Weight Goal:

What do you believe is a realistic and healthy weight for you? Write down the upper and lower limit of the weight range that you are aiming for. A five-pound difference should separate your upper and lower weight goals.

Upper Weight Limit: _____
Lower Weight Limit: _____

To establish the date when you will reach your goal, assume that you can lose one to two pounds per week on average.

I confidently expect to achieve my weight goal by: _____

If you are attempting to gain weight through weightlifting, you should follow a healthy diet and include 1.5 grams of protein each day for every 1 kilogram (2.2 pounds) you weigh. If you work hard, you can expect an average gain of 0.5 to 1 pound of muscle per month.

Waistline: I am committed to maintain a waistline of _____
Dress Size (for women):   I am committed to attain a dress size of _____
I confidently expect to attain this goal by: _____

Fitness Goal:

You have two fitness goals. The fitness program that you can see yourself doing right now is fitness goal #1. The fitness program that you are aiming for is fitness goal #2.

Aerobic Fitness Goal #1

The fitness program of gentle endurance activity to which I am committed is:

_____

Exercise Type: *(treadmill, jogging, stationary bike, etc.)* _____
Exercise Time: *(per session)* _____
Exercise Frequency: *(times per week)* _____
Exercise Distance and/or Intensity Level *(optional):* _____
(on treadmill — m.p.h. and total miles per session, walk or run — miles,
stationary bike — resistance level, stairmaster — resistance level)

Aerobic Fitness Goal #2

The fitness program of gentle endurance activity representing my long-term goal is:

_____

Type: _____

Time: _____

Frequency: _____

Distance or Intensity Level: _____

Weight-Training Program:

If you are at a level at which strength training is appropriate, write down your program.

Name of Station/Exercise *(bench press, etc.)* _____

Number of Sets _____

Number of Repetitions *(per set)* _____

The number of weight-training sessions that I plan to do each week is: _____

Dietary Strategies

- Meat: The high-fat meat products that I presently eat are: _____

_____

Solution: The low-fat flesh protein foods that I plan to eat instead because they make sense for me are: _____

_____

_____

- Dairy: The high-fat dairy products that I presently eat are: _____

_____

Solution: The low-fat dairy protein foods that I plan to eat instead because they make sense for me are: _____

_____

_____

- Pastries: The high-fat pastries, cakes, doughnuts, and chocolate products that I eat are: _____

Solution: The lower-fat solution-substitution foods that I am willing to eat instead are: _____

- Fried Foods: The fried foods that I eat are: _____

Solution: The lower-fat alternatives to these fried foods that I plan to substitute are: _____

- Sugary Beverages: The sugary beverages that tend to add more calories to my diet are: _____

  Solution: The no-calorie beverages and diluted juices that I plan to drink include:
  _____

- Candy: The candy products that I plan to reduce or eliminate are: _____
  _____

  Solution: The no-calorie or lower-calorie solutions that will help me achieve my goal are: _____

- Added Sugar: The places in my diet where I plan to reduce or eliminate added sugars are: _____

  Solution: My solution to added sugars in my diet as noted above are: _____
  _____

- Under the following complex-carbohydrate headings, list the actual foods you plan to increase in your daily life because of their health-promoting properties.

  Fruits: _____

  Green leafy vegetables: _____

  Cruciferous vegetables: _____

  Garden vegetables: _____

  Starchy vegetables: _____

  Breakfast cereals: _____

  Bread products: _____

  Other grains and noodles: _____

  Peas and beans: _____

  Soups: _____

- Supplementation: The vitamin and mineral supplementation strategy I plan to implement includes: _____

- Fibre Supplement: In addition to choosing higher-fibre foods, I plan to include a fibre supplement each day.

  Yes _____   No _____

  If yes, my strategy is: _____

- Other Supplements: In addition to the vitamin, mineral, and fibre supplements listed above, my wellness program includes the following supplements:
  _____

- Caffeine: I plan to limit my intake of coffee and tea to _____ cups per day.

- Alcohol: I plan to limit my intake of alcohol to _____ drinks per week.

Rewards

The health strategies described in my Goal-Setting Wellness Planner are designed to bring about a positive outcome for my body and to enhance my quality of life in many ways. I will be rewarded on three basic levels — my health, the appearance of my body, and my self-esteem or self-image.

The specific benefits of succeeding with this program for me are:

Fruits:

Health benefits: *(List the disease-prevention results that are most important to you.)*

_____

_____

_____

Benefits to my physical appearance: *(List the changes to your body that you are most excited about.)* _____

_____

_____

_____

Psychological benefits: *(Describe how your new, fitter, healthier, leaner body will affect your life.)* _____

_____

_____

Self-image: _____

_____

Social life: _____

_____

Willingness to participate in new activities: _____

_____

I am deeply committed to implementing these changes to experience and enjoy the rewards that this effort will bring to my life.

_____   _____
Signature   *Date*

Congratulations! If you have invested the time to complete the Goal-Setting Wellness Planner, you have taken a giant step toward including wellness as part of your daily lifestyle. You have defined how you will make the principles of fitness and nutrition fit into your life.

As you begin the program, you are strongly committed to achieving your goals, just as you were when you signed up for piano or karate lessons. You were confident that your commitment was strong enough to endure the effort required to become a concert pianist or a Bruce Lee. We all become excited at the outset because we are focused on the end product — a fitter, thinner, leaner, healthier, better-looking body. However, the effort required to maintain our initial excitement can easily give way to what appear to be the more urgent matters of day-to-day life. In the same way that most people don't have the stamina to become a piano virtuoso or a karate black belt, many people who become excited about transforming their body into a fitter, leaner, healthier machine fail to stay the course.

The following three steps will help you stay on track until your wellness program becomes a natural extension of your daily lifestyle. These steps will help you focus on your goals amid the other pressures, obligations, and activities that could otherwise divert you from your journey to better health and fitness.

Three Daily Steps to Staying on Track

STEP #1: *Briefly review your Goal-Setting Wellness Planner every day!*

Now that you have defined the benefits of the program for yourself and know exactly which strategies you will use to get there, it's important to remind yourself of them daily. With all of life's distractions, you can easily forget your plan for success.

Review the Goal-Setting Wellness Planner once a day for at least your first month on the program, and then once a week until you feel confident that you have internalized the nutrition and exercise changes that are bringing you success. This one-minute investment of your time will reawaken the enthusiasm and commitment you had when you initially outlined your strategies and rewards. Those feelings will keep you on track.

STEP #2: *Record your food intake and exercise routine in a Daily Success Journal* (see page 132).

One of the best ways to ensure your success with nutrition and exercise goals is to keep a daily record of your performance. Studies have shown that this type of self-monitoring is a very powerful instrument of change. After years on the program, we still record our exercise routine each day, and still feel the pain if we occasionally have to write "No workout today." Recording your physical activities makes you more accountable for your actions. The same principle applies when you record the foods you eat. The knowledge that you will have to acknowledge your actions at the end of the day can help you make healthier food choices and put more effort into your exercise program. In fact, you'll be amazed at how much better you do with this program if you record your day-to-day progress. You will be proud of your success and able to identify problem areas more easily.

Copy the Daily Success Journal on page 132. Record your food and beverage intake, and describe your exercise routine and any supplements you took. This process takes less than five minutes at the end of the day and can be a strong reminder of your daily performance. You can correct any problems before you risk abandoning your program. Keeping a daily nutrition and exercise journal is a proven tool to help bring about change!

Step #3: Use visualization to drive your health-promoting behaviour.

Each day, take 10 minutes to visualize the healthiest, fittest, leanest you that is within your reach. Deep down, you know how good you can look. Ask yourself how you would feel if you attained that goal.

Envision your face, arms, chest, abdominal area, waistline, thighs, and calves. See the whole image come together. Now, place yourself in a social setting, participating in an event of your choice — aerobic dance, ballroom dancing, giving a seminar, skiing, running your first marathon, cycling through the mountains.

Don't be afraid to dream. Without dreams we would have no goals — nothing to aim for. Each of us uses our dreams to direct our behaviour at some point in our lives. When I was young I dreamed that I was the quarterback for the Ottawa Roughriders and, later, the New York Jets. Although I never played professional football, I did work hard enough to be the starting quarterback of our high-school senior football team and on a semi-pro team during my university days. Visualization, which is itself a type of dream, allows you to experience in advance the feeling of success and elation associated with achieving your goals. How you feel determines whether you will remain on track during the day and how you can keep your wellness journey moving in a positive direction.

The Three Daily Steps

Step #1:
   Review your Goal-Setting
   Wellness Planner
Step #2:
   Keep a daily food
   and exercise journal
Step #3:
   Spend 10 minutes each day
   visualizing your success

Some Lifelong Strategies

Certain positive steps and resources can help you stay on track on an ongoing basis. Many of these are lifetime strategies that we use to keep our commitment to wellness at an optimal level.

• PLAN YOUR EXERCISE TIME IN ADVANCE.

At the beginning of each week, look at your plans for the next seven days. Consider your work and family commitments, social functions, appointments, and so on. Get a clear picture in advance of how your week is shaping up. Then decide when you plan to exercise; include both the day and the time. Remember, you should plan to exercise seven times per week. Write these times on your calendar or weekly planner and make a commitment to follow through.

• WRITE UP A WEEKLY WELLNESS SHOPPING LIST.

It is important to restock your kitchen with wellness foods every week. Don't buy junk food that might tempt you during a weak moment. At the same, you will be preparing healthful alternatives to disease-promoting foods for your loved ones.

Monthly Body Shape Summary

Date (Week ending):

_____

Exercise Summary:

Number of aerobic workouts:

Weight:

Waist:

Hips:

Upper Thigh:

Chest:

Bicep:

Calf:

• COMPLETE THE MONTHLY BODY SHAPE SUMMARY.

If you are trying to change your weight or figure, it is important to measure your weekly progress. The Monthly Body Shape Summary is an excellent yardstick for measuring and reviewing how your body shape is changing. If you measure these changes, you will be aware of the body transformation that is under way. Recording these measurements will help reinforce your success and strengthen your determination to continue the program.

- READ HEALTH MAGAZINES.

People who educate themselves remain more connected to a way of living that promotes wellness. As doctors who are interested in prolonging the quality of our patients' lives, we continually read the latest research materials. Yet we are also aware how reading these papers every month reinforces our own day-to-day commitment to wellness principles. You can find several excellent health magazines that translate academic findings into layperson's language. Reading positive, up-to-date information is a potent and powerful influence for staying on track from month to month.

Recommended Health Magazines

Health
In-Health
Longevity
Men's Health
Runner's World
Shape

- LISTEN TO AUDIO- AND VIDEOTAPES.

Audio- and videotapes aimed at the health, nutrition, and fitness markets provide the reinforcement you need to stay on track. If you don't want to join a fitness club, an aerobic fitness video may be a good way to work out. The more you learn about wellness, the better your chances are for succeeding in the long term.

- POST PICTURES.

Find a picture of a trim, fit person and post it somewhere you will see it at least twice a day. Remember, your goals must be believable, so choose a picture that shows a body and activity within your reach. When you see this picture, it will help you visualize your goal. Instead of someone from a magazine, a photo of yourself when you were at your peak of physical fitness could be more effective because it provides the physical evidence that you can succeed.

• RECALL POSITIVE QUOTATIONS.

Find positive quotations and put them in a prominent location. If the quotation is meaningful to you, it can inspire you to exert greater effort and can help create a positive, productive, powerful, and playful feeling that will improve your performance.

• GET SUFFICIENT REST.

Breaking out of your present comfort zone requires some energy at first. In the early stages, the extra energy you need to complete your exercise program may leave you feeling tired. If you feel tired, you may lose your initial enthusiasm and your natural tendency is to fall back on your old habits. Fight that tired feeling by either going to bed half an hour earlier or taking a power nap during the day. You'll be amazed at how much better you feel and how much easier it will be to stay on track with your wellness goals.

• ASSOCIATE WITH WINNERS.

Since the early 1970s, thousands of people have joined the wellness movement every year. These positive, high-energy people of all ages can be a tremendous source of inspiration. Although you do not have to copy their lifestyle or fitness routine, you can draw from their positive attitudes to recharge your mental battery. Joining a fitness club can also put you in contact with people who are involved in a wellness lifestyle. Make sure the club is conveniently located so you can drop in regularly. Get to know other people who are attuned to the wellness philosophy. Surround yourself with the people who can help you succeed.

- READ *BREAK THE WEIGHT-LOSS BARRIER*
AGAIN.

One of the best ways to stay on track is to read our book three or four times. Every time you read it, new information will jump off the page and new ideas will be triggered in your mind. While rereading the book, focus on how to fit the strategies we suggest into your day-to-day life.

Recipes

Low-Fat
Poultry/Fish-Protein Meals

The following recipes qualify as complete low-fat flesh-protein meals because they contain chicken, turkey or fish in combination with predominantly complex-carbohydrate foods. These recipes all derive less than 25 percent of their calories from fat and contain varying amounts of dietary fibre.

Turkey Macaroni Chili

Serves 8

This excellent low-calorie turkey dish derives a significant amount of fibre from the red kidney beans, which are famous for their cholesterol-lowering properties.

1 1/2 tsp	vegetable oil	7 mL
1 tsp	minced garlic	5 mL
1/2 cup	finely chopped carrots	125 mL
1 cup	chopped onions	250 mL
8 oz	ground turkey	250 g
1	can (19 oz [540 mL]) tomatoes, crushed	1
2 cups	chicken stock	500 mL
1 1/2 cups	peeled, diced potatoes	375 mL
3/4 cups	canned red kidney beans, drained	175 mL
3/4 cup	corn kernels	175 mL
2 tbsp	tomato paste	25 mL
1 1/2 tsp	chili powder	7 mL
1 1/2 tsp	dried oregano	7 mL
1 1/2 tsp	dried basil	7 mL
1/3 cup	elbow macaroni	75 mL

1. In large nonstick saucepan, heat oil over medium heat; add garlic, carrots, and onions and cook for 8 minutes or until softened, stirring occasionally. Add turkey and cook, stirring to break it up, for 2 minutes or until no longer pink. Add tomatoes, stock, potatoes, beans, corn, tomato paste, chili, oregano,

and basil; bring to a boil, reduce heat to low, cover and simmer for 20 minutes.

2. Bring to a boil and add macaroni; cook for 12 minutes or until pasta is tender but firm.

Sweet and Sour Turkey
Meatballs over Rice

Serves 8

Here's a great twist on meatballs. Note the high-protein contribution combined with the low percentage of calories from fat.

Tips

- If your kids don't like rice, serve this dish over 1 lb (500 g) of spaghetti.
- You can leave out the onions.
- If your children like pineapple, add 1 cup (250 mL) pineapple cubes (canned or fresh) at the end of the cooking time.

Make Ahead

Make up to 2 days ahead and reheat. Can be frozen for up to 6 weeks. Great for leftovers.

Approximately 15% fat

Per Serving

Calories	351 g
Protein	15 g
Fat, total	6 g
Fat, saturated	2 g
Carbohydrates	58 g
Sodium	558 mg
Cholesterol	54 mg
Fibre	2 g

12 oz	ground turkey	375 g
1/4 cup	finely chopped onions	50 mL
2 tbsp	ketchup	25 mL
2 tbsp	bread crumbs	25 mL
1	egg white	1
2 tsp	olive oil	10 mL
2 tsp	minced garlic	10 mL
1/3 cup	chopped onions	75 mL
2 cups	tomato juice	500 mL
2 cups	pineapple juice	500 mL
1/2 cup	chili sauce	125 mL
2 cups	white rice	500 mL

1. In bowl, combine turkey, onions, ketchup, bread crumbs, and egg white; mix well. Form 1 tbsp (15 mL) into a meatball and place on plate; set aside.

2. In large saucepan, heat oil over medium heat. Add garlic and onions and cook just until softened, approximately 3 minutes. Add tomato and pineapple juices, chili sauce, and meatballs. Cover and simmer uncovered for 30 to 40 minutes just until meatballs are tender.

3. Meanwhile, bring 4 cups (1 L) of water to a boil. Stir in rice, reduce heat, cover, and simmer for 20 minutes or until liquid is absorbed. Remove from heat and let stand for 5 minutes, covered. Serve meatballs and sauce over rice.

Teriyaki Turkey Stir-Fry
with Asparagus and Red Peppers

Serves 6

Tip

• Replace asparagus with broccoli, snow peas, or sugar snap peas.

Make Ahead

Prepare sauce up to a day ahead. Stir before using.

Approximately 14.5% fat

Per Serving

Calories	373
Protein	22 g
Fat, total	6 g
Fat, saturated	1 g
Carbohydrates	59 g
Sodium	642 mg
Cholesterol	33 mg
Fibre	2 g

Here's an excellent high-protein, low-fat recipe. The red-pepper contribution provides a rich source of beta carotene and other carotenoids.

1/2 cup	chicken stock or water	125 mL
1/4 cup	rice wine vinegar	50 mL
4 tbsp	honey	60 mL
3 tbsp	soya sauce	45 mL
1 tbsp	sesame oil	15 mL
2 tsp	minced garlic	10 mL
2 tsp	minced ginger	10 mL
2 1/2 tsp	cornstarch	12 mL
12 oz	penne	375 g
12 oz	boneless, skinless turkey breast, cut into thin strips	375 g
2 tsp	vegetable oil	10 mL
1 1/2 cups	sliced red peppers	375 mL
1 1/2 cups	asparagus cut into 1-inch (2.5 cm) pieces	375 mL

1. In small bowl, combine stock, vinegar, honey, soya sauce, sesame oil, garlic, ginger, and cornstarch; mix well.

2. In large pot of boiling water, cook penne until tender but firm. Drain and place in serving bowl. Meanwhile, in wok or skillet sprayed with vegetable spray, stir-fry turkey for

2 1/2 minutes or until just cooked at centre. Drain any excess liquid and remove turkey from wok.

3. Add oil to wok and stir-fry red peppers and asparagus for 4 minutes or until tender-crisp; stir sauce again and add to wok along with turkey. Cook for 1 minute or until slightly thickened. Toss with drained pasta.

Sautéed Turkey
with Tropical Fruit Sauce

Serves 6

With only 11% calories from fat, this is an excellent way to provide almost 30 grams of protein at one meal.

Tips

- Dates can replace the apricots.
- If fresh pineapple is available, add to sauce when you're finished cooking.

Make Ahead

Sauce can be made up to a day ahead. Reheat gently, adding more stock if too thick.

Approximately 11% fat

Per Serving

Calories	253
Protein	29 g
Fat, total	3 g
Fat, saturated	0.6 g
Carbohydrates	27 g
Sodium	668 mg
Cholesterol	66 mg
Fibre	1 g

Sauce

3/4 cup	canned pineapple bits, drained	175 mL
1/2 cup	orange or pineapple juice	125 mL
1/2 cup	chicken stock	125 mL
1/4 cup	chopped dried apricots	50 mL
2 tbsp	brown sugar	25 mL
1 tbsp	soya sauce	15 mL
1 tsp	minced garlic	5 mL
1 tsp	grated orange zest	5 mL
1	egg white	1
2 tbsp	water	25 mL
3/4 cup	seasoned bread crumbs	175 mL
1 1/2 lb	skinless, boneless turkey breasts (approximately 6) pounded until thin	750 g
1 tsp	vegetable oil	5 mL

1. In small saucepan, combine pineapple, juice, stock, apricots, brown sugar, soya sauce, cornstarch, garlic, and zest until smooth and well blended; cook over medium heat for 5 minutes, or until slightly thickened. Reduce heat to low and keep warm.

2. In shallow bowl, whisk together egg whites and water. Put bread crumbs on a plate. Between sheets of waxed paper pound breasts to 1/4-inch (5-mm) thickness.

3. Dip turkey in egg wash, then in bread crumbs. In large non-stick skillet sprayed with vegetable spray, heat oil over medium-high heat. Cook for 2 minutes per side, or until just done at centre. Serve with sauce.

Turkey Stir-Fry
with Asparagus, Bok Choy, and Oyster Sauce

Serves 4

Tips

• Serve over rice or pasta.
• Asparagus can be replaced with broccoli.
• If napa or bok choy are not available, use romaine lettuce.

Make Ahead

Prepare sauce up to a day ahead.

Approximately 16% fat

Per Serving

Calories	228
Protein	24 g
Fat, total	4 g
Fat, saturated	0.5 g
Carbohydrates	26 g
Sodium	1280 mg
Cholesterol	49 mg
Fibre	3 g

Here's a very low-fat way to serve turkey with carbohydrates. Asparagus is a rich source of carotene, vitamins C and B, including folic acid. It is one of the best health-promoting vegetables.

12 oz	skinless, boneless turkey breast, cut into thin strips	375 g
2 tsp	vegetable oil	10 mL
2 cups	asparagus cut into 1-inch (2.5 cm) pieces	500 mL
1 cup	sliced red peppers	250 mL
4 cups	sliced bok choy or napa cabbage	1 L
1 cup	water chestnuts	250 mL

Sauce

3/4 cup	chicken stock	175 mL
3 tbsp	oyster sauce	45 mL
1 1/2 tbsp	rice wine vinegar	22 mL
2 tbsp	honey	25 mL
1 tbsp	soya sauce	15 mL
1 tbsp	cornstarch	15 mL
1 1/2 tsp	minced garlic	7 mL
1 1/2 tsp	minced ginger root	7 mL
1/2 cup	chopped green onions (about 4 medium)	125 mL

1. Sauce: In bowl, whisk together stock, oyster sauce, vinegar, honey, soya sauce, cornstarch, garlic, and ginger; set aside.
2. In nonstick skillet or wok sprayed with vegetable spray, stir-fry turkey strips for 3 to 4 minutes, stirring constantly, or until just cooked at centre.
3. Heat oil in skillet over high heat. Add asparagus and red pepper strips and stir-fry for 3 minutes, stirring constantly, or until tender-crisp. Add bok choy and water chestnuts and stir-fry for 1 minute or until bok choy wilts. Stir sauce again and add to wok along with turkey strips. Cook for 2 minutes or until thickened slightly. Garnish with green onions.

Oriental Chicken Salad
with Mandarin Oranges, Snow Peas, and Asparagus

Serves 6

Tips

• Replace chicken with shrimp, pork, or steak.
• Broccoli or green beans can replace asparagus.
• Thinly sliced julienned carrots can replace bean sprouts.

Make Ahead

Prepare salad and dressing early in the day, keeping separate until ready to serve. Dressing can keep for days.

Approximately 17.4% fat

Per Serving

Calories	155 g
Protein	17 g
Fat, total	3 g
Fat, saturated	0.5 g
Carbohydrates	17 g
Sodium	434 mg
Cholesterol	33 mg
Fibre	2 g

Here's a great high-protein dish that provides an abundance of protective nutrients from mandarin oranges, snow peas, green peppers, asparagus, and bean sprouts.

12 oz	skinless, boneless chicken breasts	375 g
1 cup	asparagus	250 mL
	cut into 1-inch (2.5 cm) pieces	
1 1/4 cups	halved snow peas	300 mL
1 cup	sliced baby corn cobs	250 mL
1 cup	bean sprouts	250 mL
1 cup	canned mandarin oranges, drained	250 mL
1 1/2 cups	sliced red or green peppers	375 mL
3/4 cup	sliced water chestnuts	175 mL
2	medium green onions, chopped	2

Dressing

2 tbsp	orange juice concentrate, thawed	25 mL
1 tbsp	rice wine vinegar	15 mL
1 tbsp	soya sauce	15 mL
2 tsp	honey	10 mL
2 tsp	vegetable oil	10 mL
1 tsp	sesame oil	5 mL
1 tsp	minced ginger root	5 mL
1 tsp	minced garlic	5 mL

1. In nonstick skillet sprayed with vegetable spray, sauté chicken breasts and cook approximately 7 minutes, or until browned on both sides and just done at centre. Let chicken cook, then cut into 1/2 inch (1 cm) cubes and place in large serving bowl.
2. In bowling water or microwave, blanch asparagus for 2 minutes or until tender-crisp; refresh in cold water and drain. As well, cook snow peas for 45 seconds or until tender-crisp; refresh in cold water and drain. Place in serving bowl and chicken. Add baby corn, bean sprouts, mandarin oranges, red peppers, water chestnuts, and green onions to bowl and toss.
3. In small bowl, whisk together orange juice concentrate, vinegar, soya sauce, honey, vegetable oil, sesame oil, ginger, and garlic; pour over salad and toss.

Chicken Cacciatore
over Penne

Serves 6

Tip
- Dark chicken meat can be used but the calories and fat will increase slightly.

Make Ahead

Prepare sauce up to a day ahead. Reheat gently, adding more stock if sauce is too thick.

Approximately 10% fat

Per Serving

Calories	441 g
Protein	32 g
Fat, total	5 g
Fat, saturated	0.7 g
Carbohydrates	66 g
Sodium	283 mg
Cholesterol	48 mg
Fibre	6 g

Here is another high-protein, low-fat chicken disk that provides a generous supply of protective nutrients. Note the 6 grams of dietary fibre – providing one-fifth of your daily requirements!

12 oz	penne	375 g
2 tsp	vegetable oil	10 mL
2 tsp	crushed garlic	10 mL
1 1/3 cups	chopped onions	325 mL
1 1/4 cups	chopped sweet red peppers	300 mL
1 1/2 cups	sliced mushrooms	375 mL
1 lb	skinless, boneless chicken breasts, cubed	300 g
1/2 cup	dry red wine	125 mL
1/3 cup	chicken stock	75 mL
2 3/4 cups	fresh or canned tomatoes, crushed	675 mL
1 tsp	tomato paste	15 mL
2 tsp	dried basil	10 mL
1 tsp	dried oregano	5 mL
1/4 cup	chopped parsley	50 mL

1. Cook pasta in boiling water according to package instructions or until firm to the bite. Drain and place in serving bowl.
2. In large nonstick skillet, heat oil; sauté garlic, onions, and red peppers until soft, approximately 5 minutes. Add mushrooms and sauté until soft, approximately 5 minutes. Add

chicken and sauté on medium heat until no longer pink, approximately 5 minutes.

3. Add wine and stock; simmer for 2 minutes. Add tomatoes, tomato paste, basil, and oregano; simmer for 15 minutes, covered, on low heat, stirring occasionally. Pour over pasta. Add parsley, and toss.

Oriental Chicken Balls
over Spaghetti

Serves 6 to 8

Tips
- Replace chicken with beef, veal or pork for a change.
- Pineapple juice from frozen concentrate or the juice from canned pineapple can be used.

Make Ahead

Meatballs and sauce can be cooked up to 2 days before. Reheat gently before pouring over pasta.

Approximately 5% fat

Per Serving (8)

Calories	328
Protein	18 g
Fat, total	2 g
Fat, saturated	0.3 g
Carbohydrates	61 g
Sodium	515 mg
Cholesterol	28 mg
Fibre	5 g

Here is a super example of tasty, low-fat cooking. This dish provides a great source of protein and fibre, and contains only 5% total calories from fat. A winner!

10 oz	spaghetti	300 g
12 oz	ground chicken	375 g
1 tsp	crushed garlic	5 mL
1 tsp	minced ginger root	5 mL
3 tbsp	finely chopped onions	45 mL
3 tbsp	canned or home-made tomato sauce	45 mL
1	egg white	1
3 tbsp	seasoned bread crumbs	45 mL

Sauce

1 cup	ketchup	250 mL
1 1/2 cups	pineapple juice	375 mL
2 tbsp	brown sugar	25 mL
1 cup	thinly sliced carrots	250 mL
1 cup	thickly sliced red peppers	250 mL
1 cup	pineapple chunks	250 mL

1. Cook pasta in boiling water according to package instructions or until firm to the bite. Drain and place in serving bowl.
2. In bowl, mix together chicken, garlic, ginger, onions, tomato sauce, egg white, and bread crumbs until well combined. Form

into small balls of approximately 1 inch (2.5 cm). This will make about 32 balls.

3. Make the sauce: In large nonstick saucepan, combine ketchup, pineapple juice, brown sugar, and carrots over medium heat. Add chicken balls. Cover and simmer for 30 to 40 minutes, just until chicken balls are tender.

4. In the last 10 minutes of cooking, add red peppers and pineapple chunks. Pour over pasta, and toss.

Chicken Tortillas

Serves 4

Tip

• Boneless turkey breast, pork, or veal scallopini can replace chicken.

Make Ahead

Prepare filling early in the day and gently reheat before stuffing tortillas. Add extra stock if sauce is too thick.

Approximately 20.5% fat

Per Serving

Calories	438
Protein	21 g
Fat, total	10 g
Fat, saturated	2 g
Carbohydrates	65 g
Sodium	884 mg
Cholesterol	25 mg
Fibre	7 g

Here's a fun way to introduce your family to low-fat dishes. Note that this recipe also provides 7 grams of fibre. Red kidney beans contain cholesterol-lowering soluble fibre and colon-cleansing insoluble fibre.

Preheat oven to 375°F (190°C)

Baking sheet sprayed with vegetable spray

6 oz	skinless, boneless chicken breast, diced	150 g
1 tsp	vegetable oil	5 mL
1 tsp	crushed garlic	5 mL
1 cup	chopped onions	250 mL
1/2 cup	finely chopped carrots	125 mL
1 cup	tomato pasta sauce	250 mL
1 cup	canned red kidney beans, drained	250 mL
1/2 cup	chicken stock	125 mL
1 tsp	chili powder	5 mL
8	small 6-inch (15-cm) flour tortillas	8

1. In nonstick skillet sprayed with vegetable spray, cook chicken over high heat for 2 minutes, or until done at centre. Remove from skillet and set aside.

2. Reduce heat to medium and add oil to pan. Respray with vegetable spray and cook garlic, onions, and carrots for 10 minutes, or until browned and softened, stirring often. Add some water if vegetables start to burn. Add tomato sauce, beans,

stock, and chili powder and cook for 10 to 12 minutes or until carrots are tender, mixture has thickened, and most of the liquid is absorbed. Stir in chicken and remove from heat.

3. Put 1/3 cup (75 mL) of mixture on each tortilla, and roll up. Put on prepared baking sheet and bake for 10 minutes or until heated through.

Roasted Chicken
with Apricot Orange Glaze and Couscous Stuffing

Serves 4 to 6

Tips

- Couscous stuffing is a great dish to accompany other meals.
- Follow the instructions carefully for the apricot glaze. Glaze half of the chicken without added cornstarch, the other half with cornstarch. The extra glaze serves as gravy.
- Do not stuff chicken until ready to bake; this will avoid bacterial contamination.

Make Ahead

The glaze and couscous can be prepared earlier in the day.

Approximately 10% fat

Per Serving

Calories	429 g
Protein	23 g
Fat, total	5 g
Fat, saturated	0.9 g
Carbohydrates	74 g
Sodium	769 mg
Cholesterol	53 mg
Fibre	3 g

A great source of protein and only 10 percent total calories from fat. Note the protective nutrients provided by snow peas, carrots, red onions, and apricots, a beautiful medley of vitamins, minerals, and phytonutrients.

Preheat oven to 400°F (200°C)

Roasting pan with rack

3 lb	roasting chicken	1.5 kg

Couscous stuffing

1 tbsp	orange juice concentrate, thawed	15 mL
1 tbsp	chopped fresh coriander or parsley	15 mL
2 tsp	hoisin sauce	10 mL
1 1/2 tsp	honey	7 mL
1 tsp	minced garlic	5 mL
1/2 tsp	minced ginger root	2 mL
1 tsp	sesame oil	5 mL
1 tsp	olive oil	5 mL
1 3/4 cups	chicken stock	425 mL
1 cup	couscous	250 mL
1 cup	chopped snow peas	250 mL
2/3 cup	chopped red onions	150 mL
1/2 cup	chopped carrots	125 mL
1/2 cup	chopped dried apricots	125 mL

Apricot glaze

3/4 cup	apricot or peach jam	175 mL
1/2 cup	chicken stock	125 mL
3 tbsp	orange-juice concentrate, thawed	45 mL
1 tbsp	soya sauce	15 mL
1 tsp	minced garlic	5 mL
1 tsp	minced ginger root	5 mL
1 tbsp	cornstarch	15 mL
1 cup	chicken stock	250 mL

1. Stuffing: In small bowl whisk together orange-juice concentrate, coriander, hoisin, honey, garlic, ginger, sesame oil, and vegetable oil; set aside. Bring stock to a boil in saucepan; stir in couscous, cover and remove from heat. Let stand for 5 minutes; fluff with a fork. In bowl combine couscous, snow peas, red onions, carrots, dried apricots, and orange-juice sauce.

2. Loosely stuff chicken with some of the couscous stuffing. Place on rack in roasting pan sprayed with vegetable spray. Put remaining couscous stuffing in a casserole dish and cover. Set aside.

3. Glaze: In bowl, whisk together apricot jam, stock, orange-juice concentrate, soya sauce, garlic, and ginger. Measure out 1/2 cup (125 mL) of the glaze; combine with cornstarch and 1/2 cup (125 mL) of the chicken stock and set aside. Pour remaining 1/2 cup (125 mL) chicken stock into roasting pan under chicken. Spread some of the remaining apricot glaze (without cornstarch) over chicken; bake for 1 hour, or until juices run clear when leg is pierced at thickest point. Baste chicken with apricot glaze every 15 minutes as it roasts. Put casserole with stuffing in oven for last 30 minutes of roasting time. Let chicken rest for 10 minutes before carving.

4. Meanwhile, remove juices, if any, from roasting pan and place in saucepan. Add reserved apricot glaze-cornstarch mix-

ture; heat over medium heat for 2 minutes or until slightly thickened. Serve chicken with sauce and stuffing. Remove skin before eating.

Chicken Fagioli
(Bean Tomato Sauce)

With 8 grams of fibre, this recipe is also a spectacular contribution of protein to help repair and build your body structure. A great combination of protein, legumes, and carbohydrates.

4	chicken legs	4
1/4 cup	all-purpose flour	50 mL
2 tsp	vegetable oil	10 mL
2 tsp	minced garlic	10 mL
1/2 cup	chopped onions	125 mL
1/3 cup	chopped carrots	75 mL
1/3 cup	chopped celery	75 mL
1 1/2 cups	red kidney beans, drained	375 mL
1 cup	pureed canned tomatoes	250 mL
3/4 cup	chicken stock	175 mL
1 1/2 tsp	dried basil	7 mL
1 tsp	dried oregano	5 mL

Serves 4

Tips
- Use bone-in chicken breasts instead of legs; reduce browning time to 4 minutes and reduce cooking time to 20 minutes.
- White kidney beans or a combination of beans can be used.
- A great dish to reheat.

Make Ahead

Brown chicken earlier in the day and refrigerate until ready to cook with sauce.

Approximately 20% fat

Per Serving

Calories	316
Protein	33 g
Fat, total	7 g
Fat, saturated	1 g
Carbohydrates	31 g
Sodium	538 mg
Cholesterol	92 mg
Fibre	8 g

1. In large nonstick skillet sprayed with vegetable spray, heat 1 tsp (5 mL) of the oil over high heat. Dust chicken with flour and cook for 8 minutes, turning often, or until browned on all sides. Set aside and wipe skillet clean.

2. Reduce heat to medium. Add remaining 1 tsp (5 mL) oil to skillet. Add garlic, onions, carrots and celery; cook for 5 minutes or until softened. Mash 1/2 cup (125 mL) of the kidney beans; add mashed and whole beans, tomatoes, stock, basil, and

oregano to skillet. Bring to a boil, reduce heat to medium-low, add browned chicken pieces, cover and cook for 30 minutes or until juices run clear when legs are pierced at thickest point. Stir occasionally. Remove skin before eating.

Chicken with Rice,
Green Olives, and Tomato Sauce

Here is another fantastic high-protein, high-fibre, low-fat recipe. Remember that tomato sauce is a rich source of lycopene, which is the most prevalent carotenoid in the male prostate gland.

Preheat oven to 400°F (200°C)

9- by 13-inch baking dish (3.5 L) sprayed with vegetable spray

4	chicken legs	4
1/3 cup	all-purpose flour	75 mL
2 tsp	vegetable oil	10 mL
2 tsp	minced garlic	10 mL
1 1/2 cups	chopped onions	375 mL
1 1/2 cups	chopped green peppers	375 mL
1 cup	white rice	250 mL
1	can (19 oz [540 mL]) tomatoes, puréed	1
1 1/2 cups	chicken stock	375 mL
1/2 cup	sliced stuffed green olives	125 mL
2 tsp	drained capers	10 mL
2 tsp	dried basil	10 mL
1 1/2 tsp	dried oregano	7 mL
1	bay leaf	1

Serves 4

Tips

• Bone-in chicken breasts can be used, or a combination of both can be used. Bone-in breast will cook in less time than legs.

• A combination of wild and white rice can be used.

Make Ahead

Brown chicken earlier in the day and refrigerate until ready to complete cooking.

Approximately 17% fat

Per Serving

Calories	522
Protein	34 g
Fat, total	10 g
Fat, saturated	2 g
Carbohydrates	76 g
Sodium	964 mg
Cholesterol	92 mg
Fibre	8 g

1. In large nonstick skillet sprayed with vegetable spray, heat 1 tsp (5 mL) of the oil over high heat. Dust chicken with flour. Cook for 8 minutes, turning often, or until browned on all sides. Put in prepared baking dish.

2. In nonstick skillet, heat remaining 1 tsp (5 mL) oil over medium heat. Add garlic, onions, and green peppers; cook for 4 minutes or until softened. Stir in rice, tomatoes, stock, olives, capers, basil, oregano, and bay leaf; bring to a boil and pour over chicken. Cover tightly with aluminum foil and bake for 30 minutes, or until juices run clear when leg is pierced at thickest point and rice is tender. Remove skin before eating.

Japanese Salad
with Peanut Dressing

I love the idea of adding broccoli to these protein dishes to help you get the fibre, beta carotene, and vitamin C that account for many of its disease-preventing effects.

4 oz	spaghettini	125 g
1 cup	chopped broccoli florets	250 mL
1 cup	chopped snow peas	250 mL
1 cup	diced sweet red pepper	250 mL
1	green onion, sliced	1
2	small carrots, diced	2
1 tsp	vegetable oil	5 mL
4 oz	boneless, skinless chicken breast, thinly sliced	125 g
1 tsp	crushed garlic	5 mL

Dressing

3 tbsp	unsalted peanuts	45 mL
1 tsp	minced ginger root	5 mL
	(or 1/4 tsp [1 mL] ground ginger)	
2 tbsp	lemon juice	25 mL
1 tbsp	soya sauce	15 mL
1 tbsp	honey	15 mL
4 tsp	vegetable oil	20 mL
1 1/2 tsp	sesame oil	7 mL
2 tsp	crushed garlic	5 mL
2 tbsp	water	25 mL

Serves 4

Tips
- Turkey strips can replace the chicken.
- The dressing is also good as a marinade for other meats, chicken, or fish.
- Substitute the peanuts with pecans, cashews, or almonds.

Make Ahead

Prepare dressing up to a day before. Just before serving, complete the dish.

Approximately 13% fat

Per Serving

Calories	205
Protein	13 g
Fat, total	3 g
Fat 31 g	
Carbohydrates	31 g
Sodium	145 mg
Cholesterol	19 mg
Fibre	3 g

Chicken

1. In saucepan of boiling water, cook spaghettini according to package directions or just until firm to the bite. Drain and rinse under cold water; drain well and place in serving bowl.

2. In saucepan of boiling water, blanch broccoli and snow peas just until bright green. Drain and rinse under cold water; drain and add to noodles. Add red pepper, onion, and carrots.

3. Dressing: In food processor, combine peanuts, ginger root, lemon juice, soya sauce, honey, vegetable and sesame oils, garlic, and water; purée until smooth. Pour over vegetable mixture.

4. In nonstick skillet, heat oil; sauté chicken and garlic just until cooked. Add to vegetable mixture and combine well. Refrigerate until chilled.

Linguine with Swordfish
in Tomato Basil Sauce

The meaty texture of swordfish makes an excellent substitution for red meat and ground beef for people who enjoy that texture. This is a great low-fat pasta dish.

12 oz	linguine	375 g
1 1/2 tsp	crushed garlic	7 mL
12 oz	swordfish, cut into 1-inch (2.5-cm) cubes	375 g
14 oz	chopped tomatoes	425 g
3/4 cup	fish or chicken stock	175 mL
4 tsp	flour	20 mL
1/2 cup	chopped fresh basil	125 mL
	(or 2 tsp [10 mL] dried)	
3 tbsp	grated Parmesan cheese	45 mL

1. Cook pasta in boiling water according to package instructions or until firm to the bite. Drain and place in serving bowl.
2. In large nonstick skillet sprayed with vegetable spray, sauté garlic and swordfish until fish is just done, approximately 3 minutes. Drain and add to pasta.
3. Add tomatoes to skillet and simmer for 2 minutes.
4. Meanwhile, in small bowl combine stock and flour until smooth. Add to tomatoes and simmer on medium heat just until slightly thickened, approximately 3 minutes. Add basil; pour over pasta. Sprinkle with cheese, and toss.

Serves 6

Tips
- Tuna or Chilean seabass are good substitutes for swordfish.
- Try plum tomatoes instead of field tomatoes.

Make Ahead
Prepare sauce early in day. Reheat gently while preparing pasta, adding more stock if sauce is too thick.

Approximately 14% fat

Per Serving

Calories	374
Protein	25 g
Fat, total	6 g
Fat, saturated	2 g
Carbohydrates	54 g
Sodium	311 mg
Cholesterol	30 mg
Fibre	3 g

Bow-Tie Pasta Salad with
Shrimp, Snow Peas, and Red Peppers in Orange Dressing

Serves 6 to 8

as an appetizer

Tips

- Substitute any other seafood or firm white fish fillet such as swordfish or orange roughy.
- Fresh tarragon can replace cilantro for an unusual sweet flavour.

Make Ahead

Prepare salad and dressing early in day. Do not toss until ready to eat.

Approximately 21% fat

Per serving (8)

Calories	385
Protein	18 g
Fat, total	9 g
Fat, saturated	1 g
Carbohydrates	57 g
Sodium	522 mg
Cholesterol	71 mg
Fibre	3 g

Here's a great way not only to attain the Omega 3 fats from shrimp but also the many protective nutrients from red peppers, snow peas, mandarin oranges, and garlic.

12 oz	bow-tie pasta or rotini	375 g
12 oz	shrimp, peeled, deveined, and cut in half	375 g
1 cup	thinly sliced sweet red peppers	250 mL
1 cup	snow peas, cut in half	250 mL
1 cup	canned mandarin orange segments, drained	250 mL
1 cup	sliced water chestnuts	250 mL

Dressing

4 tbsp	olive oil	60 mL
4 tbsp	frozen orange-juice concentrate, thawed	60 mL
4 tbsp	lemon juice	25 mL
2 tbsp	balsamic vinegar	25 mL
1 1/2 tsp	crushed garlic	7 mL
1/2 cup	chopped cilantro or parsley	125 mL

1. Cook pasta in boiling water according to package instructions or until firm to the bite. Rinse with cold water. Drain and place in serving bowl.

2. In medium nonstick skillet sprayed with vegetable spray, sauté shrimp just until pink, approximately 4 minutes. Do not overcook. Add to pasta.

3. Add red peppers, snow peas, orange segments, and water chestnuts.

4. Make the dressing: In small bowl combine oil, orange-juice concentrate, lemon juice, vinegar, garlic, and cilantro. Pour over salad, and toss.

Scallops in Black Bean Sauce
with Asparagus and Oyster Mushrooms

Serves 4

Tips

- Whole black-bean sauce is less salty than the puréed version. If puréed sauce is too salty, increase honey to taste.
- Regular mushrooms are acceptable as a substitute. They give off more liquid, so drain off excess.
- Any firm seafood can be used.
- Broccoli can be substituted for asparagus.

Make Ahead

Prepare sauce up to 48 hours ahead. Keep refrigerated and stir again before using.

Approximately 24% fat

Per Serving

Calories	222
Protein	23 g
Fat, total	6 g
Fat, saturated	0.7 g
Carbohydrates	20 g
Sodium	604 mg
Cholesterol	37 mg
Fibre	2 g

Here's an innovative fish variation using scallops. Remember that asparagus is loaded with carotene, and vitamins B and C.

1 lb	scallops	500 g
1 tsp	vegetable oil	5 mL
2 1/2 cups	asparagus	625 mL
	cut into 1-inch (2.5 cm) pieces	
2 cups	sliced oyster mushrooms	500 mL
2	medium green onions, chopped	2

Sauce

3/4 cup	chicken stock	175 mL
2 tbsp	black bean sauce	25 mL
2 tbsp	honey	25 mL
2 tsp	rice wine vinegar	10 mL
2 tsp	soya sauce	10 mL
2 tsp	sesame oil	10 mL
1 tbsp	cornstarch	15 mL
1 tsp	minced garlic	5 mL
1 tsp	minced ginger root	5 mL

1. Heat a nonstick skillet sprayed with vegetable spray over high heat; add scallops and cook for 2 to 3 minutes, turning frequently, or until just cooked at centre. Remove from heat and drain any excess liquid.

2. In small bowl, whisk together stock, black-bean sauce, honey, vinegar, soya sauce, sesame oil, cornstarch, garlic, and ginger; set aside.

3. Heat oil in nonstick pan over medium-high heat. Cook asparagus and mushrooms for 5 minutes or until tender-crisp. Drain any excess liquid. Stir sauce again and add to pan. Cook for 1 minute or until bubbly and thickened slightly. Return scallops to pan and cook for 30 seconds or until heated through. Serve over rice or pasta. Garnish with green onions.

Linguine with Pecan
Oriental Sauce and Salmon

Serves 6

Tips

- Great served warm, at room temperature, or cold.
- If to be served cold, this dish can be prepared early in the day. Toss before serving.
- Sauce can be used as a marinade or in a stir-fry, or over another pasta dish.

Make Ahead

Prepare sauce up to 2 days ahead. Stir again before using.

Approximately 23% fat

Per Serving

Calories	392
Protein	18 g
Fat, total	10 g
Fat, saturated	1 g
Carbohydrates	58 g
Sodium	895 mg
Cholesterol	21 mg
Fibre	3 g

Adding fish to a pasta dish is a popular low-fat, flesh-protein meal. There are many variations on this theme. Note the inclusion of broccoli, which is a powerful, disease-fighting wonder food.

Sauce

5 tbsp	packed brown sugar	75 mL
1/4 cup	chopped pecans	50 mL
3 tbsp	chicken stock or water	45 mL
2 1/2 tbsp	soya sauce	35 mL
2 1/2 tbsp	rice wine vinegar	35 mL
2 tbsp	lemon juice	25 mL
2 tbsp	sesame oil	25 mL
2 tsp	minced garlic	10 mL
1 1/2 tsp	minced ginger root	7 mL
1 1/2 cups	chopped baby corn cobs	375 mL
1 1/2 cups	thinly sliced red or green peppers	375 mL
1/4 cup	chopped green onions (about 2 medium)	50 mL
12 oz	linguine	375 g
8 oz	salmon cut into 1/2-inch (1-cm) cubes	250 g
2 cups	broccoli florets	500 mL

1. Put brown sugar, pecans, stock, soya sauce, vinegar, lemon juice, sesame oil, garlic, and ginger in food processor; process until smooth and set aside. Put corn cobs, red peppers, and green onions in large serving bowl.

2. In large pot of boiling water, cook pasta according to package directions or until tender but firm. Drain and add to vegetables in bowl.

3. Meanwhile, in nonstick skillet sprayed with vegetable spray, cook salmon over high heat for 4 minutes or until just done at centre; put in serving bowl.

4. Cook broccoli in boiling water or microwave for 2 minutes or until tender-crisp; add to serving bowl. Pour sauce over and toss.

Seafood Tomato Stew
Over Fusilli with Fennel

Serves 6

Here's a delicious seafood-and-pasta combination that provides one-quarter of your daily fibre requirement.

Tips

- Fennel is outstanding in this dish. If it is unavailable, use 1/4 cup (50 mL) licorice liqueur or 1 tbsp (15 mL) fennel seeds. If the licorice taste is not desired, omit fennel and add 1 cup (250 mL) chopped leeks or onions.
- Any combination of seafood can be substituted to make up the total amount. Firm white fish fillets, such as halibut, snapper, or haddock, can be substituted for seafood.

Make Ahead

The sauce can be prepared a day ahead and reheated just before seafood is added.

Approximately 14% fat

Per Serving

Calories	469
Protein	32 g
Fat, total	7 g
Fat, saturated	1 g
Carbohydrates	70 g
Sodium	669 mg
Cholesterol	172 mg
Fibre	8 g

1 cup	chopped fennel	250 mL
12 oz	fusilli or rotini	375 g
2 tsp	vegetable oil	10 mL
2 tsp	crushed garlic	10 mL
1 cup	chopped red onions	250 mL
1 cup	chopped sweet green peppers	250 mL
1 cup	sliced mushrooms	250 mL
2	cans (19 oz [540 mL]) crushed tomatoes	2
1/2 cup	fish or chicken stock	125 mL
1/3 cup	sliced black olives	75 mL
1 tbsp	tomato paste	15 mL
2 tsp	dried basil	10 mL
1 tsp	dried oregano	5 mL
1	bay leaf	1
Pinch	cayenne	Pinch
8 oz	fresh mussels or clams	250 g
8 oz	shrimp, peeled and deveined	250 g
8 oz	squid, cleaned and sliced	250 g

1. Cook fennel in boiling water for 8 minutes, or just until barely tender. Drain and set aside.

2. Cook pasta in boiling water according to package instructions or until firm to the bite. Drain and place in serving bowl.

3. In large nonstick saucepan, heat oil; sauté garlic, onions, green peppers, and fennel for 5 minutes. Add mushrooms and cook for 3 minutes. Add tomatoes, stock, olives, tomato paste, basil, oregano, bay leaf, and cayenne. Simmer on medium-low heat for 15 minutes, stirring occasionally.

4. Add seafood. Cover and simmer for 3 minutes, or until mussels are open and seafood just cooked. Pour over pasta.

Seafood Kebabs
with Pineapple and Green Pepper in Apricot Glaze

Serves 4

Tips

- Swordfish, shrimps, or scallops are a good choice for fish.
- Peach jam can substitute for the apricot jam.
- If fresh pineapple is unavailable, use canned.

Make Ahead

Prepare kebabs and the glaze up to 24 hours ahead, keeping separate until just ready to cook.

Approximately 14% fat

Per Serving

Calories	317
Protein	23 g
Fat, total	5 g
Fat, saturated	0.6 g
Carbohydrates	47 g
Sodium	118 mg
Cholesterol	54 mg
Fibre	3 g

Here's a great variation of seafood in kebab form. It provides a great opportunity to add vegetables to the menu in a fun, distinctive form.

Start barbecue or preheat oven to 425°F (220°C)

1 lb	firm white fish, cut into 2-inch (5-cm) cubes	500 g
16	dried apricots	16
1	green pepper, cut into 16 chunks	1
16	pineapple chunks	16

Glaze

1/3 cup	apricot jam	75 mL
2 tbsp	lemon juice	25 mL
1 tbsp	vegetable oil	15 mL
1 tbsp	water	15 mL
1 tbsp	chopped fresh coriander or parsley	15 mL
1 tsp	Dijon mustard	5 mL
1 tsp	minced garlic	5 mL
3/4 tsp	curry powder	4 mL

1. Alternately thread fish cubes, apricots, green pepper, and pineapple chucks onto 4 long or 8 short barbecue skewers.
2. Glaze: In small bowl whisk together apricot jam, lemon juice, oil, water, coriander, mustard, garlic, and curry. Brush

kebabs with some of the sauce; reserve remainder of sauce to serve with cooked kebabs.

3. Barbecue or bake kebabs for 5 to 8 minutes, turning once, or just until seafood is opaque.

Fettuccine with Mussels,
Shrimp, and Parsley

Serves 6

Tips
- Substitute clams for mussels for a variation or use a combination of both.
- Shrimp can be replaced with scallops or a firm white fish fillet such as halibut or monkfish.

Make Ahead

The processed sauce in Step 2 can be made up to a day ahead.

Approximately 25% fat

Per Serving

Calories	436
Protein	27 g
Fat, total	12 g
Fat, saturated	2 g
Carbohydrates	52 g
Sodium	182 mg
Cholesterol	107 mg
Fibre	2 g

Here's a tasty and unique combination of seafood and pasta. The use of olive oil and garlic can help to lower blood cholesterol.

12 oz	fettuccine	375 g
2 1/2 slices	stale bread	2 1/2
3 tbsp	red wine vinegar	45 mL
2 tbsp	water	25 mL
2 cups	chopped parsley leaves	500 mL
2 tsp	capers	10 mL
4	anchovy fillets	4
2 tsp	crushed garlic	10 mL
1/4 cup	olive oil	50 mL
1 tbsp	chicken or seafood stock	15 mL
24 (approx.)	mussels	24
1/2 cup	dry white wine	125 mL
1 1/2 tsp	crushed garlic	7 mL
12 oz	shrimp, peeled, deveined, and cut in half	375 g

1. Cook pasta in boiling water according to package instructions or until firm to the bite. Drain and place in serving bowl.
2. In small dish, soak bread in vinegar and water until saturated, approximately 2 minutes. Place bread mixture in food processor. Add parsley, capers, anchovies, and garlic. Process

until smooth. Add oil and stock and process until smooth. Set aside.

3. In large covered saucepan, steam mussels with wine and garlic just until open, approximately 5 minutes. Discard any that do not open. Remove mussels from shells and save liquid.

4. In large nonstick skillet sprayed with vegetable spray, sauté shrimp just until pink, approximately 3 minutes. Add mussels, reserved liquid, and parsley purée. Heat for 1 minute. Toss with pasta.

Salmon Over
White-and-Black-Bean Salsa

Serves 4

Tips

• Swordfish or tuna can be substituted for salmon.
• Other varieties of beans can be substituted if black or white navy beans are unavailable.
• If you're not using canned beans, 1 cup (250 mL) dry yields 3 cups (750 mL) cooked.

Make Ahead

Prepare bean mixture earlier in the day and keep refrigerated. Stir before serving.

Approximately 25% fat

Per Serving

Calories	319
Protein	32 g
Fat, total	9 g
Fat, saturated	2 g
Carbohydrates	29 g
Sodium	313 mg
Cholesterol	56 mg
Fibre	9 g

Who says fibre has to be dry and tasteless? This dish contains 9 grams of fibre!

Start barbecue or preheat oven to 425°F (220°C)

1 lb	salmon steaks	500 g

Salsa

1 cup	canned black beans, drained	250 mL
1 cup	canned white navy beans, drained	250 mL
3/4 cup	chopped tomatoes	175 mL
1/2 cup	chopped green peppers	125 mL
1/4 cup	chopped red onions	50 mL
1/4 cup	chopped fresh coriander	50 mL
2 tbsp	balsamic vinegar	25 mL
2 tbsp	lemon juice	25 mL
1 tbsp	olive oil	15 mL
1 tsp	minced garlic	5 mL

1. Salsa: In bowl combine black beans, white beans, tomatoes, green peppers, red onions, and coriander. In small bowl whisk together vinegar, lemon juice, olive oil, and garlic; pour over bean mixture and toss to combine.

2. Barbecue fish or bake uncovered for approximately 10 minutes for each 1-inch (2.5 cm) thickness of fish, or until fish flakes with a fork. Serve fish over bean salsa.

Vegetarian
Meals

The following recipes contain no animal protein. They are excellent choices for your vegetarian meal, and use a wide variety of complex carbohydrates. They are low in fat and provide varying amounts of dietary fibre.

Polynesian
Wild Rice Salad

Serves 4 to 6

Tips

• This recipe can be prepared using all wild rice or all white rice.

• Great salad for brunch or picnic. Keeps well for hours.

Make Ahead

Prepare up to a day ahead. Keep refrigerated and stir well before serving.

Approximately 10.6% fat

Per Serving

Calories	169
Protein	5 g
Fat, total	2 g
Fat, saturated	0.2 g
Carbohydrates	36 g
Sodium	388 mg
Cholesterol	0 mg
Fibre	2 g

One of the great features of this vegetarian meal is its very low fat content. Here's a delicious and nutritious rice salad that is full of protective nutrients.

2 cups	chicken stock	500 mL
1/2 cup	white rice	125 mL
1/2 cup	wild rice	125 mL
1 cup	halved snow peas	250 mL
1 cup	chopped red peppers	250 mL
3/4 cup	chopped celery	175 mL
2/3 cup	sliced water chestnuts	150 mL
1/2 cup	canned mandarin oranges, drained	125 mL
2	medium green onions, chopped	2

Dressing

2 tsp	orange-juice concentrate, thawed	10 mL
2 tsp	honey	10 mL
1 tsp	soya sauce	5 mL
1 tsp	olive oil	5 mL
1/2 tsp	sesame oil	2 mL
1/2 tsp	lemon juice	2 mL
1/2 tsp	minced garlic	2 mL
1/4 tsp	minced ginger root	1 mL

1. Bring stock to boil in medium saucepan; add wild rice and white rice. Cover, reduce heat to medium low and simmer for 15 to 20 minutes, or until rice is tender and liquid is absorbed. Rinse with cold water. Put rice in serving bowl.

2. In a saucepan of boiling water or microwave, blanch snow peas for 1 or 2 minutes or until tender-crisp; refresh in cold water and drain. Add to serving bowl along with red peppers, celery, water chestnuts, mandarin oranges, and green onions; toss well.

3. In small bowl, whisk together orange-juice concentrate, honey, soya sauce, vegetable oil, sesame oil, lemon juice, garlic, and ginger; pour over salad and toss well.

Pasta Salad
with Apricots, Dates, and Orange Dressing

Serves 6 to 8

Tips

• A delicious sweet pasta salad that goes well with a grilled fish or chicken entrée.
• Prunes can replace apricots or dates or use in combination.

Make Ahead

Prepare salad and dressing early in day. Toss just before serving.

Approximately 17.5% fat

Per Serving

Calories	307
Protein	7 g
Fat, total	6 g
Fat, saturated	0.8 g
Carbohydrates	58 g
Sodium	8 mg
Cholesterol	0 mg
Fibre	4 g

Note the contribution of fibre from the dried dates and the disease-fighting nutrients from peppers, onions, and garlic.

12 oz	medium shell pasta	375 g
1 1/2 cups	diced sweet red or green peppers	375 mL
3/4 cup	diced dried apricots	175 mL
3/4 cup	diced dried dates	175 mL
1/2 cup	chopped green onions	125 mL

Dressing

3 tbsp	balsamic vinegar	45 mL
3 tbsp	frozen orange-juice concentrate, thawed	45 mL
3 tbsp	olive oil	45 mL
2 tbsp	lemon juice	25 mL
2 tbsp	water	25 mL
1 1/2 tsp	crushed garlic	7 mL
1/2 cup	chopped parsley	125 mL

1. Cook pasta in boiling water according to package instructions or until firm to the bite. Rinse with cold water. Drain and place in serving bowl.
2. Add sweet peppers, apricots, dates, and green onions.
3. Make the dressing: In small bowl combine vinegar, orange-juice concentrate, oil, lemon juice, water, garlic, and parsley. Pour over salad, and toss.

Corn and Three-Bean
Salad

Here is a super way to add more legumes to your diet. Note the 7 grams of fibre that the legumes provide.

8 oz	pasta wheels or small shell pasta	250 g
1 cup	canned black beans or chick peas, drained	250 mL
3/4 cup	canned red kidney beans, drained	175 mL
3/4 cup	canned white kidney beans, drained	175 mL
3/4 cup	canned corn niblets, drained	175 mL
1 1/4 cups	diced sweet red peppers	300 mL
3/4 cup	diced carrots	175 mL
1/2 cup	diced red onions	125 mL

Dressing

1/4 cup	lemon juice	50 mL
3 tbsp	olive oil	45 mL
3 tbsp	red wine or cider vinegar	45 mL
2 tsp	crushed garlic	10 mL
1/2 cup	chopped coriander or parsley	125 mL

1. Cook pasta in boiling water according to package instructions or until firm to the bite. Rinse with cold water. Drain and place in serving bowl.

2. Add all three beans, corn niblets, red peppers, carrots, and onions.

3. Make the dressing: In small bowl combine lemon juice, oil, vinegar, garlic, and coriander. Pour over dressing, and toss.

Serves 6 to 8

Tips
- Use any combination of cooked beans.
- For a sweeter salad, try balsamic vinegar.

Make Ahead

Prepare salad and dressing separately up to a day ahead. Pour dressing over top just before serving.

Approximately 22.7% fat

Per Serving

Calories	277
Protein	10 g
Fat, total	7 g
Fat, saturated	0.6 g
Carbohydrates	46 g
Sodium	293 mg
Cholesterol	0 mg
Fibre	7 g

Sweet Potato, Apple,
and Raisin Casserole

Increasing your intake of squash and sweet potatoes is a fantastic way to naturally increase your intake of beta carotene and its sister, carotenoids.

Preheat oven to 350°F (180°C)

Baking dish sprayed with nonstick vegetable spray

1 lb	sweet potatoes, peeled and cubed	500 g
3/4 tsp	ground ginger	4 mL
1/4 cup	honey or maple syrup	50 mL
3/4 tsp	ground cinnamon	4 mL
2 tbsp	margarine, melted	25 mL
1/4 cup	raisins	50 mL
2 tbsp	chopped walnuts	25 mL
3/4 cup	cubed, peeled sweet apples	175 mL

1. Steam or microwave sweet potatoes just until slightly underdone. Drain and place in baking dish.

2. In small bowl, combine ginger, honey, cinnamon, margarine, raisins, walnuts, and apples; mix well. Pour over sweet potatoes and bake, uncovered, for 20 minutes or until tender.

Wild Rice, Snow Peas,
and Almond Casserole

Here's a great way to make a casserole with very little fat. A good vegetarian alternative.

2 tsp	margarine	10 mL
1/2 cup	chopped onion	125 mL
1 tsp	crushed garlic	5 mL
1/2 cup	wild rice	125 mL
1/2 cup	white rice	125 mL
3 1/4 cups	chicken stock	800 mL
3/4 cup	chopped snow peas	175 mL
1/4 cup	diced sweet red pepper	50 mL
1/4 cup	toasted sliced almonds	50 mL

1. In large nonstick saucepan, melt margarine; sauté onion and garlic until softened. Add wild and white rice; stir for 2 minutes.
2. Add stock; reduce heat, cover and simmer just until rice is tender and liquid is absorbed, 30 to 40 minutes.
3. Add snow peas, red pepper, and almonds; cook for 2 minutes. Place in serving bowl.

Serves 4

Tips
- This is delicious served warm or cold.
- Toast almonds in small skillet on top of stove or in 400°F (200°C) oven for 2 minutes.
- For a special dinner menu, use 1 cup (250 mL) wild rice and omit the white rice.

Make Ahead

If serving cold, prepare early in day and stir just before serving.

Approximately 23.6% fat

Per Serving

Calories	305
Protein	13 g
Fat	8 g
Carbohydrates	43 g
Sodium	1425 mg
Cholesterol	1 mg
Fibre	3 g

Vegetable Hoisin
Fried Rice

A great rice dish that encompasses a whole meal. With only 14% calories from fat, this dish is loaded with protective nutrients from carrots, red peppers, snow peas, garlic, and onions.

1 cup	white rice	250 mL
1/4 cup	chicken stock	50 mL
2 tbsp	soya sauce	25 mL
2 tbsp	hoisin sauce	25 mL
1/2 cup	chopped carrots	125 mL
1 tbsp	vegetable oil	15 mL
1 tsp	minced garlic	5 mL
1 tsp	minced ginger root	5 mL
3/4 cup	chopped red peppers	175 mL
3/4 cup	chopped snow peas	175 mL
2	green onions, chopped	2

1. Bring 2 cups (500 mL) water to a boil in a saucepan; stir in rice, cover, reduce heat to medium and cook for 20 minutes or until liquid is absorbed. Remove from heat.
2. In small bowl, whisk together stock, soya sauce, and hoisin sauce; set aside.
3. Cook carrots in boiling water or microwave for 4 minutes or until tender-crisp. Drain. Heat oil in wok or skillet over high heat. Add garlic, ginger, red peppers, snow peas, and carrots;

cook, stirring for 2 minutes. Add rice; cook, stirring, 2 minutes longer. Add hoisin-soya mixture and cook for 1 minute longer. Serve garnished with green onions.

Barley, Tomato,
and Olive Casserole

Serves 4 to 6

Tips
- If you don't like the taste of coriander (chinese parsley), substitute basil or dill.
- If plum tomatoes are unavailable, use field tomatoes – deseeded to eliminate excess liquid.
- The combination of flavours is delicious and unusual.

Make Ahead

Prepare early in the day and reheat gently before serving. Tastes great next day.

Approximately 19% fat

Per Serving

Calories	140
Protein	5 g
Fat, total	3 g
Fat, saturated	0.4 g
Carbohydrates	27 g
Sodium	761 mg
Cholesterol	0 mg
Fibre	6 g

Remember that whenever you combine tomatoes with olive oil, the fat in the olive oil carries the disease-fighting lycopene from tomatoes into the body. A recent study correlated higher lycopene levels with lower risk of prostate cancer.

1 tsp	vegetable oil	5 mL
2 tsp	minced garlic	10 mL
1 cup	chopped red peppers	250 mL
1 cup	chopped green peppers	250 mL
3 cups	chicken stock	750 mL
3/4 cup	barley	175 mL
1/3 cup	sliced black olives	75 mL
1 tbsp	drained capers	15 mL
1 1/2 tsp	dried basil	7 mL
3/4 tsp	dried oregano	4 mL
1	dried bay leaf	1
1 1/2 cups	chopped plum tomatoes	375 mL
1/4 cup	chopped fresh coriander	50 mL
1/4 cup	chopped green onions (about 2 medium)	50 mL

1. In large nonstick saucepan, heat oil over medium heat; add garlic and red and green peppers and cook for 5 minutes, or until softened. Add stock, barley, olives, capers, basil, oregano, and bay leaf; bring to a boil and cover. Reduce heat to low and

cook covered for 35 minutes or until barley is tender. Add tomatoes, coriander, and green onions and cook for 5 minutes longer.

Couscous with Raisins,
Dates, and Curry

Serves 4

Tips

- This dish is fine served at room temperature.
- Try adding 1/4 cup (50 mL) diced carrots to vegetables.

Make Ahead

Prepare up to the day before, then gently reheat over low heat.

Approximately 11% fat

Per Serving

Calories	243
Protein	6 g
Fat	3 g
Carbohydrates	47 g
Sodium	239 mg
Cholesterol	0 mg
Fibre	3 g

Note that this dish contains only 11% calories from fat and provides 3 grams of dietary fibre.

1 1/4 cups	chicken stock	300 mL
3/4 cup	couscous	175 mL
1 tbsp	margarine	15 mL
3/4 cup	finely chopped onions	175 mL
1 tsp	crushed garlic	5 mL
1 cup	finely chopped sweet red pepper	250 mL
1/4 cup	raisins	50 mL
1 tsp	curry powder	5 mL
5	dried dates or apricots, chopped	5

1. In small saucepan, bring chicken stock to boil. Stir in couscous and remove from heat. Cover and let stand until liquid is absorbed, 5 to 8 minutes. Place in serving bowl.

2. Meanwhile, in nonstick saucepan, melt margarine; sauté onions, garlic, and red pepper until softened, approximately 5 minutes. Add raisins, curry powder, and dates; mix until combined. Add to couscous and mix well.

Chili Bean Stew

Who says chili requires meat? This excellent, low-fat vegetarian chili is fortified with a variety of protective nutrients.

1 1/2 tsp	vegetable oil	7 mL
1 tsp	crushed garlic	5 mL
1 cup	chopped onion	250 mL
8 oz	tofu dried	250 g
1	can (19 oz [540 mL]) tomatoes, crushed	1
2 cups	chicken stock	500 mL
1 1/2 cups	diced peeled potatoes	375 mL
3/4 cup	drained canned red kidney beans	175 mL
3/4 cup	corn niblets	175 mL
2 tbsp	tomato paste	25 mL
1 1/2 tsp	chili powder	7 mL
1 1/2 tsp	each dried oregano and basil	7 mL
1/3 cup	small shell pasta	75 mL

Serves 4 to 6

Tip
• Other cooked beans can be used.

Make Ahead
Make and refrigerate up to a day before. Reheat gently, adding more stock if too thick.

Approximately 23% fat

Per Serving
Calories	232
Protein	15 g
Fat 6 g	
Carbohydrates	30 g
Sodium	580 mg
Cholesterol	22 mg
Fibre	5 g

1. In large nonstick saucepan, heat oil; sauté garlic and onion until softened, approximately 5 minutes.
2. Add tofu and cook for 3 minutes.
3. Add tomatoes, stock, potatoes, kidney beans, corn, tomato paste, chili powder, oregano, and basil. Cover and reduce heat; simmer for 40 minutes, stirring occasionally.
4. Add pasta; cook until firm to the bite, approximately 10 minutes.

Vegetarian Three-Bean Chili

Serves 6

Tips
- Use other vegetables of your choice.
- Fresh chili pepper (1 tsp [5 mL] chopped) can replace chili powder.
- Six ounces (170 g) sautéed tofu can be added at the end of the cooking time.
- Serve over rice or pasta.

Make Ahead

Prepare up to 2 days ahead and gently reheat.

Approximately 11.4% fat

Per Serving

Calories	236
Protein	12 g
Fat	3 g
Carbohydrates	47 g
Sodium	773 mg
Cholesterol	0 mg
Fibre	13 g

This chili contains 13 grams of fibre — almost half of your daily requirement. Don't miss the chance to include this super vegetarian chili often in your diet.

1 tsp	vegetable oil	5 mL
2 tsp	minced garlic	10 mL
1 cup	chopped onions	250 mL
1 cup	chopped green peppers	250 mL
1 cup	chopped carrots	250 mL
1 cup	chopped zucchini	250 mL
1 tbsp	chili powder	15 mL
1 tsp	dried basil	5 mL
1 tsp	dried oregano	5 mL
2	cans (19 oz [540 mL]) tomatoes, crushed	2
1 tbsp	tomato paste	15 mL
1 cup	canned black beans drained	250 mL
1 cup	canned red kidney beans, drained	250 mL
1 cup	canned chick peas, drained	250 mL

1. Over medium heat, heat oil in large nonstick saucepan sprayed with nonstick vegetable spray. Add garlic, onions, green peppers, and carrots; cook for 5 minutes or until onion is softened. Add zucchini, chili powder, basil, and oregano; cook for 2 minutes longer.

2. Add tomatoes and tomato paste; bring to a boil, reduce heat to medium-low, stir in beans and chick peas, cover and cook for 35 minutes, or until thickened and carrot is tender.

Complex-
Carbohydrate Soups

The following soup recipes are an excellent way to capitalize on the many benefits of complex-carbohydrate foods. To create a complete vegetarian meal, have a bowl of one of the following soups with a garden or cruciferous vegetable salad.

These soup recipes are low in fat and provide varying amounts of dietary fibre.

Leek Split-Pea Soup

Here's a low-fat vegetarian meal that is both filling and delicious.

1 tbsp	vegetable oil	15 mL
2 tsp	minced garlic	10 mL
2 cups	chopped leeks	500 mL
1/2 cup	chopped carrots	125 mL
5 1/2 cups	chicken stock	1.375 L
1 cup	peeled diced potatoes	250 mL
3/4 cup	split peas	175 mL
1/4 tsp	ground black pepper	1 mL

1. In nonstick saucepan sprayed with vegetable spray, heat oil over medium heat. Add garlic, leeks, and carrots; cook for 4 minutes or until onion is softened. Add stock, potatoes, split peas, and pepper; bring to a boil. Cover, reduce heat to low and simmer for 40 minutes, or until peas are tender.

2. Transfer soup to food processor or blender; purée.

Serves 6

Tips

- Leeks can contain a lot of hidden dirt. To clean thoroughly, slice in half lengthwise and wash under cold running water, getting between the layers where dirt hides.
- Mushrooms make a tasty addition to this soup. While soup is cooking, sauté 2 cups (500 mL) of sliced mushrooms in a nonstick skillet. Add to soup before serving.

Make Ahead

Prepare and refrigerate up to a day ahead and reheat gently before serving, adding more stock if too thick.

Approximately 16% fat

Per Serving

Calories	165
Protein	8 g
Fat, total	3 g
Fat, saturated	0.3 g
Carbohydrates	28 g
Sodium	980 mg
Cholesterol	0 mg
Fibre	1 g

Vegetable Bean Soup

Serves 6

This bean soup is a floating sea of antioxidants, protective nutrients, and dietary fibre.

Tips

- Napa or Chinese cabbage can replace bok choy. Otherwise, substitute romaine lettuce.
- Leeks can have a lot of hidden dirt. To clean thoroughly, slice in half lengthwise and wash under cold running water, getting between the layers where dirt hides.
- Any canned beans can replace the red kidney beans.
- If green beans are unavailable, substitute chopped broccoli or zucchini.

Make Ahead

Prepare soup up to a day in advance, but leave Step 2 until just before serving.

Approximately 17% fat

2 tsp	vegetable oil	10 mL
1 1/2 tsp	minced garlic	7 mL
3/4 cup	chopped onions	175 mL
1 cup	chopped leeks	250 mL
1 cup	chopped carrots	250 mL
5 cups	chicken stock	1.25 L
1 1/4 cups	peeled, chopped potatoes	300 mL
2	bay leaves	2
1/2 tsp	dried basil	2 mL
1/2 tsp	dried oregano	2 mL
2 cups	chopped bok choy	500 mL
1 cup	drained, canned red kidney beans	250 mL
1 cup	trimmed green beans	250 mL
1/3 cup	chopped fresh parsley	75 mL
1/4 tsp	ground black pepper	1 mL

Per Serving

Calories	160
Protein	12 g
Fat, total	3 g
Fat, saturated	0.3 g
Carbohydrates	24 g
Sodium	934 mg
Cholesterol	16 mg
Fibre	5 g

1. In nonstick saucepan sprayed with vegetable spray, heat oil over medium heat. Add garlic, onions, leeks, and carrots; cook 4 minutes or until onions are softened, stirring occasionally. Add stock, potatoes, bay leaves, basil, and oregano; bring to a boil.

Cover, reduce heat to low and simmer for 20 minutes or until potatoes are tender.

2. Stir in bok choy, kidney beans, and green beans. Cover and cook for 5 minutes. Stir in parsley and pepper and serve.

Vegetable, Sweet Potato,
and Bean Minestrone

Here's a minestrone with some of the world's most health-promoting factors — all in one bowl.

2 tsp	vegetable oil	10 mL
2 tsp	crushed garlic	10 mL
1 1/2 cups	finely chopped onions	375 mL
1/2 cup	finely chopped carrots	125 mL
1/2 cup	finely chopped celery	125 mL
4 1/2 cups	chicken or vegetable stock	1.125 L
1 1/2 cups	sweet potatoes, peeled and finely chopped	375 mL
1 1/2 cups	sliced zucchini	375 mL
1	can (19 oz [540 mL]) tomatoes, crushed	1
3/4 cup	canned white or red kidney beans, drained	175 mL
1	bay leaf	1
2 tsp	dried basil	10 mL
1 tsp	dried oregano	5 mL
	Pepper	
1/3 cup	orzo or small shell pasta	75 mL

1. In large nonstick saucepan, heat oil; sauté garlic, onions, carrots, and celery until softened, approximately 5 minutes.
2. Add stock, potatoes, zucchini, tomatoes, kidney beans, bay leaf, basil, and oregano; cover and simmer for approximately 40

minutes or until vegetables are tender, stirring occasionally.
Remove bay leaf. Season with pepper to taste.
3. Add pasta; cook for 10 to 15 minutes, stirring often, or until
orzo is firm to the bite. Sprinkle with pepper.

White-Bean Spinach
Pasta Soup

Serves 6

Tips

- Chick peas or navy beans can replace white kidney beans.
- Half a 10-oz (300 g) package of fresh chopped spinach can be used instead of frozen.

Make Ahead

Prepare soup early in day, but do not add pasta until 10 minutes before serving.

Approximately 14% fat

Per Serving

Calories	188
Protein	9 g
Fat, total	3 g
Fat, saturated	0.7 g
Carbohydrates	33 g
Sodium	1040 mg
Cholesterol	2 mg
Fibre	8 g

Like other beans and peas, white beans contain cholesterol-lowering fibre and colon-cleansing fibre. Also, the spinach is an excellent touch.

2 tsp	vegetable oil	10 mL
1 1/2 tsp	chopped garlic	7 mL
1 cup	chopped onions	250 mL
2/3 cup	finely chopped carrots	150 mL
1/2	package (10 oz [300 g]) frozen spinach (chopped, thawed, and squeezed dry)	1/2
4 cups	chicken broth	1 L
1	can (19 oz [540 mL]) crushed tomatoes	1
1 1/2 cups	canned white kidney beans, drained	375 mL
1 1/2 tsp	dried basil	7 mL
1	bay leaf	1
1/3 cup	macaroni	75 mL

1. In nonstick saucepan sprayed with vegetable spray, heat oil; sauté garlic, onions, and carrots until softened, approximately 5 minutes.

2. Add spinach, broth, tomatoes, beans, basil, and bay leaf; cover and simmer for 15 minutes. Add pasta and cook for 10 minutes or until pasta is just tender.

Curried Broccoli
Sweet Potato Soup

Adding broccoli to this low-fat, high-fibre soup provides a strong disease-fighting benefit.

2 tsp	vegetable oil	10 mL
1 1/2 tsp	minced garlic	7 mL
1 1/2 cups	chopped onions	375 mL
1 tsp	curry powder	5 mL
4 cups	chicken stock	1 L
4 cups	broccoli florets	1 L
3 cups	peeled, diced sweet potato	750 mL
2 tbsp	honey	25 mL

1. Heat oil in nonstick saucepan over medium heat. Add garlic, onion, and curry; cook for 4 minutes or until softened. Add stock, broccoli, and sweet potatoes; bring to a boil. Cover, reduce heat to low and simmer for 30 minutes or until vegetables are tender.

2. Transfer soup to food processor or blender; add honey and purée.

Serves 6

Tip

Increase curry to 1 1/2 tsp (7 mL) for more intense flavour.

Make Ahead

Prepare and refrigerate up to a day ahead and reheat gently before serving, adding more stock if too thick.

Approximately 12% fat

Per Serving

Calories	150
Protein	4 g
Fat, total	2 g
Fat, saturated	0.3 g
Carbohydrates	31 g
Sodium	684 mg
Cholesterol	0 mg
Fibre	4 g

Carrot, Sweet Potato,
and Parsnip Soup

Serves 4

Tip

- You can substitute carrots for parsnips or vice versa.

Make Ahead

Make and refrigerate up to a day before and reheat before serving, adding more stock if too thick.

Approximately 24% fat

Per Serving

Calories	149
Protein	6 g
Fat	4 g
Carbohydrates	23 g
Sodium	692 g
Cholesterol	0 mg
Fibre	4 g

Here is a nice carotenoid boost, which includes both carrots and sweet potatoes in the same bowl.

2 tsp	vegetable oil	10 mL
1 tsp	crushed garlic	5 mL
1 cup	chopped onion	250 mL
3 1/2 cups	chicken stock	825 mL
1	small potato, peeled and chopped	1
3/4 cup	chopped carrots	175 mL
3/4 cup	chopped, peeled sweet potato	175 mL
1/2 cup	chopped, peeled parsnip	125 mL
2 tbsp	chopped fresh dill	25 mL
	(or 1 tsp [5 mL] dried dillweed)	

1. In medium nonstick saucepan, heat oil; sauté garlic and onion for approximately 5 minutes or until softened.

2. Add stock, potato, carrots, sweet potato, and parsnip; reduce heat, cover and simmer for 30 to 40 minutes or until vegetables are tender.

3. Purée in food processor until creamy and smooth. Stir in dill.

Mexican Corn, Bean,
and Pasta Soup

This is a great combination of protective nutrients with a generous contribution of dietary fibre.

2 tsp	vegetable oil	10 mL
2 tsp	crushed garlic	10 mL
1 cup	chopped onions	250 mL
1 1/2 cups	chopped sweet green peppers	375 mL
1	can (28 oz [796 mL]) crushed tomatoes	1
2 1/2 cups	chicken stock	625 mL
2 cups	canned red kidney beans, drained	500 mL
1 cup	corn niblets	250 mL
1 tbsp	chili powder	15 mL
1/4 tsp	cayenne pepper	1 mL
1/2 cup	macaroni	125 mL
	Coriander	

1. In large nonstick saucepan, heat oil; sauté garlic, onions, and green peppers until soft, approximately 5 minutes.
2. Add tomatoes, stock, beans, corn niblets, chili powder, and cayenne. Cover and simmer on low heat for 20 minutes.
3. Add pasta, simmer for 10 to 12 minutes or until pasta is al dente (firm to the bite). Garnish with fresh coriander.

Serves 6 to 8

Tips

- Chick peas or other beans can replace kidney beans.
- Any small shell pasta can be used.

Make Ahead

Prepare soup up to a day ahead, but do not add pasta until 10 minutes before serving.

Approximately 14% fat

Per Serving

Calories	187
Protein	7 g
Fat, total	3 g
Fat, saturated	0.2 g
Carbohydrates	37 g
Sodium	682 mg
Cholesterol	0 mg
Fibre	7 g

Black Bean Soup

Serves 4 to 5

Tips

- A small dollop of low-fat sour cream or yogurt with a sprinkling of coriander gives this soup an elegant look.
- Canned black beans can sometimes be difficult to find. Use 12 oz (375 g) cooked beans. One cup (250 mL) of dry beans yields approximately 3 cups (750 mL) cooked.

Make Ahead

Prepare and refrigerate up to a day ahead and reheat gently before serving, adding more stock if too thick.

Approximately 18% fat

Per Serving

Calories	147
Protein	8 g
Fat, total	3 g
Fat, saturated	0.3 g
Carbohydrates	25 g
Sodium	741 mg
Cholesterol	0 mg
Fibre	8 g

North Americans have an extremely poor intake of beans and peas. Here's the perfect solution that also tastes phenomenal.

2 tsp	olive oil	10 mL
2 tsp	minced garlic	10 mL
1 cup	chopped onions	250 mL
1 cup	chopped carrots	250 mL
1	can (19 oz [540 mL]) black beans, drained (or 12 oz [375 g] cooked beans)	1
3 cups	chicken stock	750 mL
3/4 tsp	ground cumin	4 mL
1/4 cup	chopped coriander or parsley	50 mL

1. In a nonstick saucepan sprayed with vegetable spray, heat oil over medium heat; add garlic, onions, and carrots and cook, stirring occasionally, for 4 minutes or until the onion is softened.

2. Add beans, stock, and cumin; bring to a boil. Cover, reduce heat to medium low and simmer for 20 minutes or until carrots are softened. Transfer to food processor and purée until smooth.

3. Ladle into bowls; sprinkle with coriander.

Curried Carrot
Orange Soup

Check out the total fat content at 7.5% and only 11 grams of total calories. A great soup to help you lose excess fat while feeling content.

1 tsp	vegetable oil	5 mL
1 1/2 tsp	minced garlic	7 mL
1 tsp	curry powder	5 mL
1 cup	chopped onions or sliced leeks	250 mL
1 lb	carrots, peeled and sliced	500 g
3 3/4 cups	chicken stock	925 mL
1 cup	peeled, diced sweet potatoes	250 mL
1/2 cup	orange juice	125 mL
2 tbsp	honey	25 mL
1 tbsp	grated orange zest (1 large orange)	15 mL

1. In nonstick saucepan sprayed with vegetable spray, heat oil over medium heat. Add garlic, curry, onions, and carrots; cook for 5 minutes or until onions are softened. Add stock and sweet potatoes; bring to a boil. Cover, reduce heat to low and simmer for 25 minutes or until carrots and sweet potatoes are tender.
2. Transfer soup to food processor or blender; purée. Return to saucepan and stir in orange juice, honey, and zest.

Serves 6

Tips
- Leeks can contain a lot of hidden dirt. To clean thoroughly, slice in half lengthwise and wash under cold water, getting between the layers where dirt hides.
- For an elegant presentation, serve with a small dollop of low-fat sour cream or yogurt.
- When grating zest of an orange, be careful not to scrape the bitter white pith underneath the zest.

Make Ahead

Prepare and refrigerate up to a day ahead and reheat gently before serving, adding more stock if too thick.

Approximately 7.5% fat

Per Serving

Calories	119
Protein	2 g
Fat, total	1 g
Fat, saturated	0.1 g
Carbohydrates	26 g
Sodium	624 mg
Cholesterol	0 mg
Fibre	3 g

Index

Mastering
Break the Weight-Loss Barrier

DR. BARRY SIMON'S PLAN:

AUDIO TAPE SERIES 1: MASTERING YOUR OVERWHELMING MOMENT

This audiotape series helps you apply chapters one to four to your own overwhelming moments. This "how-to" system is the natural companion to the knowledge in the book. Dr. Simon will talk you through the universal overwhelming moments of opening the cupboard or the refrigerator, ordering from the menu or drive-through, or facing your late-night urges or mid-afternoon hunger. By listening to Dr. Simon describe success stories, you will overcome your doubt and uncertainty as he describes exactly how to create your own real solutions.

The series includes three audiotapes and a one-month success journal that guides you in creating your personal solution to your overwhelming moments. This includes a quick start audiotape on adopting a winning attitude entitled "Becoming a Weight-Loss Expert." One set will cost $29.95 (U.S. funds) plus $4.95 shipping and handling.

AUDIO SERIES 2: OVERCOMING EMOTIONAL EATING...STARTING NOW!

If, after reading Dr. Simon's section, you recognize yourself but are left feeling frustrated and helpless, you might need to go beyond the book. In this series, Dr. Simon guides you through nine sessions as if you were working with him one-on-one. With him, you will delve deeply into your own inner conversations and discover your own activators. By discovering how your feelings and needs determine what you eat and do, you will finally be prepared to master your overwhelming moments.

This comprehensive system includes six audiotapes, a success manual, and a free six-month subscription to his newsletter. The entire system is $69.95 (regular price) minus $10 for mentioning you have read our book plus $6.95 shipping and handling.

Please make the check or money order (U.S. funds only) payable to: Simbahealth Consultants.

To order simply send your name, address, zip code, and identify which program you are ordering to Simbahealth Consultants, c/o Dr. Barry Simon, 36 Madison Avenue, Toronto, Canada M5R 2S1.

For further information about these audiotape series, write to the address above or visit Dr. Barry Simon at his web site (www.healthexchange.com/drsimon.html).

DR. JAMES MESCHINO'S PLAN:

Dr. Meschino offers various nutritional resources and information. For example, he provides a series of audiotapes and videotapes covering topics ranging from wellness for women to nutritional and athletic performance. In addition, he has developed a comprehensive program entitled "The 20/20 Vision of You," which is a twenty-day program that combines education and coaching in addition to nutritional supplements to improve your personal health. For further information about these programs, contact Dr. Meschino at 1-888-meschino.

Acquisitions Editor: Sara Borins
Production Editor: Kelly Dickson
Substantive Editor: Jennifer Glossop
Copy Editor: Dianne Broad
Production Coordinator: Julie Preston
Art Direction: Kyle Gell
Cover and Interior Design: Counterpunch/Linda Gustafson
Cover Image: Nicholas Vitacco
Page Layout: Linda Gustafson

The text is set in Walbaum, a Modern (or Romantic) typeface first cut about 1805 by Justus Erich Walbaum, a contemporary of Beethoven. It was revived under Stanley Morison's direction by Monotype in 1933. The display is set in FC Racer, and in News Gothic, a 1908 attempt by Morris F. Benton to modernize the American Gothics of the nineteenth century.